PRESIDENTIALIZING THE PREMIERSHIP

Presidentializing the Premiership

Sue Pryce
Department of Politics
University of Nottingham

First published in Great Britain 1997 by
MACMILLAN PRESS LTD
Houndmills, Basingstoke, Hampshire RG21 6XS and London
Companies and representatives throughout the world

A catalogue record for this book is available from the British Library.

ISBN 0–333–68185–1

First published in the United States of America 1997 by
ST. MARTIN'S PRESS, INC.,
Scholarly and Reference Division,
175 Fifth Avenue, New York, N.Y. 10010

ISBN 0–312–17554–X

Library of Congress Cataloging-in-Publication Data
Pryce, Sue, 1947–
Presidentializing the premiership / Sue Pryce.
p. cm.
Includes bibliographical references and index.
ISBN 0–312–17554–X (cloth)
1. Executive advisory bodies—Great Britain.   2. Cabinet system–
–Great Britain.   3. Prime ministers—Great Britain.   4. Great
Britain—Politics and government—1964–1979.   5. Great Britain–
–Politics and government—1979–   6. Executive advisory bodies–
–United States.   7. Cabinet system—United States.   8. Presidents–
–United States.   9. United States—Politics and government.
I. Title.
JN405.P79 1997
352.7'43'0941—dc21   97–7101
                                                           CIP

To Ken

'The first opinion that is formed of a ruler's intelligence is based on the quality of the men he has around him. When they are competent and loyal he can always be considered wise, because he has been able to recognize their competence and to keep them loyal. But when they are otherwise, the prince is always open to adverse criticism; because his first mistake has been in the choice of his ministers.'

Machiavelli

Contents

Preface

This book was inspired by the political and constitutional fuss that erupted when Nigel Lawson resigned as Chancellor in 1989. He attributed a large measure of the blame for his sudden departure from the exchequer, to the fact that Mrs Thatcher was listening to alternative economic advice. The implication was that there were rules about advice that the prime minister was not observing. Controversy about advice had erupted from time to time ever since Mrs Thatcher entered No.10 and it was often linked with claims that the prime minister was behaving 'presidentially'. I remembered that similar complaints had been made during Harold Wilson's premierships, especially when, in 1967, George Brown resigned as Foreign Secretary. This prompted me to investigate whether there were indeed constitutional rules circumscribing advice to the prime minister, and to examine what, if any, connection existed between prime ministerial advisory strategies and the claims that British politics was becoming presidentialized. Had the presidentialization of electoral politics in Britain brought about a change in constitutional and institutional relationships at the heart of British government?

This book is my own work but it would never have been completed without support and practical assistance. I am grateful to Mrs Jan Beckett, the librarian at Harlaxton College, for the help she gave me with my research. She took a keen interest in the progress of my work and always made me feel welcome even on occasions when my queries must have been tiresome. Thanks are also due to Sunder Katwala and Karen Brazier of Macmillan Press for providing me with guidance on the intricacies of publishing. I am greatly indebted to my friend and mentor, Dr John McClelland of the Politics Department of the University of Nottingham, for reading early drafts of this work, providing inspirational advice and for setting standards to which I shall always aspire. Finally, I would like to thank my husband, Ken Pryce, for using his considerable expertise and infinite patience to produce this work in camera ready form; for always encouraging me, providing me with emotional support and for sharing my priorities.

1 Introduction

> There is a great difficulty in the way of a writer who attempts to sketch a living Constitution – a Constitution that is in actual working and power. The difficulty is that the object is in constant change . . . The difficulty is the greater because the writer who deals with a living Government naturally compares it with the most important other living Governments, and these are changing too . . [1]

> The theme of 'the power behind the throne' . . . has long exerted as strong a hold on the imagination of people without power as it has on the minds of those with power.[2]

The rise of the British presidency in electoral terms[3] has led to the presidentialization of the premiership, at least in respect of advice. Advice to the executive in Britain is a constitutional matter, to change the advisory system is to change the constitution. This is rarely achieved without resistence from those who stand to lose their former prerogatives.

Controversy about advice has always been a feature of British politics. On 26 October 1989 Nigel Lawson resigned from his position as Chancellor of the Exchequer. A difference of opinion over the conduct of economic policy that had divided Nos 10 and 11 Downing Street during the previous year was fast becoming a matter of public scandal. The Chancellor's abrupt departure raised broad questions about economic policy and Britain's position in Europe, but more specifically it drew attention to the part played in government by special advisers and their impact on cabinet and collective responsibility. Mr Lawson complained in his resignation speech that the prime minister was failing to observe conventions of cabinet government, in particular that she was listening to alternative advice from Professor Alan Walters, her personal economic adviser. He justified his resignation in terms of constitutional principle. The question was not whether this or that policy was correct, but to whose advice the prime minister should be obliged to listen.

Nigel Lawson clearly thought that there were known rules about advice to the prime minister and that they were being broken. He not only echoed the complaints of some of his contemporaries in Mrs Thatcher's governments, but also joined in a continuous dialogue about rights of advice to the executive that has been one of the hallmarks of British constitutional evolution.

Power attracts advice and advisers attract attention. Such attention partly springs from curiosity: an interest in trying to identify the 'power behind the throne'. It also arises from a need to identify lines of communication to decision-makers by those who wish to influence public policy. Advisers also arouse suspicion and rivalry, and may become the centre of controversy stirred up by those who feel themselves illegitimately excluded from positions of influence. Constitutions attempt to establish rules circumscribing the exercise of government power. It seems inevitable that constitutions should seek to extend such rules to establish the legitimacy of those having influence on the exercise of that power. Since it is often not possible to identify the point at which a policy decision is taken, let alone isolate one particular influence upon such decisions, influence is assumed to be proportionate to access. One of the things constitutions are expected to do is establish rules about who should have access to supposed decision-makers.

If the next best thing to being king was to have the king's ear, then the question: 'Who advises the king?' becomes urgent. The British constitution developed out of attempts, on the one hand, to force monarchs to act only on advice, and on the other, to prescribe the sources of that advice. But this very process of institutionalizing sources of advice was partly self-defeating. Institutionalization, whilst legitimizing advisers by making them permanent, also reduced their usefulness, since the position of the adviser then ceased to depend solely upon mutual loyalty or the quality of the advice offered. British constitutional history, therefore, charts a continuous story of monarchs agreeing, often reluctantly and sometimes under duress, to consult prescribed sources of advice, whilst secretly seeking counsel elsewhere.

During Queen Victoria's reign, this vexed question of advice seemed to be settling down. By this time the generally accepted constitutional position was that the monarch should only act on the advice of a cabinet minister, usually the prime minister. This did not, however, settle the question; it simply changed the terms of the debate.

By means of advice, the royal prerogatives came to be exercised by a collective executive, the cabinet. It was a collective executive in which the prime minister was recognized to have a dominant role. The question therefore became, on whose advice should the cabinet, and more specifically the prime minister, exercise these powers? It was a question to which the Northcote-Trevelyan Report (1854) attempted to provide an answer. It led to the establishment of a permanent government of politically impartial, anonymous bureaucrats appointed on merit, who would advise the elected government and at the same time represent some continuity of policy in the face of the expected whimsicalities of mass democracy. The radicalism and political expediency of cabinets, exposed to the risks of the ballot box, would be tempered by the moderation and wisdom of senior policy advisers in the civil service. Government, which had once been a discourse between King and Parliament, executive and legislature, would become instead, a dialogue between permanent bureaucrats and transient politicians. Public policy would be the outcome of negotiation between these two parts of the executive. The civil servants would advise, and ministers would decide. Prime ministerial advice was supposed to come from senior political colleagues in the cabinet, who were themselves well known to the public and accountable to Parliament, and were in their turn advised by their departmental civil servants.

In Britain the debate about advice to the executive centred both on the quality of the advice and upon the legitimacy of its source, controversy typically occurring when a supposedly illegitimate source is also the source of advice which appears to be bad. In contrast, in America there has been less sensitivity about sources of advice and more concern that presidents trawl widely in order to catch the 'best' advice available. The American constitution-makers were able to be selective about what they imported from the British system. The model on which they drew was the British constitution at its eighteenth century stage of development and they were able to overlook Britain's legacy of trouble about 'advice politics' stretching back at least to 1215. It was the election of Andrew Jackson in 1828 that placed questions about presidential advice on the American political agenda. Advice did not, however, become an important constitutional issue until the chief executive assumed the position of chief legislator: that is, not until the presidency of Franklin D. Roosevelt. It was FDR who succeeded in persuading Congress to legitimize a new advisory system which institutionalized a number of competing presidential advisory bodies.

In Britain, despite the Northcote-Trevelyan attempt at a settlement, public policy failure periodically re-opens questions about advice. The common interests of Whitehall and Downing Street diverge when the policy advice of the former seems unlikely to deliver electoral success to the latter. At these times politicians seek alternative advisers to radicalize policy initiatives and, at the same time, coerce the permanent government. Both world wars provide examples of this pattern. Whitehall was obliged to cooperate with temporary 'irregulars' introduced to expedite the war effort and cabinets had to acquiesce to alternative prime ministerial advisers in the form of the 'Garden Suburb' and the Statistical Section. Such failures to observe what seems to have been accepted constitutional propriety about advice were countenanced partly because desperate times legitimized desperate measures and partly because they were assumed in any case to be temporary.

After the Second World War governments everywhere were forced to shoulder vastly increased responsibilities for the welfare of their citizens. This gave rise to the need for new kinds of advice. The civil service succeeded in safeguarding its former monopoly by claiming exclusive rights to mediate the advice of experts and interest groups. The post war period also saw a change taking place in the political system. By the 1960s election campaigns in Britain were fast becoming highly personalized affairs which invited comparison with American presidential elections. The personality and style of the leaders had become at least as important, if not more important, than party or policy. These political changes prompted changes in the institutional relationships within the government. If prime ministers were expected to bear responsibility for winning or losing elections, they needed to be certain that the advice they received was advice which was advantageous to them, and this often meant advice that would enable them to challenge the accepted wisdom of departmental civil servants mediated by their cabinet colleagues.

Prime ministers, in a manner similar to American presidents, began casting their nets more widely for advice. They seemed less inclined to observe accepted constitutional proprieties, and more willing to undermine the traditional monopolies of Whitehall and Westminster by seeking to institutionalize alternative sources of advice. As a consequence of this, by the 1990s the cabinet was beginning to look uncomfortably like its American counterpart. It could be seen as just one among many advisory bodies orbiting the prime minister, and its members were becoming frontmen who were expected to sell the prime minister's policies to the political nation and the public. Prime ministers seemed to consider themselves free to exploit tensions between their cabinets, advised by Whitehall, and the various alternative advisers on their personal staff, in a way which reminds us of the way American presidents exploit the tensions between the White House staff, the rest of the Executive Office and the cabinet and line departments. There were signs that the prime minister's advisory system was being presidentialized and the public fuss this provoked indicated that all was not well in the unwritten constitution.

This book examines the constitutional position in respect of advice to the British prime minister and joins in the presidentialization debate that has been an enduring theme in the study of British politics for at least the last three decades. It argues that the presidentialization of electoral politics has opened up a gap between the political and constitutional position of the prime minister. The prime minister has become a president in the eyes of the electorate but remains a prime minister according to the constitution. To bridge this gap prime ministers have been forced to stretch the constitutional rules about advice and presidentialize their advisory systems.

The contents of subsequent chapters may be described briefly. Chapter two examines the history of the politics of advice to the executive in Britain to establish the constitutional position about advice. Chapter three examines the politics of advice in America. It describes the way in which the changing political role of the president prompted a presidentialization of American government, which in turn led to questions about advice acquiring constitutional significance. This permits the construction of a model of the presidential advisory system. Chapters four to eight examine the advisory systems of four British prime ministers: Harold Wilson 1964–70; Edward Heath 1970–74; Harold Wilson 1974–76; James Callaghan 1976–79 and Margaret Thatcher 1979–90, within the context of both the British model and the American presidential model in order to show both that the constitution is evolving and that the direction of change is one of convergence with the American model. Chapter nine reflects on the history of advice politics and explores the constitutional and political obstacles that, for the present at least, stand in the way of further presidentialization.

A note about style: the terms 'aide', 'assistant' and 'adviser' have been used interchangeably. American spellings are left intact when quoted or used in titles. EOP (Executive Office of the President); WHO (White House Office); CPRS (Central Policy Review Staff) and DEA (Department of Economic Affairs) are the only frequently used abbreviations.

Notes

1. Bagehot, Walter, *The English Constitution* Fontana edn., (London: Fontana, 1963) p. 267.
2. Benn, Stephen, 'The White House Staff' (unpublished doctoral thesis, University of Keele, 1984) p. vii.
3. Foley, Michael, *The Rise of the British Presidency* (Manchester University Press, 1993).

2 Constitutional Propriety and the Politics of Advice to the Executive in Britain

'On all great subjects,' says Mr Mill, 'much remains to be said,' and of none is this more true than of the English Constitution. The literature which has accumulated upon it is huge. But an observer who looks at the living reality will wonder on the contrast to the paper description. He will see in the life much which is not in the books, and he will not find in the rough practice many refinements of the literary theory.[1]

British political history does not provide a fixed model of constitutional propriety in respect of advice, but it does confirm that the right of advice has always been contentious and that advice has been a motor of constitutional change. When advice becomes an important issue on the political agenda it is often a signal that the constitution is shifting and changes are meeting resistance from those who stand to lose.

Britain has evolved a system of government by conversation. It is a conversation in which certain institutions claim a right to a voice. If the executive appears to be conversing exclusively with 'outsiders' fears are aroused that rule by dictation may be the result. Controversy about advice to the executive lies at the very heart of the unwritten constitution. The powers of, and relationships between, the different parts of the state are governed primarily by conventions. There is little in the way of written law to substantiate claims of constitutional impropriety. Instead, fundamental rules have evolved as a result of a process of challenge and response between executive and legislature over almost a thousand years. Whether, and from whom, the executive is obliged to seek advice has formed a major part of this unending dialectic. An unwritten assumption of the constitution would seem to be that the responsibility for government is shared between the executive and legislature. The executive, once in fact, now only in name, the monarch, determines policy but policy is legitimated and, if necessary funded, by being acceptable to Parliament. Acceptability is best gained by basing policy on Parliament's advice or on pursue a policy that is unacceptable to Parliament. Questions are then raised about the policy's origins and about the sources of advice upon which it is based, the assumption being that not only should the executive seek advice before determining policy, but that there is a connection between the propriety of the source and value of the advice.

This discourse about advice, though perceived as a problem to the participants, can be seen as forming a necessary part of the ordinary processes of English politics. By the end of the eighteenth century what has come to be known as the Whig view of English history emerged. Whigs believed England to be fortunate because the political nation was divided between defenders of authority, institutionalized in the monarchy, and defenders of liberty, institutionalized in Parliament. The liberties of Englishmen were guaranteed by the unending dialectic within the political community that this entailed.

The resignation of a Chancellor might be regarded as proof enough of the seriousness with which advice politics are regarded in Britain; regicide underlines the matter. This is not to claim that the question of advice was the only one that drove Cromwell and his supporters to the extreme remedy of executing a king. But the king's stubborn belief that he could disregard the advice of Parliament did form an important part of the dispute concluded, for Charles at least, on the scaffold.

The execution of Charles I in 1649 marked the end of the English Civil War, but not the end of the argument about advice that had been high on the political agenda since the Stuarts had ascended to the English throne. Charles's beliefs about the unlimited nature of kingly power had been shaped by his father's theories on divine right monarchy. These theories were rejected by parliamentarians as incompatible with English constitutional precedents and regarded as dangerous foreign nonsense that the Stuarts had acquired from their continental in-laws.

In the 1620s Parliament was outraged by James I's refusal to wage war against Spain to assist his son-in-law, the Protestant Elector Palatine, to regain territories lost to Spain during the Thirty Years War, which started in 1618. James ignored Parliament's advice and instead courted Spain, attempting to arrange a marriage between his son Charles and the Spanish Infanta. Parliament's quarrel with the King focused not only on the policy itself but on the source of that policy. The King was being counselled, not by the great interests of the realm as represented in Parliament, but by the court favourite, Buckingham.[2] Parliament demanded James abandon his planned Spanish marriage for Charles. When he ignored them they sent a petition (3 December 1621) containing the veiled threat that supply would be withheld until their advice was accepted.

Parliament claimed that precedents, traceable back to Anglo-Saxon times, confirmed that although executive power was exercised personally by the monarch, it was never absolute. Whilst there was no formal constitution, Anglo-Saxon kings had sought, and had been expected to seek advice from the Witanagemot. This practice was confirmed by the Normans whose feudal structure imposed on tenants-in-chief the duty of advising the king, if called upon to do so. By the thirteenth century the duty of advising had been transformed, by custom, into a right, with powerful landowners and clerics demanding that monarchs act only after consultation. Such expectations were supposed to have found documented expression in Magna Carta 1215. The magnates' claim to prerogative over advice to monarchs led to virtual 'civil war' following the establishment of the Oxford Parliament,[3] 1258, and to the enforced abdication of the King in 1326.[4] Even the powerful Tudor dynasty appeared to have conformed to these assumptions. Whilst the Tudors claimed absolute freedom to select their counsellors, dominated the Great Council and gave disproportionate weight to the advice of favoured advisers such as Wolsey, Thomas Cromwell and Cecil, they nevertheless recognized that policy should be based on advice and that its source should be recognized by, and acceptable to, the powerful estates of the realm.

James I attempted to refute Parliament's claim to the right to give advice. He rejected theories of medieval kingship with all its contractual implications. In *The Trew Law of Free Monarchies* (published anonymously in 1598) James repudiated any limitations on sovereignty. He claimed instead that monarchs ruled by divine hereditary right. The king was God's vice-regent on earth. As God's anointed, he was already mysteriously qualified to rule; he was neither bound to seek, nor bound to heed, advice from any source. If he wanted advice, he chose the advisers. The function of Parliament was to give advice, but only if asked: it had no right to advise.

James's absolutism was more tempered in practice than it was in theory. He took his coronation oath, to respect the laws and customs of England, seriously. Neither this, nor the practices of his predecessors, diluted his theoretical claims. He asserted that whilst the power of kings was unlimited, kings of settled states, though not obliged to respect the rights and customs of their subjects, would normally do so since if they did not God would be displeased.[5]

The parliamentary magnates were only too well aware that Buckingham, as is usual with favourites of no recognized provenance beyond their patron, had a vested interest in encouraging James in his absolutist claims. The death of James in 1625 did not improve this state of affairs. When Charles I succeeded to the throne he inherited not only his father's theory of divine right, but also Buckingham. Charles did not, however, continue his father's cautious practice.

Political ineptitude, exacerbated by bad advice, eventually brought direct conflict between Parliament and Charles. Parliament was concerned not only that the king was listening to Buckingham but that he appeared to be listening only to Buckingham. In 1626 Sir William Walter moved that '. . . the cause of all the grievances is that all the King's council ride upon one horse, therefore the Parliament shall advise the King to take unto him assistants.'[6] What could Parliament do when it thought the king was getting bad advice but the king would not listen to advice telling him his advisers gave bad advice? In 1626 Parliament resorted to impeaching[7] Buckingham. But Charles intervened on his friend's behalf by rejecting Parliament's right to question his servant: 'I must let you know I will not allow any of my servants to be questioned amongst you, much less such as are in eminent place and near to me':[8] a claim to 'executive privilege' by any other name.

In 1628 an assassin rid Parliament of the unsavoury influence of Buckingham. This did not remove the perennial problem of influence. Charles now turned more towards his wife for counsel. However, not only had Henrietta Maria been reared in the absolutist court of France, she also lent heavily on the French Catholic advisers who surrounded her. This reinforced Charles's absolutist tendencies and aroused fears about his commitment to the protestant faith.

By 1629 Parliament and the king had a series of confrontations over the failure of his foreign policy, over the fiscal expedients needed to finance that policy, over the use of imprisonment to enforce these expedients, and over his sponsorship of a catholic-leaning minority group within the Church. As a result of all this squabbling, the king dissolved Parliament in 1629 and did not recall if for the next eleven years. Parliament's fears were realized. It was excluded from the dialogue of government; the king was determined to rule alone.

Parliamentarians failed to instruct the king on the limits of his prerogative, and this eventually became one of the causes of the Civil War. The question was who had the right to give the monarch advice and subsequently whose advice was the monarch duty bound to listen to:

> If kings be so inclinable to follow private advice rather than public, and to prefer that which closes with their natural impotent ambition before that which crosses the same, (and) are without all limits, then they may destroy their best subjects at pleasure, and all charters and laws of public safety and freedom are void; and God hath not left human nature any means of sufficient preservation. But, on the contrary, if there be

any benefits in laws to limit princes when they are seduced by privados (favourites) and will not hearken to the great council of the land, doubtless there must be some court to judge of the seducement and some authority to enforce that judgement, and that court and authority must be the Parliament . . .[9]

In the Petition Accompanying the Grand Remonstrance presented to the King (1 December 1641), the second prayer claimed, for Parliament, the right to determine the acceptability of sources of the king's public policy advice:

That your Majesty will likewise be pleased to remove from your council all such as persist to favour and promote any of these measures and corruptions wherewith your people have been aggrieved, and that for the future your Majesty will vouchsafe to employ such persons in your great and public affairs, and to take such to be near you in places of trust, as your Parliament may have cause to confide in . . [10]

This was a right roundly rejected by the King in his response to the Petition, (23 December, 1641) in which he claimed: '. . . it is the undoubted right of the Crown of England to call such persons to our secret counsels to public employment and our particular service as we shall think fit . . . '[11] Throughout the Civil War Parliament insisted it fought not against the king but against evil his counsellors. It was not until 1642 that the king was for the first, and only time, named in Parliament's criticisms of the executive. The House of Commons made the following vote: 'that the King, seduced by evil counsel, intended to levy war against his Parliament and people, to destroy the fundamental laws and liberties of England and to introduce an arbitrary government . . .'[12]

The Civil War and the ensuing periods of Commonwealth and Protectorate failed to settle this question of the constitutional relationship between executive and legislature. Cromwell lived no more easily with Parliament than his Stuart predecessors. It was not, therefore, just a 'divine right' problem.

The year 1660 witnessed the unconditional restoration of the monarchy. Charles II still espoused divine right theory. He was strongly drawn to Catholicism and recognized that where Catholicism thrived the monarchy was strong, as in France and Spain. He was too circumspect to reveal his Catholicism until his deathbed, but throughout his reign he flirted with support for religious toleration of catholics. This, and his obvious admiration for his cousin, Louis XIV of France, caused growing alarm. In France the Estates General had not been summoned for almost fifty years (since 1614) and Parliament feared that if Charles's financial position permitted, he also would dispense with representative institutions and rule without Parliament. The secret Treaty of Dover, concluded in 1670, fuelled Parliament's fears. Its promise of a French pension, plus traditional taxes, would give the king financial independence; he would not need to call a parliament ever again.

Parliament sought to curtail the king's activities by, on the one hand, limiting his finances and, on the other, insisting he always act on advice, and taking steps to control the advisers. To this end Parliament prevailed upon the king to return to a system of guidance by the whole Privy Council instead of relying exclusively on the advice of a few favourites. Financial difficulties forced Charles to make concessions. On 20 April 1679 he agreed to dismiss his old Privy Council and said '. . . he hath resolved to lay aside the use he may have hitherto made of any single ministry of private advices or Foreign Committees for the conduct of his affairs'.[13] On the same day a new Privy Council was sworn in, the majority of whom had been opponents of absolutism. Charles in private repudiated this arrangement and only complied with it in public to gain time: 'God's fish! they have put a set of men about me, but they shall know nothing'.[14]

Parliament, fearing a further drift towards Catholicism and absolutism, attempted unsuccessfully to exclude James II, Charles's brother and heir, from the throne. In 1685 James inherited his brother's throne, his Privy Council and a cabinet of advisers, all of whom were holders of offices of state, but reverted to consulting secret advisers (Sunderland and the Jesuit, Edward Petre) once he had determined to press the Catholic cause. The growing crisis this engendered was only averted by the arrival of protestant, Dutch William of Orange (James's son-in-law) and James's subsequent flight to France.

In retrospect, the Civil War seemed to have had little immediate effect on the power of the Crown or on the monarchy's attitude to government in general. Although the loss of lucrative feudal rights and royal lands had increased the monarch's financial dependence on Parliament, Parliaments had shown themselves quite unable to defeat the king in the sense of imposing on him restrictions and conditions that he disliked or taking away from him powers he had hitherto enjoyed. The royal prerogatives in the 1680s were practically indistinguishable from those of the early 1600s. The king could veto bills, he could dispense individuals from the operation of the law, especially anti-catholic laws, pardon whom he chose, select his own councillors and dismiss them at will. He was not bound to take anyone's advice. It took the threat of invasion by Louis XIV and possibly the return of the exiled James II after 1689, which would have introduced popery and absolutist government at a stroke, to effect finally changes in the constitutional relationship between executive and legislature.

In 1688 William and Mary were offered the throne on condition that they accept the Declaration of Rights. This latter insisted that the consent of Parliament meeting frequently and in freedom, was necessary for taxation, suspending statutes and maintenance of a standing army in peacetime. The principle of divine right kingship was formally abandoned. Although William never actually agreed to the Declaration of Rights, he accepted it by implication. He and Mary promised at their coronation to rule 'according to the statutes in Parliament agreed on', the result being the substantive acceptance of constitutional monarchy and a permanent adjustment in the relationship between Crown and Parliament.

But advice continued to be a problem. William, in compliance with expectations, consulted the Cabinet Council, but it did not have his full confidence. Why should he trust or even like people who had already killed one king and forced the abdication of another? His closest advisers continued to be his Dutch compatriots, especially Bentinck. In the Act of Settlement of 1701, Parliament attempted to address this problem by inserting a provision that, when the House of Hanover succeeded, important matters of state should be dealt with in the Privy Council and that resolutions were to be signed by the councillors who had indicated their agreement. Advice to the monarch was to be institutionalized and the practice of consulting secret advisers was to end.

Under the Georges, the terms of the argument about advice began to shift. It was not merely the source of royal advice that was controversial, but the additional issue was raised about linking of the questions of advice and responsibility. George I showed little love for Britain or its politics. He continued to immerse himself in German affairs and surround himself with German advisers. The disinclination of the first two Georges to attend meetings of the Cabinet gave impetus to the evolution of the office of prime minister. The convention developed that the minister appointed First Lord of the Treasury, but sometimes Secretary of State, chaired cabinet meetings in the absence of the king and undertook the role of go-between in relations between monarch and Parliament.

Sir Robert Walpole is traditionally regarded as Britain's first prime minister. The title was intended to be pejorative. In 1741, Mr Sandys accused Walpole of misconduct in assuming a role of 'prime minister':

> according to our constitution, we can have no sole and prime minister: we ought always to have several prime ministers or officers of state: every such officer has his proper department; and no officer ought to meddle in the affairs belonging to the department of another. But it is

publicly known, that this minister, having obtained a sole influence over all our public counsels, has not only assumed the sole direction of all public affairs, but has got every officer of state removed that would not follow his direction, even in the affairs proper to his own department. By this means he hath monopolized all the favours of the crown, and engrossed the sole disposal of all places, pensions, titles and ribbons, as well as of all preferments, civil, military or ecclesiastical.[15]

This charge was vigorously denied by Walpole: 'but while I unequivocally deny that I am sole and prime minister, and that to my influence and direction all measures of government must be attributed, yet I will not shrink from the responsibility which attaches to the post I have the honour to hold . . . '[16]

Although Walpole may be regarded as the first prime minister, his office and powers were still a far cry from those of a modern counterpart. His long period of supremacy (1721–42) can be attributed more to his skill at manipulating the system of royal patronage, that was the key to delivering the support of Members of Parliament at that time, than to any clear political programme. Walpole owed his appointment to the political skills that first gained him the confidence of George I and subsequently, George II, his eventual fall from power was the result of his failure to retain the confidence of Parliament. It was this that signalled a shift in relationships, both within the executive branch of government, and between the executive and the legislature.

During the reign of George III the battle for the Whig constitution was rejoined. Once again the focus of the struggle was the question of whether executive authority was a personal prerogative of the monarch, and on whose advice the monarch was expected to exercise power. The new king did not feel obliged to accept restrictions on his choice of advisers. He attempted to regain the traditional royal prerogatives over the choice of ministers that appeared to have slipped to parliamentary leaders during the latter part of his grandfather's reign. He chose the Earl of Bute, his ex-tutor and favourite, to become first minister. Bute was neither a member of Parliament, nor in the cabinet. The king tried to legitimize Bute's position by appointing him Secretary of State. In 1763 Bute resigned. The ostensible cause of his premature departure was the unpopularity of his cider tax, but the underlying cause was his inability to command support of the majority in Parliament. His short tenure was testament to the limits that now circumscribed royal choice.

The debacle over the appointment of Bute, however, failed to resolved the question of who should advise the executive. In 1782, a Whig-dominated Commons refused to support the administration of Lord

Shelburne, the king's chosen first minister. The king, stubbornly defending his freedom to choose his own advisers, refused his confidence to a coalition headed by Fox and North, and two years later effected the downfall of their ministry by inducing the Lords to reject Fox's India Bill. In the subsequent election in 1784, a hundred Fox supporters lost their seats. In terms of royal power this was a pyrrhic victory marking only a temporary respite in the decline of personal hereditary executive. The Fox ministry was succeeded by that of Pitt. Although according to Keir: 'throughout Pitt's long ministry George III continued in countless ways to rule as well as to reign',[17] by the end of Pitt's period in office the king's personal choice was considerably diminished: ' . . . the dominant personality of Pitt gradually ensured that Cabinet deliberations must be confined to persons actually holding office and in agreement with the views of their colleagues'.[18] Thus the foundations were laid for the developing convention of collective responsibility that was to shape modern cabinet government.

By the end of the eighteenth century government, though still in name the job of kings, was in practice rapidly becoming the business of the leaders of the dominant political party in Parliament, especially the Commons. This process was accelerated by the 1832 Reform Act which effectively destroyed the control over Parliament which the Crown had exercised, for more than half a century, by means of patronage and influence.

Parliament not only secured its right to advise the executive, it was also able to determine who would exercise executive power. An evolving advisory system had enabled the formally unchanged constitutional position of an hereditary monarchy to adjust to the changes in the political system that accompanied the rise of the democratic state. When Bagehot revealed the 'secret constitution' in 1867, he was almost correct in concluding that executive power was no longer the personal prerogative of monarchs. The 1832 Reform Act, in extending the suffrage to the middle classes, marked the beginnings of the democratization of the state, a process extended in 1867 and 1884, and reinforced by the Secret Ballot Act of 1872. Henceforth, the legitimacy of government passed from being a favour conferred according to the personal preferences of an hereditary monarch, and became instead the prerogative of a House of Commons chosen by an expanding, and increasingly differentiated, electorate. Executive power had all but ceased, except in name, to be the business of kings. By 1913 Asquith was able to proclaim in a memorandum on the rights and obligations of the Crown: 'we have now a well-established tradition of two hundred years, that, in the last resort, the occupant of the Throne accepts and acts on the advice of his ministers . . . '[19]

Having realized its aim of obliging monarchs to act only on advice and determining the sources of that advice, Parliament had to come to terms with the fact that though the political and constitutional orders may change, the problems might not. The shift in the location of sovereignty simply entailed a shift in the problem. How could the 'advisers' who now in effect exercised royal power be rendered accountable? Northcote-Trevelyan provided some of the answers. Monarchs only exercised power on the advice of Ministers of the Crown, who were themselves responsible to Parliament and advised by a known legitimate source, the professional bureaucracy.

Northcote-Trevelyan, however, only provided a temporary solution. By the early twentieth century the problem of advice re-emerged. Like their royal predecessors, prime ministers soon began to seek advice outside those sources recognized as legitimate by Parliament. It soon became apparent not only that bureaucrats, like all political actors, had policy preferences and vested interests in particular policies, but that their anonymity shielded them from accountability. This placed a question mark over the neutrality of their advice. Prime ministers felt the need for alternative advice to act as a counter-balance to Whitehall departmentalism. They needed advice which came from sources whose primary loyalty was to the prime minister and his policies.

Lloyd George exploited the opportunities provided by war to initiate changes in the advisory system. In 1916 he transformed the Secretariat to the Committee for Imperial Defence into the Cabinet Secretariat, thus providing both prime minister and the cabinet with a team of advisers masquerading as a secretariat. He effected greater changes in the Private Office at No.10. This office, established to support the prime minister, had existed since the middle of the nineteenth century. Lloyd George appointed personal political friends to key posts within the Private Office.[20] In addition, he established the 'Garden Suburb', a group of five specially selected people from outside Whitehall, to provide him with alternative advice.[21]

Parliament initially accepted these innovations in wartime conditions but disquiet was soon expressed about Lloyd George's very personal style of government. He seemed to many to be 'out of control'. Much criticism focused on his sale of honours and use of patronage, and the relationship of these to his election fund. It was felt that the prime minister was relying on dubious and constitutionally improper sources of advice. According to Jones, 'Lloyd George's premiership seemed to many very close to personal dictatorship and after his fall there was a reaction to his style. The 'Garden Suburb' was abolished and the Cabinet Secretariat was considerably reduced in size.'[22]

Prime ministers continued to appoint personal political advisers loyal only to themselves but it was not until Churchill established the prime minister's Statistical Section[23] that the politics of advice again became sensitive. The exigencies of war reconciled Whitehall and Westminster to Churchill's innovations in the advisory system, but Whitehall soon reclaimed its former monopoly when Churchill left office.

A mass electorate permitted a presidentialization process to creep into the 'premierization' of government which had gradually occurred since at least the time of Walpole. Democratization of the state prompted the shift in the location of executive power from hereditary to representative institutions and thereby changed the terms of the dialogue about advice. It also gave impetus to the development of mass parties. The political parties inside Parliament soon recognized the need to gain the support of a mass electorate and set about establishing grass-root structures to acquire it. The extension of the suffrage saw the bureaucratization of the party system and the development of hierarchical, cohesive, disciplined parliamentary parties, intent on capturing the executive.

By the middle of this century the executive in Britain was organized in a command structure with the cabinet at the top. But cabinet members are appointed and dismissed (within political restraints of balancing party support, rather than any constitutional limits) by the prime minister, who is the leader of the majority party of the House of Commons. The prime minister chairs meetings of the cabinet, sets its agenda and sums up its decisions. The prime minister determines the number of, and terms of reference of, cabinet committees, and appoints their chairmen and members. In addition the prime minister exercises a wide power of patronage through the honours list, and diplomatic, civil service, ecclesiastical and quango appointments.

The extent of prime ministerial power and the dominance of the prime minister in British government had, by the 1960s, become a matter of debate among the politically aware.[24] The shift in emphasis in electoral politics that appeared to be taking place by the 1960s, partly a response to this perceived growth in prime ministerial power, and in part a cause of it, gave rise to the thesis that British politics had become presidentialized.

In 1974 Butler and Stokes noted that 'the increasing complexity of government and the extension of the system of Cabinet committees have made the Premier appear more and more presidential. His share of the moulding of his party's image is much enhanced by the coming of new styles in journalism and even more by the advent of television.'[25] Not only was the prime minister now clearly the dominant actor in the executive, but the changing nature of electoral politics had resulted in the mass media encouraging the mass electorate to focus attention on the executive, but the changing nature of electoral politics had resulted in the mass media encouraging the mass electorate to focus attention on the prime minister. From about the time of the Macmillan premiership (1957–63) voters seemed to be less interested in party and programme and more swayed by personality and style of party leaders. The cause of this shift has been attributed to the advent of 'telly-politics'. Anthony Eden was the first prime minister to make use of television, but Harold Macmillan was the first to capitalize upon the asset of a strong television image. Harold Wilson was quick to exploit the potential of this new medium, to which he attributed Macmillan's success and Douglas-Home's failure. The premiership of Margaret Thatcher provided further evidence in support of this 'personalization of politics' thesis. Cockerel, Hennessy and Walker claim that

> 1983 was, above all, a television election. The major current affairs programmes on BBC and ITV concentrated almost exclusively on the party leaders and forsook reporting or analysis of the election issues . . . She (Mrs Thatcher) has brought prime ministerial use of television into a new age: Sir Harold Wilson's pipe and firesides and Mr Callaghan's avuncular displays for the cameras appear in comparison like the performance of silent movie actors. For Mrs Thatcher, television is vital and using it she has become like an American politician for whom political life is a permanent election campaign.[26]

This change that was taking place in the nature of electoral politics not only served to enhance the powers of the prime minister, but also promoted changes in institutional relationships. The past provides examples of party leaders, like Gladstone and Lloyd George, who appear to have commanded personal electoral support. In the immediate post-war period, however, electors' loyalties seemed to be to parties rather than personalities.[27] By the 1970s political analysts noted a growing trend towards partisan-dealignment.[28] The advent of television politics in the 1960s, seemed at least partly to blame for the undermining of traditional loyalties to parties. This growing volatility among the electorate, coupled with the use of sophisticated campaigns orchestrated by media experts, has enabled party leaders to be regarded as delivers of parliamentary majorities – a fact recognized by the parties. No longer, it seems, is the prime minister elected because he or she leads the party offering a programme most favoured by the electorate. Instead, the winning party is the beneficiary of the prime minister's personal popularity with the voters. Berkley writing in 1968 noted that 'the party machines, which have increasingly become the personal property of the party leaders, so far from today.'[29] By the 1980s the Conservatives' electoral successes were being attributed mainly to the personality of Mrs Thatcher, and likewise the demise of the Labour Party was blamed on the poor leadership images of Michael Foot, and, subsequently, Neil Kinnock. Electoral logic was changing the relationship between party and leader in ways that considerably increased the power of the leader when the latter was able to deliver electoral victory. Important features of the British system of government were, by the late twentieth century, coming to resemble parts of the American political system, a system in which a singular executive, the president, claims an electoral mandate gives him the right to bully other institutions of government.

The history of British constitutional practice reveals that advice has been a contentious matter. It clearly indicates what the problem is but does not easily provide a settled and acceptable model of constitutional propriety. Instead it offers a continuous discourse about the constitutional position with regard to advice. When advice appears to lead to the 'wrong' policies, that is, policies unacceptable to an important section of the political nation, then questions are asked about the sources of that advice. Is it constitutionally legitimate?

The development of British constitutional practice at least since the early seventeenth century makes the following things clear:

1. The politics of advice is contentious and forms part of the continuing power struggle between the executive and the legislature.
2. At certain moments advice becomes politically and constitutionally controversial. Such moments also coincide with times when the executive appears to be attempting to rule alone, that is, when alternative advisers enable the executive to ignore the constitutionally accepted sources.
3. These periods of constitutional controversy lead to temporary settlements of the advice question, in which one side or the other gains some ground and attempts to constitutionalize and institutionalize the new position.

It is difficult to be precise about the exact dates of such periods, but in post-war British politics 1964 seems to have ushered in a period of change and controversy. On becoming prime minister, Harold Wilson promised reappraisal of, and innovation in, the machinery of government, part of which would be the introduction of a greater number of political advisers. The process was continued by Edward Heath and subsequently by Wilson when he regained the premiership in 1974. It was during the three administrations of Mrs Thatcher, however, that questions about the politics of advice took on much greater significance and at times topped the political agenda.

It was also about 1964 when the debate about the presidentialization of British politics began to interest political scientists. This book joins in that debate by arguing that the presidentialization of British politics has brought about a presidentialization of British government, in particular, that the prime ministerial advisory system is becoming presidentialized. In chapters four to eight the advisory systems of the four British prime ministers who held office between 1964–90 will be examined to show the way in which the constitutional position in respect of advice was changing during this period and that the direction of change showed convergence with the American presidential model. But what is the advisory system of an American president like? The task of the next chapter will be to answer that question by constructing a model of the American presidential advisory system.

Notes

1. Bagehot, W., *The English Constitution* Fontana edn (London: Collins, 1963) p. 59.
2. George Villiers, First Duke of Buckingham 1592–1628. The son of minor gentry whose subsequent meteoric rise in rank (cup bearer in 1614 at the age of 22; Gentleman of the Bedchamber 1615; Viscount Villiers 1616; Earl of Buckingham 1617; Marquess 1618 and Duke 1623) was attributed to his striking good looks and a homosexual relationship with the King.
3. Henry III's controversial scheme for providing for his son Edmund involved an alliance with the Pope in a campaign to oust Frederick II's illegitimate son from Sicily. John Gillingham notes that 'this expensive and absurd commitment in 1258 provoked the barons into taking the government out of the King's hands and to initiate a far reaching programme of reform: the Provisions of Oxford 1258 and those of Westminster 1259. Taking the power out of the hands of the King and handing it to an unelected aristocratic council was a revolutionary step and for the next five years England teetered on the brink of civil war. When in the spring of 1264 war finally came, the issue at stake had been narrowed down to one question: was, or was not, the King free to choose foreigners to be his counsellors?' Cit. Morgan, Kenneth, ed. *Oxford Illustrated History of Britain* (Oxford: University Press, 1984) p. 134.

4. Edward II sought advice from ambitious favourites such as Pierre Galvaston and Hugh Despenser, who were regarded as unworthy by the King's magnates. Civil War 1321-2 and the King's 'abdication' (the King having no option but to consent to his own deposition), were the fateful outcome of the failure of the King to govern by cooperation. See ibid, p. 176.

5. Speech to Parliament 21 March 1610, cit. Kenyon, J.P., ed. *The Stuart Constitution 1603-1688* (Cambridge: University Paperback, 1976) p. 7.

6. Cit. Sharpe, Kevin, ed. *Faction and Parliament - essays on early Stuart history* (London: Metheun, 1978) p. 41.

7. Impeachment itself, being a process first used by Parliament in its attempt to eradicate the influence of undesirable advisers of Edward III. During the latter part of his reign (1327-77), continued military campaigns in France were proving costly and unsuccessful. Questions were raised, especially in the Commons, about the honesty, as well as the competence, of the King's advisers and officials. In the 'Good Parliament' of 1376, corrupt and incapable ministers, and even the old King's influential mistress, Alice Perrers, were accused by the Commons and tried before the Lords in (what was then) a novel and highly effective procedure, impeachment. See *Oxford Illustrated* op.cit., p. 178.

8. Cit. Tanner, J.R., *English Constitutional Conflicts of the Seventeenth Century 1603-89* (Cambridge: University Press, 1971) p. 65.

9. Henry Parker (1642), cit. Hughes, Ann, ed. *Seventeenth Century England: A Changing Culture Volume 1* (London: Ward and Lock in Assoc. with O.U. 1980) pp. 99-100.

10. Cit. ibid., p. 77.

11. Cit. ibid., p. 78.

12. Cit. Neville, Henry, 'Plato Redovovis 1681' in Robbins, Caroline, ed. *Two English Republican Tracts* (Cambridge: University Press, 1969) p. 150.

13. Privy Council Register Vpl. LXVII, cit. Mackintosh, John, *The British Cabinet* 2nd edn. (London: Metheun, 1968) p. 39.

14. Cit. ibid., p. 39.

15. Cit. Williams, E.N., *The Eighteenth Century Constitution* (Cambridge: University Press, 1960) p. 127.

16. Cit. ibid., p. 129.

17. Keir, D.L., *The Constitutional History of Modern Britain* 9th edn (London: Black, 1969) p. 380.

18. Ibid., p. 382. In 1782 Pitt obtained the dismissal from office of Lord Thurlow, who, although Lord Chancellor, opposed him in Parliament.

19. Cit. Jennings, Sir Ivor, *Cabinet Government* (Cambridge: University Press, 1969) p. 336.
20. John T. Davies, a Welsh-speaking teacher; Francis Stevenson, his daughter's former teacher, and William Sutherland, a former civil servant at the Board of Trade.
21. For a more detailed discussion of the 'Garden Suburb', see Jones, G.W., 'The Prime Ministers' Secretaries: Politicians or Administrators?' in Griffith, J.A.G., ed. *From Policy to Administration* (London: Allen & Unwin, 1976) p. 27. See also, Moseley, R.K., *The Story of the Cabinet Office* (London: Routledge & Kegan Paul, 1969) pp. 19–22.
22. Jones, ibid., p. 28.
23. A small group of alternative advisers under the leadership of Professor F.A. Lindeman. For a fuller discussion of Churchill's experiment, see Jones, G.W., 'The United Kingdom' in Plowden, William, ed. *Advising the Rulers* (Oxford: Blackwell, 1987) pp. 36–66, p. 44.
24. See Mackintosh, op.cit., pp. 428–53, Crossman, R.H.S., *Introduction to the English Constitution* Bagehot, op.cit. and Gordon-Walker, Patrick, *Cabinet* (London: Cape, 1970) pp. 85–91.
25. Butler, David and Stokes, Donald, *Political Change in Britain* (London: Macmillan, 1974) p. 351.
26. Cockerel, Michael, Hennessy, Peter and Walker, David, *Sources Close to the Prime Minister* (London: Macmillan, 1984) p. 189 and p. 191.
27. See Thomson, David, *England in the Twentieth Century* (London: Pelican, 1969) p. 219.
28. See Butler, D. and Stokes, D., *Political Change in Britain* (1974); Sarlvik, B. and Crewe, I., *Decade of Dealignment* (1983).
29. Berkley, Humphrey, *The Power of the Prime Minister* (London: Allen & Unwin, 1966) p. 23.

3 An American Presidential Model

> Now, after bitter experience, we are having to learn all over again that no single man or institution can ever be counted upon as a reliable or predictable repository of wisdom and benevolence; that the possession of great power can impair a man's judgement and cloud his perception of reality, and that our only protection against the misuse of power is the institutionalized interaction of a diversity of independent opinions.[1]

In America controversy about advice has been a comparatively recent phenomenon. From time to time the question 'who advises the president?' has been a matter of interest and occasionally disquiet, but it was the Watergate scandal of 1973–4 that transformed the presidential advisory system into a subject of urgent public debate.

In Britain controversy about advice has formed a continuous theme in evolving the unwritten constitutional rules governing the powers of, and relationship between, the executive and legislature. In America, in 1787, specially elected state conventions were deliberating acceptance of the American Constitution, a written document spelling out some of the powers and functions of the institutions of state. Such written rules and procedures can only be regarded as providing a set of guidelines. Actual powers and relationships in the American system have also evolved, over the last two hundred years, as a result of a dialectic of challenge and response between executive and legislature, sometimes adjudicated by the judiciary. Whilst controversy about presidential advisers erupted during the incumbency of Andrew Jackson (1829–37), and can be said to have continued intermittently ever since, it is only in the last fifty years that the politics of advice has formed an important part of the discourse on the constitution between the branches of government.

America's written Constitution, which customarily provides a convenient starting point for the scholar of American government and politics, remains silent on the question of advice to the executive.[2] We can therefore assume questions about advice were not pressing. The advisory system of the American president forms part of the unwritten constitution that has evolved over the last two hundred years. A static description of the contemporary presidential advisory system would provide a model with which to compare that of the British prime minister, but it would be of only limited use. What is needed is an examination of the way in which the presidential model has evolved to its present state, in order to establish a pattern against which the evolving British system can be examined for any signs of convergence.

In 1974, in the face of impending impeachment, Richard Nixon resigned as president of the United States. Ostensibly the reason for the proposed impeachment was the president's suspected involvement in the attempted cover up of the Watergate scandal.[3] Watergate, however, can be seen as a 'Trojan Horse' concealing Congress's determination to cure a much deeper malady within the policy-making community: a breakdown of communication and cooperation between the president and congressional leaders, and a growing imbalance of power in favour of the presidency.

There can be little doubt that the Founding Fathers intended the president to play a prominent part in American government. They did not anticipate that political pressure would subvert their carefully constructed system of checks and balances and allow the presidency to become the dominant instituion of government. The Constitution drawn up by the Founding Fathers in Philadelphia in 1787 was designed to establish a system of government in America that would be limited in scope and representative in nature. It incorporated two seemingly contradictory doctrines: the separation of powers, involving division and independence, and checks and balances, involving interaction and dependence. Of the two doctrines, checks and balances, or interaction and dependence of the branches, seems to have been ascendant.[4] The powers of the executive, vested in the presidency, were to be exercised with the 'advice and consent' of the great interests in the nation represented in the Senate. The voice of the masses was to be checked by the wisdom and moderation of the oligarchy. The constitution-makers provided for a political order in which English Whigs of 1688 would have felt at home. It was an order in which the political nation was identified with the holders of property and in which an enlightened patrician elite ruled through the Senate, the Presidency and the Court, with the consent or acquiescence of the masses, muted in the lower house of the legislature.

The Constitution established a system of separate institutions sharing powers.[5] This was an arrangement designed to prevent the tyranny of either the majority or of one man. There was to be no sovereign: no institution would exercise supreme power. Cooperation between different parts of the system would be a prerequisite for government to do anything much at all. The Founding Fathers recognized that concentration of power was a recipe for arbitrary rule and that liberties were best guaranteed by forcing separate institutions to share powers, thereby creating the need for a permanent conversation within the policy-making community. The rules of the written constitution assumed a network of relationships, not clearly specified, but nevertheless implied.

By the time Richard Nixon left the White House it seemed that the president assumed he could dispense with congressional advice; he appeared, at least for a time, to be able to rule alone and had developed the means to do so. The president had acquired extensive powers to act independently of Congress and, for that matter, any other important constituency in the policy-making community.[6] The elected chief executive had become surrounded by a large and growing coterie of advisers, aides and assistants, who, in contrast to members of the cabinet, were beyond the reach of congressional confirmation and investigation. Cronin notes that the president had become the centre of '. . . a powerful inner sanctum of government, isolated from traditional constitutional checks and balances' and that it had become '. . . common practice for anonymous unelected and unratified aides to negotiate sensitive international commitments by means of executive agreements which were free from Congressional oversight. Other aides wielded fiscal authority over funds appropriated by Congress for one purpose but redirected by the administration to another, free from accountability and public scrutiny.'[7]

The Senate Select Committee on Watergate exposed the involvement of close presidential aides in the sponsoring of, and subsequent attempt to cover up, a number of illegal activities. Eventually, release of White House tapes revealed that the president himself had knowledge of the cover-up. The holder of the highest office in the land, who had solemnly sworn to faithfully execute the Office of President of the Unites States and to uphold the laws, and who was himself a lawyer by profession, clearly appeared to be implicated in a conspiracy to subvert the course of justice. The Watergate scandal, with its allegations of presidential staff involvement in illegal activities, subsequent resignation of key political advisers and administrators, and the indictment of presidential aides and appointees, cast a harsh light on the whole system of presidential advising. Questions were asked about the nature and sources of presidential advice: 'should a political system that has made a virtue of periodic electoral accountability accord an ever increasing policy-making role to White House counsellors who neither are confirmed by the US Senate, nor, because of the doctrine of 'executive privilege'[8] subject to questioning by Congress?'[9]

The ignominious end of the Nixon presidency demonstrated the dangers inherent in a presidential advisory system that had become detached from the wider policy-making community. The president, it appeared, had only listened to those who confirmed him in the view '. . . that the American President, like the English King, could do no wrong.'[10]

The debacles of the Nixon presidency should not be viewed in isolation but can be seen as representing the culmination of developments that had already aroused considerable congressional disquiet about advice to presidents. The politics of advice in America became controversial as a result of two fundamental changes: the democratization of the presidency under Andrew Jackson and the institutionalization of the presidency under Franklin D. Roosevelt (FDR).

The democratization of the presidency prompted the presidentialization of American government. In 1787 the Founding Fathers designed constitutional arrangements that intended the forces of democracy to be safely neutralized by being channelled through the elaborate institutional filters of state and federal legislatures. They had not anticipated that the masses would find more effective representation by channelling demands through the oligarch of the oligarchies, the president.[11] The masses 'captured' the presidency, and gave presidents the chance to colonize the political system.

In 1829, 'King Andrew the First',[12] denied the presidency by the 'magnates' in 1824,[13] became President of the United States by 'acclamation' of the people. Jackson was the first popularly elected president.[14] His incumbency introduced a change in the nature of the American political system. The Jackson era was designated that of 'the rise of the common man', and according to Binkley, 'this common man was beginning to look to the one official of the federal government who was not only chosen by his vote but could speak the voice of the people of the whole nation.'[15] The president was forced to find ways of circumventing anti-democratic constitutional restraints in order to substantiate his claim to be the 'tribune of the people'.

Whilst it was clearly the intention of those gathered at Philadelphia to create a strong executive[16] to check the unrestrained power of popular assemblies, what is unclear is the interpretation placed upon the words 'strong' and 'energetic'. The opening words of Article II Section 1 of the Constitution: 'The executive Power shall be vested in a President of the United States of America' can at best be regarded negatively: executive power was to be in the president and nowhere else. The substance of the office, its power and authority, was left to the practice of future incumbents and the process of challenge and response that could be expected to ensue.

The Constitution then left much that could be contested between the executive and legislature. But the debate or conflict this initiated was not a problem to be solved, but a permanent energising force in the system:

The doctrine of the separation of powers was adopted by the convention of 1787, not to promote efficiency but to preclude the exercise of arbitrary power. The purpose was not to avoid friction, but, by means of the inevitable friction incident to the distribution of the government powers among three departments, to save the people from autocracy.[17]

The constitution-makers did not spell out what was to be the motor force of government; the constitution was silent on the questions of what was to be the source of legislative initiative. A written constitution cannot be too long if it is to be presented to the people for ratification, but such detail would in any case be unnecessary among a group of politicians who shared an understanding about how constitutional government worked.[18] Madison's discussion of factions in 'Federalist Paper X' would seem to imply an assumption that factions would lobby state and federal legislatures, and that the president would be responsible for executing the laws that emerged from this process. There is no indication that the initiative for legislation was expected to arise through the presidency. Hamilton clearly distinguished between tasks appropriate to the legislature and those appropriate to the executive:

The essence of legislative authority is to enact laws, or in other words to prescribe rules for the regulation of the society; while the execution of the laws and the employment of the common strength, either for this purpose or the common defence, seem to comprise all the functions of the executive magistrate.[19]

The president then, was expected to preside over the federal government, not to be its motor. The president was expected to be '. . . its chief executive, but an executive in the eighteenth century sense of one who executes the laws which are the will of another, and not in the modern sense of the active manager of an enterprise who makes its day-to-day decisions and plans for its future.'[20] What brought about a transformation in the nature of the presidency? What changed the president from an eighteenth century chief executive into an active interventionist manager? According to Binkley,

It was the awaking of the American masses in the 1820's, their revolt against what they considered the failure of a government dominated by the rural and urban gentry entrenched in Congress, to satisfy their need and their consequent turning with passionate devotion to a party messiah in Andrew Jackson, that ended the hegemony of Congress

. . . The common man found the presidency to be the most convenient organ for achieving its desires, and it has ever since turned to the presidency for redress of grievances.[21]

Jackson was the embodiment of what was to become the 'American Dream'. He made the transition from humble beginnings, the log cabin, to the most prestigious house in the land. Whilst it is true that the transition involved the long process of soldiering and money-making in the interim, Jackson was not by birth part of the aristocracy of wealth. He was closer to the people than any of his predecessors and saw himself as the special defender of the plebian interest.[22] Though by temperament a democrat, Jackson's economic doctrine was *laissez-faire*. He was against government economic intervention. He did not believe in positive economic policy to promote the well-being of the masses, but he strongly objected to what he perceived to be the contemporary practice of the government adopting economic policies that favoured the privileged few. His stand on economic affairs provided the impetus for institutional innovation. President Washington had seen the cabinet as an institution for reconciling antagonistic economic interests.[23] Jackson, however, wanted to surround himself with men who shared his conviction that '. . . economic problems, and the balance of class power, overshadowed all other questions of the day'.[24] To this end he reorganized his cabinet in 1831, but this failed to transform it into a united team convinced as to the merits of his programme. He therefore sought alternative advice and support and found it in a group of like-minded friends, soon pejoratively christened the 'kitchen cabinet' by his political opponents.[25]

Jackson's 'kitchen cabinet' became an object of deep suspicion. It was criticized for being '. . . an influence at Washington . . . unknown to the Constitution and to the country'.[26] Amos Kendall, in particular, was singled out for criticism. Kendall had come from nowhere. He was a provincial newspaperman having neither political pedigree nor wider constituency. Complaints were raised that, though officially given an appointment as Fourth Auditor of the Treasury, he was rarely to be found in his office, the implication being that he was occupied elsewhere as Jackson's closest adviser. In 1838 an exasperated Representative, Henry A. Wise, said in the House that Kendall was '. . . the President's thinking machine, and his writing machine – aye and his lying machine . . . he was chief overseer, chief reporter, amanuensis, scribe, accountant, general man of all work . . . '.[27] This was a view endorsed in 1840 by the aging John Quincy Adams, who observed of Jackson and Van Buren:'both. . . have been for twelve years the tool of Amos Kendall, the ruling mind of their dominion'.[28] The close relationship between Andrew Jackson and

Amos Kendall, chief executive and newspaperman (or former newspaperman), established a precedent that was to be repeated in the future on both sides of the Atlantic.[29]

The place of the presidency in the American constitutional system may be said to have been the outstanding constitutional question posed by the incumbency of Jackson.[30] The office was transformed into the agency of the common man and the president was forced to employ novel means of working within constitutional constraints[31] if he was to meet the new demands placed upon the executive resulting from this shift that had taken place within the political system. The Founding Fathers had not anticipated the presidency would come to be seen as the prize of the parties, let alone that it would be a prize bestowed by the people. The fear of democracy, once so threatening in the state legislatures, with the incumbency of Jackson was transferred to the presidency. If the president had become the dominant source of public policy, then the question of who advised, and who was entitled to advise, the president became the most pressing constitutional issue.

The presidency became the focus of democratic pressure which prompted an expansion of executive power. This in turn provoked opposition within the legislature. A period of oscillation between energetic presidents and assertive Congresses ensued. Between Jackson and Lincoln, with a series of 'weaker' incumbents, Congress held the executive in check but failed to regain lost ground. Abraham Lincoln introduced a new period of executive energy. Elected at a time of national emergency and imminent civil war, he resorted to the novel doctrine of presidential 'war powers', and built upon the presidency enlarged by Jackson. Though Lincoln did not surround himself with a coterie of unofficial advisers, he did extend the executive territory, and this gave questions about advice added significance when successors to his office continued to build on precedents set by him, but turned to less legitimate sources of advice. Lincoln's assassination ushered in a renewed period of insurgency by the legislature, and Congress was able to regain command over the political arena. It was not until Vice-President Theodore Roosevelt succeeded to office after the assassinated President William McKinley in 1901, that this trend was reversed.

Theodore Roosevelt was a romantic nationalist who extolled the virtues of the soldier and the frontiersman and cast himself in the role of the austere warrior waging a moral crusade against fat materialism and the trusts. Roosevelt believed in enlightened capitalism and used the presidency to take on both big business and labour. To this end Roosevelt pressed for reform in his Square Deal programme.

Roosevelt cited constitutional precedents for his interventionist role by adopting views of the presidency that were in the Hamiltonian tradition:[32]

> I decline to adopt the view that what was imperatively necessary for the Nation, could not be done by the President unless he could find some specific authorization to do it. My belief was that it was not only his right but his duty to do anything that the needs of the Nation demanded unless such action was forbidden by the Constitution or by the laws. Under this interpretation of executive power I did and caused to be done many things not previously done by the President and the heads of the departments.[33]

This claim that the president's prerogative also derived from residual powers about which the Constitution was silent, provided justification for Roosevelt to pioneer presidential leadership in legislation: 'in theory the executive has nothing to do with legislation; in practice, as things now are, the executive is or ought to be peculiarly representative of the people as a whole.'[34]

Roosevelt also pioneered the use of public pressure to bully the Congress. In his autobiography he claims he 'tried to get along with Congress', found it was impossible, and so '. . . appealed over the heads of the Congress to the people, who are the masters of both the Congress and the President.'[35] This was a stratagem that was to be considerably enlarged and refined by his cousin, Franklin D. Roosevelt. It was, indeed, the foundation upon which the imperial presidency was built: the president claiming that a mandate from the electorate at large gave him the right to ride rough-shod over other institutions.

FDR is credited with being the creator of the modern presidency. National crisis followed by war provided a unique opportunity for presidential leadership. FDR accepted the challenge and sought the wherewithal to enable the president to meet his new responsibilities. In doing so he institutionalized the presidency and permanently transformed the power ratio between president and Congress. It was FDR who completed the process of presidentializing American government that had continued intermittently since the days of Andrew Jackson.

By the 1930s the minimal programme for government envisaged by the Founding Fathers in the eighteenth century[36] had been transformed by civil war, economic crisis and international interdependency, so that by the twentieth century governments were held responsible for ensuring the survival of capitalism and expected to deliver a wide variety of services. Solutions to complex problems in modern society, it seemed, could not be left to the vagaries of the market-place. Citizens' expectations of government rose and the executive branches of national government appeared best placed to initiate and coordinate rapid responses and shoulder new responsibilities. Like the states of old Europe, America was not immune to these trends. When Roosevelt became president in 1932 he took over the job on almost the same formal terms as that prescribed by the Founding Fathers in 1787, but one vastly changed in political terms. The president's range of responsibilities was increasing dramatically, but the resources at his disposal to meet new demands and expectations had not changed in proportion since the late eighteenth century.

The convergence of several forces account for the remarkable transformation in the role of the presidency effected by Roosevelt. In the first place, dire economic crisis followed by war virtually paralysed Congressional initiative. In addition, Roosevelt developed *ad hoc* administrative procedures for the collection of data, publishing of proposals, drafting of bills and steering of them through Congress, all of which served to expedite his programme. Thirdly, Roosevelt developed to a fine art the skill of persuading Congressmen to concur with his proposals: if political sympathy failed to elicit sufficient supporters, the patronage and 'pork barrel', greatly increased by the New Deal, might serve to seduce others. If these methods proved inadequate, Roosevelt coerced the legislators by means of public pressure. He used his 'Fireside Chats' to arouse public opinion in favour of his policies. The public would in turn lobby their congressmen. Lastly, Roosevelt increased the institutional support for the president by persuading Congress to accept the recommendations of the Brownlow Report and pass the impeccably constitutional Reorganization Act 1939, which created the Executive Office of the President (EOP), providing the presidency with a bureaucracy to facilitate performance of its greatly increased responsibilities. In particular the WHO, which was to be part of the EOP, confirmed the dominant role of the presidency in the political system. It formalized the existence of 'kitchen cabinets' and it legitimized the role of a number of individuals close to, and influential with, the president.

The WHO was an institutional but at the same time *ad hoc* attempt to aid a president facing government departments resistant to new initiatives and radical policies. The WHO was not expected to have a policy-making role. Brownlow in his report, and Executive Order 8248, went to great lengths to constrain the role of the new administrative assistants in relation to policy matters.

The President needs help. His immediate staff assistance is entirely inadequate. He should be given a small number of executive assistants who would be his direct aides in dealing with the management agencies and administrative departments of the government . . . These aides would have no power to make decisions or issue instructions in their own right. They would not be interposed between the President and the heads of his departments. They would not be Assistant Presidents . . They would remain in the background, issue no orders, make no decisions, emit no public statements. Men for these positions should be carefully chosen by the President from within and without the government . . . They should be possessed of high competence, great physical vigour and a passion for anonymity.[37]

Such expectations were based on the false premise that policy initiatives and making the machinery of government work, could be separated, and on the notion that 'gate-keeping' is simply a neutral activity of making sure that vital presidential time is wisely spent. The WHO in the post-Brownlow period has increased its power in the political arena, has acquired significant policy-making powers and at the same time provided presidents with the means of legitimating cronies and campaign aides by assigning them positions in the WHO.[38] Theodore Sorensen's description of the role of WHO staff during Kennedy's administration is a far cry from the limited expectations of Brownlow:

Two dozen or more Kennedy assistants gave him two dozen or more sets of hands, eyes and ears, two dozen or more minds attuned to his own. They could talk with legislators, newsmen, experts, Cabinet members, politicians – serve on inter-departmental task forces – review papers and draft speeches, letters and other documents – spot problems before they were crises and possibilities before they were proposals – screen requests for legislation, Executive Orders, jobs, appointments with the President, patronage and presidential speeches – and bear his messages, look out for his interests, carry out his orders and make certain his decisions were executed.[39]

All too soon the solution became, if not part of the problem, at the very least the cause of a new set of problems. Roosevelt was able to avoid the problems of bureaucratization of the WHO partly as a result of his own style of what Koenig describes as 'competitive administration',[40] in which he played off different advisers one against the other. Roosevelt is said to have liked creative tension. He used his aides as extra eyes and ears to provide information but, by making each answerable to only himself, and frequently changing their areas of responsibility, he denied them the chance of constructing their own power bases or 'going into business for themselves'. His practice of divide and rule enabled him to retain the power of decision.

During the Eisenhower presidency, disquiet was already being voiced about the role of Special Assistant to the President, Sherman Adams, and he was soon referred to pejoratively as 'Assistant President'.[41] Concern came to be expressed about the fact that growth in the power of the presidential establishment had largely been at the expense of traditional sources of executive power and policy making, the cabinet members and their departments. Presidential cabinets had never acquired the status of their British namesake: few of their members were well known political figures and they did not share collective responsibility for the executive. As presidents turned more to their White House team the status of the cabinet declined further. According to Cronin 'several of President Kennedy's cabinet members regularly battled with White House aides who blocked them from seeing the President.'[42] Cabinet secretaries began to feel as if they were simply the salesmen of policies made by presidential advisers who barely had the courtesy to pretend to consult the departments.

The tenure of Franklin Roosevelt was obviously the decisive turning point in the role of the presidency in the political system. Roosevelt made effective use of public opinion to overcome the resistance of other institutions. By the end of his long tenure, the presidency exercised a vast range of powers unimagined by the constitution-makers, and against which the hackneyed old institutional checks and balances were no longer effective. Roosevelt left a presidency with much greater opportunities for abuse of power in the future, so leaving a time bomb in the shape of sources of advice. Brownlow's institutional reforms left the presidency better provided with administrative support but failed to ensure that advice would be legitimized by being visible, and, therefore, at least notionally accountable.

The legacy of FDR was an institutionally expanded presidency which implicitly recognized that the chief executive of the written constitution had become the chief legislator of the unwritten constitution. The presidential advisory system that FDR established can be described as a 'wheel model'(see appendix). It was accepted that the president at the hub would receive advice from a wide range of competing sources, all of which were assumed to be part of the wider policy-making community, and none of which had claim to exclusive right of advice.

Under Roosevelt the new institutional arrangements served to increase the range and sources of presidential advice and assistance; under subsequent incumbents it served to replace traditional sources and to insulate the president from knowledge of realities which would have been gained by more direct contact with other policy constituencies. Schlesinger, for instance, points out that under Nixon

White House aides were no longer channels of communication. They were powerful figures in themselves, making decisions and issuing instructions in their own right, more powerful than members of the Cabinet. Henry Kissinger was more powerful than the Secretary of State or Secretary for Defence, Haldeman and Ehrlichman were more powerful than the forgotten men who headed domestic departments. But they were not, like members of the Cabinet, subject to confirmation by the Senate or to interrogations by committees of the Congress.[43]

The history of the presidency then, has been one of an accretion, even if spasmodic, of power and responsibility. A large share of the impetus for this has arisen from a combination of, on the one hand, electoral pressures of the masses seeking, and finding, a more effective channel through which to press their demands, and on the other hand a series of office-holders willing to accept this new role and seeking the power to perform it. A president at the centre now shoulders responsibilities well beyond the scope of his original constitutional power to deliver. Incumbents have been forced to 'push' the constitution to its limits in their attempt to bridge this gap.

One source of power which has placed the executive at an advantage *vis-à-vis* the institutions designed to check and balance it, is what George Reedy describes as ' . . . the ability . . . to make commitments which could not easily be revoked'.[44] Another measure to which president's have resorted has been an expansive, 'creative' use of the veto power in order to prevent Congress passing unwelcome measures, or in threatening to veto measures dear to Congress's heart in order to expedite the passage of bills desired by the president. Presidents have also been forced to exploit the inviting elasticity of constitutional language in order to justify presidential initiatives in legislation. Interpreting Article II Section 3 of the Constitution,

> He shall from time to time give to the Congress Information of the State of the Union, and recommend to their consideration such Measures as he shall judge necessary and expedient. . .

as the constitutional authority for executive initiative in legislation, using the 'speech from the throne' to recommend specific legislative proposals for Congress's 'consideration'. In addition, Congress has undoubtedly colluded in the process of aggrandizement of the executive. Apathy or lack of taste for shouldering new burdens on the part of the legislature has facilitated executive imperialism.[45]

Congress's accommodation of the executive in respect of legislation can, however, partly be attributed to 'compulsory co-operation'. Presidents have become adept in the use of public opinion to appeal over the heads of Congress and the Court[46] to enforce their cooperation. Binkley points out that 'the President's power in shaping policy and getting policy translated into statutes is chiefly the power of publicity rather than power invested in him by the letter of the Constitution.'[47] It was the first Roosevelt who stumbled upon the effectiveness of using the news media as a tool for persuading recalcitrant congressmen to support his programme, an asset honed to perfection by his cousin, Franklin. Greenstein notes:

> Roosevelt was heard over the radio and seen through newsreels. Eisenhower was the first president to employ a White House television consultant. Kennedy was the first gifted television president. Reagan innovated further, using state-of-the-art techniques to make himself a ubiquitous media presence. During Reagan's tenure it came to appear that 'going public' had replaced bargaining among Washington actors as the engine of presidential leadership.[48]

In the post-war era concern has arisen about the overt use of this asset. Many of the president's new powers rely on demonstrating that they have public support. This has made the president a hostage to the pollster and image-makers, privy to the secrets of public opinion manipulation and presidential image enhancement. The presidentialization of American government is in part attributable to the democratization of the presidency and the claim by presidents that they speak for the nation. Woodrow Wilson once hailed the presidency's capacity to speak with the 'Voice of the People':

> His is the only national voice in affairs. Let him once win the admiration and confidence of the country, and no other single force can withstand him, no combination of forces will easily over-power him. His position takes the imagination of the country . . . If he rightly interprets the national thought and boldly insists upon it, he is irresistible.[49]

Substantiating this claim to be the 'voice of the people' has necessitated institutional support, 'eyes' and 'ears' to transmit and process the 'nation's will' to the president; but it has also necessitated a means for communicating, and justifying, the president's responses. It was in response to the former need that the EOP was created in 1939; in attempting to address the latter need, presidents have come to rely increasingly on the expertise of public relations professionals able to orchestrate public opinion and enhance and exploit the public image of the president.

The post-war period witnessed a disintegration at national level of the American party system.[50] Research in California indicated that people's opinions were influenced less by political parties, churches, trade unions and the like; instead opinions were increasingly formed by exposure to television. John F. Kennedy was the first presidential candidate to utilize this new knowledge when he ran for the White House in 1960. In doing so he ushered in an era of media politics which has led to an emphasis on image and style at the expense of substance and depth. The message has become tailored to the medium. 'Sound bites' and photo-opportunities substitute for policy and programme. Exposure to the rough and tumble of the hustings is replaced by a safe, and carefully orchestrated, monologue. The candidate becomes hermetically sealed behind a TV screen and a phalanx of media men.[51] Political brokerage, formerly performed by the old institutions of party, cabinet, line departments and congressmen, becomes the prerogative of a new breed of functionary injected into presidential politics from the outside – advertizing and marketing specialists and opinion manipulators, whose comprehension of, and commitment to, the assumptions and practices of democratic politics may be frail. The political indebtedness of presidents, therefore, on entering the White House, is not to political machines, or intermediary institutions having recognized constituencies, but to campaign financiers and 'ad-men' who have facilitated their rites of passage. The key staff with which the new incumbent surrounds himself tend to be the 'heroes of the campaign'. Nixon's appointment of H.R. Haldeman, his chief advance man of the 1968 campaign, as his White House chief of staff demonstrates the dangers inherent in this practice. Theodore White points out that

> In the campaign there is no conflict between ends and means. The end is to win victory, and, as in war, the means do not matter - deception, lying, intelligence operations are common in all campaigns; a campaign is no place for the squeamish. But what happens . . . when advance men become the government? What happens when they all sit in the same room in Washington and the President trusts them and nobody is squeamish, nobody is there to say 'wait a minute, is it right or wrong?'.[52]

Presidents may become isolated within a circle of advisers who

> Typically are young people with few obligations and limited experience
> who will gamble for a chance on a ticket to the White House. . . .
> Most candidates will do as Carter did and take his campaign staff to
> the White House with them. And they will find . . . that these aides
> are people who are more adept at, and more interested in, running the
> campaign than they are in running a government.[53]

This is a view supported by the prominent role played in the White House
by Jody Powell, President Carter's resident press secretary[54] and the
similar prominence of Michael Deaver[55] who oversaw President Reagan's
diary and coordinated appointments to meet the dictates of his publicity.

The decline of party and the advent of 'tele-democracy' has led to a
union between the new institutional structures erected to provide policy
inputs and the new breed of advisers upon whom presidents have come to
rely. The 'ad-men' and pollsters have colonized the WHO. They not only
determine what image the public receives of the president but they also
determine what and whom the president will see, the result being that'...
political decisions are made on the basis of one criterion: what is best for
the political standing, prestige, reputation and re-election of the
President.'[56] If it is assumed that the president's effective power is a
function of his standing in the polls, then it is inevitable that it is to the
pollsters and image manipulators that he turns for advice.

The presidentialization of American government occurred in response
to democratic pressure. A faction of the majority, frustrated by institutions
and procedures deliberately designed to divide and rule its will, found an
alternative input to the political process through the presidency. Accepting
the role of representative of the majority, the president was then obliged
to find ways of circumventing the checks and balances intended, not only
to obstruct majority rule, but also, to prevent the exercise of extra-
constitutional power by the executive. Electoral pressure impelled the
president to subvert the Constitution in favour of the democracy the
Founding Fathers feared. This was achieved by assuming new
responsibilities and taking over some of the functions allocated by the
original Constitution to other institutions. These additional powers claimed
by the executive were legitimated, not by Constitutional authority, but by
public support. This in turn gave rise to new methods of measuring public
opinion, and birth to a new group of professionals expert in their use. The
democratic legitimation of the presidency, however, makes it worth
lobbying by interest groups. The president, therefore, needed additional
'eyes' and 'ears' to process the inputs from lobbyists: a new presidential
advisory system was created in the White House to meet this need. At the
same time television hastened the demise of traditional intermediary

channels.

The Nixon presidency represented a culmination of this process. The new presidential advisory system created by FDR had become bureaucratized and its inner-most circle peopled by the president's cronies and creatures who rushed to the barricades against the legitimate policy-making community. Cabinet members were relegated to the role of salesmen for policies decided elsewhere. Cabinet, party, bureaucracy, congressional leaders and the media were forced to inhabit the outer circles having little or no access to an increasingly invisible president.[57]

During the Nixon presidency a 'corrupted model'(see appendix) of the presidential advisory system emerged, in which Haldeman and Ehrlichman became a 'Berlin Wall'[58] that insulated and isolated the president from the rest of the policy-making community.[59]

What model of an evolving presidential advisory system does the above analysis provide?

1. The American Constitution vested executive power in the president but said little about advice; advice was not a pressing constitutional question. There was an unwritten assumption that executive power would be exercised on the advice of other institutions, particularly Congress, which, it was assumed, would be the source of legislative initiative.

2. A perceived failure of the institutions of representative government, the legislature, prompts a search for alternative channels of input into the political system. The presidency becomes the institution of democracy.

3. The democratization of the presidency prompts a presidentialization of American government.

4. The president's new responsibilities give rise to a need for additional sources of advice and assistance. The presidency becomes institutionalized and the WHO legitimizes 'kitchen cabinets' of personal political aides.

5. A 'wheel model' advisory system emerges according to which it is accepted that the president at the hub will be bombarded with advice down every spoke from a wide variety of sources.

6. The president needed to acquire new powers to fulfil his new role. Accumulation of power was legitimized, not by constitutional authority, but by public support. Public appeal is used to coerce the cooperation of other institutions in the political system.

7. Professionals develop expertise in the understanding of, and management of, public opinion.

8. The inner circles of the new presidential advisory system soon become controlled by those able to correlate the presidential image with public support. Traditional sources of advice are forced into the outer circles, having little or no access to the man in the White House.
9. The evolving presidential advisory system has a potential for presidential isolation and may give rise to a 'corrupt model'. The man in the White House may become the captive of his cronies and creatures, who, lacking wider legitimacy, have a vested interest in reassuring their patron that he can ignore other institutions with impunity and rule alone. Questions about advice then acquire constitutional significance.

Having constructed a model of the evolving American presidential advisory system we can now return to our examination of the British system, and in particular, the advisory systems of four British prime ministers who held office between 1964 and 1990. What kind of changes did they introduce in the prime ministerial advisory system? Did the changes arouse the kind of controversy and public fuss that signals constitutional change is occuring? Can similarities be discerned between the changes in the prime ministerial adivsory and the kind of changes that took place in the presidential advisory system as it evolved to meet the needs of the modern president?

Notes

1. Fulbright, J.W., (Senator) 'The Decline and Possible Fall of Constitutional Democracy in America' in Bach, Stanley and Sulzner, George, T., eds *Perspectives on the Presidency* (New York: D.C.Heath & Co., 1974) pp. 355–64, p. 357.
2. It specified that important executive appointments would be made with the advice and consent of the Senate but in other respects the position with regard to sources of presidential assistance and advice was left more implicit than explicit by the Founding Fathers. Whilst rejecting the developing British model of cabinet government within the legislature, some had wished to establish a presidential advisory council. There was no reference to either a council, cabinet or any other collective institution to aid the president, in the Constitution submitted for ratification. Article II Section 2 stated that the president 'may require the Opinion, in writing, of the principal Officer in each of the executive Departments, upon any Subject relating to the Duties of their respective Offices.' George Washington began consulting with his department heads collectively and this gave rise to the convention

of a presidential cabinet.
3. Congressional investigation exposed the involvement of people on the White House pay-roll in the illegal entering and bugging of the Democratic presidential candidate's campaign headquarters, in the Watergate Building, Washington. Controversy raged concerning the extent of the president's personal involvement.
4. Koenig, Louis W., *The Chief Executive* 5th edn (New York: Harcourt Brace Janovich, 1986) p. 80.
5. Neustadt, Richard E., *Presidential Power – Politics of Leadership with Reflections on Johnson and Nixon* (New York: Wiley & Sons, 1976) p. 101.
6. See Cronin, Thomas, 'A Resurgent Congress and the Imperial Presidency' *Political Science Quarterly* Vol.95, No.2, Summer 1980, pp. 209–37, particularly pp. 211–16.
7. Cronin, Thomas, 'The Swelling Presidency' in Bach and Sulzner, op.cit., pp. 179–89, p. 179.
8. The very existence of, or at least legitimacy of, the doctrine of executive privilege has informed much of the dialectic between the executive and legislature. Presidents have claimed, and Congress rejected, that certain kinds of information fall within the scope of executive privilege and are thus beyond the reach of Congressional investigation. The written constitution is silent about this matter, but presidents have invoked this doctrine ever since George Washington protested the investigation by Congress of the Saint Clair expedition during his first term. The first official use of the term 'executive privilege' is attributed to Attorney General William P Rogers in 1958, when he attempted a comprehensive justification of the increasing practice of denying Congress access to records and documents. The doctrine, by placing limits on information available, limited Congress's ability to advise the executive and influence policy. Richard Nixon claimed executive privilege extended to all members of his personal staff past and present and used it to justify none surrender of tape recordings of discussions with his White House staff, to the Watergate hearings. Executive privilege, once confined to 'national security' matters, now seemed to extend to everything else, including tenure of presidential aides. For a full discussion of 'executive privilege' see Schlesinger, Arthur, Jr., *The Imperial Presidency* 2nd edn (Boston: Houghton Miffen Co., 1989) p. 158, and Vile, M.J.C., *American Historical Documents: The Presidency* (London: Harrap, 1976) pp. 130–1.
9. Cronin, 'The Swelling Presidency', op.cit., p. 181.

10. Schlesinger, *The Imperial Presidency* op.cit., p. 273. Lewis J. Paper, a Nixon aide acknowledged that 'during the time I served in the White House I rarely questioned a presidential order. Infrequently did I question the President's judgment. I had one rule – to get done that which the President wanted done.' Cit. Koenig, *The Chief Executive* op.cit., p. 197.

11. An exception being Gouveneur Morris, who spoke of the executive as 'the guardian of the people' against the tyranny of the 'great and wealthy who in the course of things will necessarily compose the legislative body.' Cit. Rossiter, Clinton, *The American Presidency* 2nd edn (London: Harvest Books, 1960) p. 88.

12. A pejorative title bestowed on President Andrew Jackson by members of the 'Whig' opposition in Congress.

13. In 1824 the electoral college produced no clear winner. Of the four candidates Jackson won a plurality of the popular vote and ninety-nine electoral college votes. John Quincy Adams gained eighty-four electoral college votes   William H. Crawford and Henry Clay receiving forty-one and thirty-seven respectively. Since none of the four polled a majority in the Electoral College, the choice had to be made by the House of Representatives from among the three leading candidates. Clay, who had come in forth was thus eliminated from the competition, serious illness forced Crawford to withdraw. The choice was, therefore between Adams and Jackson. When the House voted backstairs politicking ensured Adams of a majority.

14. The Constitution ratified in 1787 had prescribed the indirect election of the president. The president was to be elected by an electoral college, the members of which would be chosen in a manner directed by state legislatures (Article II Section 1). Whilst initially electors had been chosen by the state legislatures, the enlargement of the Union led to a democratization of electoral practices. In 1800 only six out of sixteen states held popular elections for choosing electors. By 1828 South Carolina was the only one out of twenty-four in which the legislature still performed this function. The development of political parties served to further subvert the electoral college. Electors soon ceased to be representatives exercising their own political judgement and wisdom as envisaged by the constitution-makers and became delegates, or automatons, casting all their votes for the first-past-the-post candidate in their respective states. By 1800 it was common practice for electors to be chosen on the basis of their pledge to vote for the candidate of a particular party and this practice soon became a convention of the unwritten constitution. By the middle of the nineteenth century every state had adopted the state-wide ticket system

which gives all the state's electoral votes to the candidate with a simple majority state wide.

15. Binkley, Wilfred, E., *President and Congress* (New York: Vintage Books, 1962) p. 103.

16. See Hamilton, Alexander, 'Federalist Paper LXX', *The Federalist Papers* (London: Penguin, 1987) p. 402.

17. Justice Brandeis cit. Bach and Sulzner eds op.cit., p. 359.

18. The Founding Fathers could draw upon a wealth of experience and tradition: a heritage of British constitutional and political arrangements; the experiences of five generations of colonial assemblies; the drafting of state constitutions and the rudiments of national government under the Articles.

19. Hamilton, 'Federalist Paper LXXV', op.cit., p. 425.

20. McClelland, J.S., *The Crowd and the Mob* (London: Unwin, 1989) p. 107.

21. Binkley, Wilfred, E., *The Man in the White House* (New York: Greenwood Press, 1978) p. 149.

22. Opinion borne out by his inauguration celebrations: an occasion on which, according to some eye witnesses, a mob ran riot through the White House. Events which prompted Justice Story to comment 'The reign of King "Mob" seemed triumphant'. Cit. Schlesinger, Arthur M. Jr., *The Age of Jackson* (Boston: Little Brown & Co., 1945) p. 4.

23. As was demonstrated by his appointment of Jefferson to one post and Hamilton to another.

24. Schlesinger, *Age of Jackson* op.cit., p. 66.

25. Though not a cabinet in a formal sense, more an informal shifting group of men in whom Jackson had confidence, including Martin Van Buren, Major William B Lewis (who lived in the White House) Francis Preston Blair of Kentucky, who came to Washington to edit the *Washington Globe* as an Administration organ; Isaac Hill, editor of the *New Hampshire Patriot*; and Amos Kendall, whom Jackson appointed Fourth Auditor of the Treasury.

26. Schlesinger, *Age of Jackson* op.cit., p. 67.

27. Cit. ibid., p. 72.

28. Cit. ibid., p. 73.

29. For example, Richard Nixon and Ronald Ziegler; Winston Churchill and Lord Beaverbrook; Harold Wilson and Joe Haines, and Margaret Thatcher and Bernard Ingham.

30. Binkley, *President and Congress* op.cit., p. 84.

31. Increased use of the veto, powers of appointment and dismissal etc.

32. 'The general doctrine of our constitution, then, is that the Executive power of the nation is vested in the President, subject only to the exceptions and qualifications which are expressed in the instrument.' Alexander Hamilton cit. Binkley, *President and Congress* op.cit., p. 236.
33. Cit. Haight, David E. and Johnson, Larry D., eds *The Presidents Roles and Powers* (New York: Rand McNulty & Co., 1965) p. 128.
34. Theodore Roosevelt cit. Binkley Wilfred E., 'The President as Chief Legislator' in Bach and Sulzner, op. cit., pp. 302–19, p. 304.
35. Cit. ibid., p. 306, see also p. 305.
36. In the eighteenth century governments were generally expected to maintain law and order at home and provide protection against aggression from abroad. The expectations of the Founding Fathers were minimal even by these standards in that they envisaged the United States to have only limited requirements for foreign policy.
37. Brownlow Report, cit., Vile, J.M.C., *The Politics of the USA* 4th edn (London: Unwin, 1987) pp. 205–6.
38. Hart notes that the White House soon became '. . . a dumping ground for campaign specialists who were given specially created jobs to keep them occupied for four years. One doubts, for example, that the jobs and titles President Carter bestowed on WHO staffers Peter Bourne (Special Assistant for Health Issues) Joseph Aragon (Ombudsman) and Grey Schneiders (Special Assistant for Special Projects) had much to do with the day to day work of WHO.' Hart, D., 'The President and his Staff' in Shaw, Malcolm, ed. *Roosevelt to Reagan: Development of the Modern Presidency* (New York; C. Hurst & Co., 1987) p. 173.
39. Theodore Sorensen, cit., Vile, *The Politics of the USA* op.cit., p. 202.
40. Koenig, *The Chief Executive* op.cit., p. 184.
41. Vile notes that '. . . access to the president was channelled through Adams, who saw his function as that of 'shielding the president from problems that could be settled on the lower echelons', and assuring that the work of 'secondary importance' should be kept off the president's desk. Although Adams strongly denied that this position represented in any way a usurpation of authority, it inevitably meant that it was his judgement that determined what was, and what was not, of secondary importance.' Vile, *The Politics of the USA* op.cit., pp. 202-3.
42. McGeorge Bundy, Kennedy's chief assistant for national security affairs simply side-stepped the State Department in one main area of departmental communications. He had all important incoming State Department cables transmitted simultaneously to his office in the

White House. Under Nixon, Henry Kissinger, continued this practice and, Cronin points out that '. . . indeed we recently witnessed the bizarre and telling spectacle of Secretary of State, William Rogers, insisting that he did have a role in making foreign policy.' Cronin, 'The Swelling Presidency' op.cit., p. 182.

43. Schlesinger, *The Imperial Presidency,* op.cit., p. 222.
44. Reedy points out for instance, that although the constitution-makers balanced the president's power as commander-in-chief by granting power of supply to Congress, they had not reckoned with the president being able to coerce Congress's cooperation. He cites the example of Theodore Roosevelt forcing Congress to vote the required appropriations for a 'good will' world tour of the American fleet in 1907. See Reedy, George, *The Twilight of the Presidency* (New York: NAL Books, 1970) p. 37.
45. Cronin asserts that 'Congress, which has grown increasingly critical of the burgeoning power of the presidency, must take some of the blame itself for the expansion of the White House. Divided within itself and ill-equipped, or simply disinclined to make some of the nation's toughest political decisions in recent decades, Congress has abdicated more and more authority to the presidency.' Cronin, Thomas, 'The Swelling Presidency' op.cit., p. 187. See also Schlesinger *Imperial Presidency*, op.cit. pp. 326–7.
46. Lees points out that until FDR Presidents rarely challenged judicial authority directly but the conjunction of a popular, interventionist, Democratic President and a 'constitutional', predominantly Republican, Supreme Court provided the ingredients for conflict. Elected to the Presidency along with a large Democratic majority in both Houses of Congress, Roosevelt was given a mandate to deal with the domestic crisis. The Court saw itself in the role of protector of interests adversely affected by the New Deal legislation. The New Deal legislation did not percolate to the Court until January 1935, but in the sixteen months that followed the Court ruled eight out of ten cases considered against the Executive, including ruling, in May 1935, the National Recovery Act to be unconstitutional. After his 1936 electoral endorsement Roosevelt accepted a 'court packing' plan, ostensibly to relieve congestion. The necessary legislation was rejected by the Senate but the threat, it seemed, was sufficient to make the Court look more favourably on the New Deal programme. See Lees, D., *The President and the Court* (London: British Association for American Studies, 1980) p. 16.
47. Binkley, *President and Congress*, op.cit., p. 318.

48. Greenstein, Fred I., *Leadership in the Modern Presidency,* (Harvard: University Press, 1988) p. 348.
49. Cit. Koenig, *The Chief Executive,* op.cit., p. 91.
50. See Hodgson, Godfrey, 'After the Parties Break Up', *Independent* 17 June 1992, p. 23.
51. Nixon's 1968 campaign is a classic example of this kind of tightly controlled 'media-friendly' campaign. For a detailed account, see McGuinnis, Joe, *The Selling of the President 1968* (London: Trident, 1968).
52. White, Theodore, *Breach of Faith: the fall of Richard Nixon* (New York: Atheneum, 1975) p. 92.
53. Brodner, David S., 'Let 100 Single-Issue Groups Bloom' *Washington Post* 7 January, 1979, cit. Hodgson, Geoffrey *All Things to All Men* (New York: Simon & Schuster, 1980) p. 218. This is a view endorsed by, Chester et al, who point out that aside from Henry Kissinger '. . . there was nobody within close range of the President who could be remotely classed as an intellectual and, perhaps more important, even those with experience of elective office were at a premium . . . Lacking any experience in the exercise of political power or even the intellectual's capacity to speculate about it, their limited understanding of politics derived from the salesmanship of the campaign trail. They were . . . essentially apparatchiks - men whose destiny and identity depended on advancing the interests of a particular politician, President Richard Nixon. These were not necessarily the interests of the institution of the Presidency.' Chester Lewis et al, *Watergate: The Full Story* (London: Deutsch, 1973) p. 6. Richard J. Whalen, a conservative intellectual who had worked for Nixon in the preconvention stage of the 1968 campaign, lamented that 'The once-prestigious title of "Special Assistant to the President" was bestowed wholesale on ex-advance men who had proved their fitness to govern by releasing the balloons precisely at the moment that the candidate's arms shot skywards in a V.' cit. Chester, et al p. 7.
54. Carter also maintained a resident image adviser, Gerald Rafshoon, an Atlanta advertizing entrepreneur, who quickly acceded to the small circle of the President's closest senior advisers.
55. A former head of a California public relations firm and long time confidant of Reagan.
56. Hodgson, *All Things to All Men,* op.cit., p. 219.
57. See Koenig, Louis W., *The Invisible Presidency* (New York: Rinehart, 1960) pp. 15–22.

58. Chester et al, note that 'Haldeman and Ehrlichman were openly described by pressmen and politicians, of both parties alike, as "the two Germans". The isolation of the President himself was attributed to the construction of a "Berlin Wall" round him by his closest aides.' Chester et.al., op.cit., p. 13.

59. Theodore White points out that in the final days: 'In seclusion with his children, his wife and Bebe Rebozzo, Richard Nixon was seeing from outside almost no one but Ronald Ziegler [his press secretary] and Alexander Haig.' White, op.cit., p. 13.

4   Harold Wilson 1964-70: A Presidential Premier

I am rather against the idea of bringing in series of *éminences grises* or Rasputins or Court favourites to advise a Prime Minister.[1]

I resigned as a matter of fundamental principle, because it seemed to me that the Prime Minister was . . . introducing a 'presidential' system into the running of the Government that is wholly alien to the British constitutional system . . . and far too often outsiders in his entourage seemed to be almost the only effective 'Cabinet'.[2]

In retrospect the 1960s can be seen as marking a transition in the British political system. The growing dominance of the prime minister coincided with the advent of television politics to 'presidentialize' electoral politics in Britain in the American manner. Harold Wilson understood the implications of this. Prime ministers were becoming presidents in the eyes of the electorate but remained prime ministers according to the constitution. They were expected to bear an increasing individual share of responsibility for winning or losing elections, but their constitutional powers remained formally static and were shared collectively with their cabinet colleagues. In order to bridge this gap between the political and constitutional position of the prime minister Wilson changed the prime ministerial advisory system. This aroused public fuss and claims that constitutional propriety was not being observed, and provoked traditional advisers to 'counter-revolutionary' tactics in their attempt to safeguard their prerogative of advice. It ensured that controversy about advice became one of the hallmarks of the Wilson years.

On 15 March 1968 George Brown, Foreign Secretary in the Labour Government, resigned from his post in what seemed at the time to be a fit of pique[3] at being excluded from an emergency meeting of the Privy Council held in the early hours of that day.[4] In subsequent explanations for his behaviour, Brown claimed that it was constitutional principle, and not personal pique in response to a perceived slight by the prime minister, that prompted his action. In his resignation speech he implied that his premature departure from office could be attributed to the prime minister's leadership and ways of doing business. Brown asserted that '. . . it is essential for Cabinet Government to be maintained if democracy is to be assured. . . . Power can very easily pass not merely from the Cabinet to one or two Ministers, but effectively to sources quite outside the political control altogether.'[5] In his letter of resignation to the prime minister he maintained he was unable to remain in the government because of '. . . the way this Government is run, and the manner in which we reach our decisions.'[6] In his autobiography, discussing the events leading up to his resignation, Brown specifically accuses Wilson of introducing a presidential system and he implies that there had been a failure to observe constitutional propriety in the ways in which decisions were reached and the sources of advice upon which they were based.[7] Brown draws a distinction between legitimate advisers, 'insiders', and those of dubious legitimacy, 'outsiders'. He goes on to explain more fully his particular problems with Wilson's conduct of government and his (Brown's) misgivings about innovations in the advisory system:

> I came to feel that Mr Wilson preferred something akin to the presidential system, that he really did prefer to have his own outfit at No.10, rather like the way in which the President in the United States has his own outfit in the White House. In my view, one of the arguments against the White House system . . . is that it places too much power in the hands of one man. It also places power where it shouldn't be, in the hands of friends or unofficial advisers to the President or Prime Minister, who are not accountable to Congress or Parliament while reducing the real Cabinet to the levels the others should occupy. And indeed, the greater the pressures . . . the greater the chances are that the effective decisions will be taken by these friends or unofficial advisers.[8]

Brown's explanations of, and justifications for, his resignation were, then, couched in constitutional terms. He was claiming that the prime minister was acting unconstitutionally, the assumption being that constitutional government in Britain was cabinet government predicated on known and accepted principles and rules of procedure. Cabinet government rested on the principle of collective responsibility. Ministers were collectively responsible for, and publicly bound to defend, cabinet decisions. It was accepted that such decisions were based upon civil service advice and agreed after full and confidential discussion in cabinet. George Brown claimed such procedure was no longer being observed. British cabinet ministers were coming to resemble their American counterparts: they were being reduced to the role of salesmen for policies determined elsewhere.[9] Ministers were still answerable in the public arena; they were expected to defend decisions which they had not been party to but which had been made by the prime minister based on advice from unofficial and unaccountable sources.

At the time Brown's was a lone voice crying in the political wilderness,[10] the subsequent publication of diaries and biographies of his cabinet colleagues[11] has gone some way towards substantiating Brown's claims. Such accounts are liberally sprinkled with disgruntled complaints about Harold Wilson's conduct of cabinet relations. At the time of Brown's resignation Crossman, for instance, grumbles about the disadvantages of being excluded from the conversation of government:

> If I was ever to resign it would be precisely because I can't stand the way cabinet is run. It's because of Harold's inability to create a firm inner group with whom to work consistently, and his determination to keep bilateral relationships with each one of us, and arbitrarily leave us out of absolutely vital conversations just because we don't happen to be in No.10 or because we're out of favour that afternoon.[12]

As early as January 1965, Crossman complained that despite being a member of the cabinet he did not learn of the cancellation of the TSR2 project until he read about it in the press, and he asserts that it had probably been discussed and decided at Chequers '. . . with George Wigg and his pals present and people like me completely excluded.'[13] In July 1966 he further complained that Wilson conducted the government by:

> . . . arbitrating between George Brown and Callaghan, and in every other field retaining the right of final decision and, in this particular crisis [run on sterling] working directly with Permanent Secretaries behind the backs of their Ministers. As for his own personal decisions, they've been taken in consultation with a very small inner private circle. In the first place there is the real inner group, the real Kitchen Cabinet – that is Marcia Williams, Gerald Kaufman and Peter Shore. And in addition there are three independent personalities – George Wigg, Tommy Balogh and, last but not least, Burke Trend, the one really powerful force in this entourage.[14]

George Wigg, Paymaster General in the cabinet, and a Wilson crony, complained after his own fall from grace, that he felt increasing disquiet about the way things were run at No.10 and asserted that it was '. . . shared by many. It became all too clear that civil servants and ministerial colleagues had a formidable competitor for the prime minister's ear in Mrs

Williams.'[15] Wiggs claims: '. . . the influence exerted by Mrs Williams inside No.10 was great and pervasive, for there was no doubt the Prime Minister rated her opinions as important and on many issues her reactions markedly influenced his thinking.'[16]

Tony Benn, Minister of Technology 1966-1970, in his diary entry for 3 January 1968, describes a dinner at the Crossmans' which had started with '. . . a great gripe about the absolute exclusion of Cabinet Ministers from important decisions.'[17] More specifically, Benn noted in his diary on 11 February 1968 that Crossman was '. . . bitterly contemptuous of Gerald Kaufman, Trevor Lloyd-Hughes [both press officers at No.10] and Marcia, a little inner group who, with John Silkin [Chief Whip], didn't give Harold good advice.'[18] Initially Benn himself had been a great admirer of Marcia Williams. In 1965 he noted in his diary, 'I do like Marcia, she's got all the right instincts and she does Harold a great deal of good'[19] and he described her as '. . . infinitely the most able, loyal, radical and balanced member of Harold's personal team.'[20] By 1970 he had changed his mind: 'My view that Marcia's instinct was something on which Harold ought to rely has largely collapsed. She is now almost a courtier in a fading court. .'[21]

Questions about Harold Wilson's conduct of government and the role of, and constitutional status of, his unofficial advisers in general, and of Marcia Williams, his Personal and Political Secretary, in particular, were not confined merely to Whitehall gossip and the odd disgruntled outburst of former colleagues and/or favourites. These questions formed part of a wider public debate at the time.[22] Academic evaluation of these first two Wilson governments usually includes at least some reference to the questionable role played by Wilson's 'kitchen cabinet'.[23] In addition a number of recently published political biographies (in the 1990s) spanning the 1964–70 period[24] have re-opened questions about Harold Wilson's conduct of government. Press reviews and serializations of these works have focused on extracts describing and questioning the role of Marcia Williams and that of the 'kitchen cabinet'.[25] Harold Wilson's death in 1995 provided a further opportunity for airing these questions in the obituary columns.

The accounts of former participants in the political arena are invariably partial. A close study of these accounts provides ambiguous evidence about Wilson's advisory strategies. Some complainants only complain when they themselves have lost their own privileged place in the charmed circle (eg. R.H.S. Crossman; George Wigg). Nevertheless, the references by participants, academics and journalists, to Wilson's 'kitchen cabinet' in general and to Marcia Williams in particular, occur too frequently to be ignored. The Wilson governments of 1964–70 raised questions that contemporary and more recent commentators regard as being of constitutional importance. Wilson's conduct of business, his apparent failure to observe accepted procedures, his penchant for conspiracy and intrigue,[26] his reputed preference for favourites and unofficial advisers, and his self-proclaimed admiration for President Kennedy and possible self-conscious cultivation of a similar image in the same way, gave rise to discontent and criticism which typically became articulated in constitutional terms.

In order to evaluate the constitutional implications of changes in the advisory system introduced by Harold Wilson in his first two governments and to assess the extent to which such changes followed the American model, it is first necessary to answer some preliminary questions. What was the accepted constitutional position in respect of advice to the executive when Wilson took office? What did this mean in practical terms for a prime minister seeking advice? Why did Wilson want to change the system? What kind of changes did he introduce?

What was the constitutional position in respect of advice to the prime minister when Wilson took office? This question is difficult to answer, partly because of the fluid nature of the British constitution, particularly in respect of the executive branch of government, and partly because there are two, interconnected but different constitutions operating simultaneously. Excepting the Ministers of the Crown Act 1937, which primarily concerns ministerial titles and salaries, little exists by way of statutory evidence to explain the workings of cabinet government and the principles upon which it is based. Rules of behaviour governing the executive branch have arisen as part of the evolutionary process by which former royal prerogatives have become powers exercised by representative institutions. Reference has to be made to the memoirs of political actors and the writings of constitutional theorists in order to discover what was the generally accepted procedure in any particular period. This task is itself complicated by the dual nature of the British constitution. Since Bagehot revealed the existence of an efficient constitution in the 1860s, the British political class has recognized that the British have one constitution for public consumption which provides a dignified facade obscuring the efficient workings of a network of power relationships framed by a secret constitution, known only to insiders. Constitutional theorists and political commentators frequently shift between these constitutions when establishing the reference points from which they attempt to judge the constitutionality of political behaviour. It is partly because the dual and largely uncodified nature of the British constitution gives rise to much contention and debate that evidence is provided of the constitution's existence: it is argued about, therefore it is.

The public facade or dignified constitution by 1964 had changed since Bagehot's day. In the 1860s Bagehot revealed that the Queen and Parliament were a dignified facade obscuring the real government, the Cabinet. By the 1960s it was being suggested that the cabinet itself was now part of the dignified constitution.[27] The constitution now understood by the public was that a cabinet, selected and led by a prime minister, supported by a majority in the House of Commons, decided public policy questions in the name of the monarch. Government policy was based on manifesto promises endorsed by the electorate. Civil servants advised ministers on the implementation of policy and executed the instructions arising from ministerial decisions reached in cabinet.

The secret constitution was a more complex arrangement. It took account of blurred lines between policy and administration, it recognized that much policy is incremental and that election pledges were at best only general pointers as to the direction of government policy. In effect there were two governments, one, permanent and anonymous, consisting of senior civil servants, was responsible not only for administration and execution of policy but also for much of its formulation. The other government was transitory and public. It consisted of politicians in the cabinet, whose function it was, after full discussion in cabinet, to take final policy decisions based on civil service advice and subsequently to defend those decisions in the public arena. Senior civil servants were anonymous, politically neutral, generalist administrators, who were deemed to have a monopoly over the giving of policy advice. The advice of specialists, experts in any particular field of government activity, was filtered up to the political masters via senior civil servants. The process of public policy advice was therefore: specialists advised senior civil servants, senior civil servants in each department mediated all advice to their political head, who in turn advised the prime minister in cabinet. Sir John Hunt, a former Cabinet Secretary, confirmed that '. . . in theory advice to the prime minister is given by departmental ministers.'[28] Prime ministers performed the role of selecting and coordinating their team. Policy was the outcome of cabinet decisions for which ministers were then collectively responsible. Ministers were each individually responsible for the conduct of their own departments. The Cabinet Secretariat was there to serve the whole cabinet, ensure its instructions were transmitted to the appropriate departments and to help the prime minister in the task of the overall coordination of government. Prime ministers had few executive functions; they were not individually responsible for any particular aspect of government. Prime ministers were not expected to formulate government policy by taking individual decisions based on proposals

arising from an *alternative* advisory system (advice to the prime minister
unmediated by either the cabinet or Whitehall). Such behaviour would not
only place a severe strain on the known constitutional convention of
collective responsibility upon which the whole cabinet system was based,
it would also be tantamount to usurping the functions of the permanent
government, that is, undermining the secret constitution.

Behind the facade of cabinet government was the efficient reality of rule
by a permanent government. Marcia Williams asserts that 'in the offices
of Whitehall and in the clubs of Pall Mall lies immense power. The
electorate believes that on Polling Day it is getting a chance to change
history. The reality is that in many cases the power remains with the civil
servants who are ensconced in Whitehall, rather than with the politicians
who come and go at elections.'[29] By the end of the nineteenth century
the monarch exercised the royal prerogative only on the advice of the
elected government. By the middle of the twentieth century the elected
government primarily exercised those same executive powers only on the
advice of senior civil servants. It was this secret constitution that
Crossman hoped to reveal by the publication of his *Diaries*.[30] Crossman
intended to expose the reality of civil service power.[31] Just as the
monarch's power had gradually slipped to those on whose advice it was
exercised, now those one-time royal advisers had in their turn let power
slip to those on whose advice they were now expected to rely.

If this was the constitutional context in respect of advice, what did it
imply in everyday terms for prime ministers seeking advice? What
advisory system-in-place did Wilson inherit upon entering No.10 in 1964?

Then as now, when a new prime minister crosses the threshold of 10
Downing Street he is immediately taken into the civil service's
embrace.[32] The prime minister is served by a Private Office manned by
a small number of civil servants located in No.10. Most of these 'high-
flyers' serve a short period of secondment to the prime minister before
returning, often on promotion, to work within the departments of
Whitehall. Headed by the Principal Private Secretary, the Private Office
is responsible for organizing the prime minister's official life: arranging
his appointments; dealing with his correspondence; preparing briefs for
answers to his Parliamentary questions; accompanying him on all official
visits; listening into, and making notes on all his phone calls, and
providing him with a 'bush telegraph' linking him with the private offices
of all his ministers.[33] In addition to the support and advice from this
source, the prime minister is also closely served in his roles of chairman
of the cabinet and First Lord of the Treasury, by the two most senior civil
servants in Whitehall: the Permanent Secretary to the Cabinet and the
Permanent Secretary to the Treasury. Whilst the cabinet secretary serves

the whole cabinet and is not the prime minister's exclusive servant, he is the prime minister's closest most senior adviser and the relationship that exists can be likened to that between a departmental minister and the permanent secretary.[34] The prime minister is also advised by a Press Secretary, a civil servant responsible for liaison between the prime minister and the media and for overseeing the coordination of media relations for the government as a whole. In 1964 there was also recent precedent for prime ministers to introduce a political element into the advisory system of No.10: Harold Macmillan in 1957 appointed John Wyndham to be his political secretary.[35] Prime ministers also, of course, received advice from cabinet colleagues.

Turning now to the third of our preliminary questions, we need to explore why Harold Wilson was dissatisfied with the system in place. What kinds of advice were not provided for and why were they necessary?

In the first place, Wilson wanted to introduce change and the civil service was designed to check radical initiatives and temper political expediency. Secondly the advisory system-in-place failed to cater for the kind of advice required by a premier expected to shoulder responsibility for the electoral fortunes of his party.

On 16 October 1964 Harold Wilson became, at the age of forty-eight, the youngest prime minister this century. Sked and Cook note that 'it is difficult to exaggerate the degree to which the new Labour government was dominated by Harold Wilson. During the election campaign he had shown himself to be a politician of the first rank. He was extremely good on television and a brilliant performer in the House of Commons.'[36] Wilson had been very impressed with President Kennedy, on whom he reputedly modelled his own election campaign and to some extent his image. George Wigg recalls how Wilson had been ' . . . fascinated by his visit to the late John Kennedy. He had been enthraled by the White House set-up.'[37] Marcia Williams recounts how they had '. . . forced the pace Kennedy-fashion throughout the run-up to the election and through the campaign itself, . . . [and] had to face a Kennedy-type hundred days of urgent and instant action.'[38] Wilson cast himself in the role of technocrat and modernizer. According to Ramsay, 'Wilson . . . brought hope of a new dawn, one in which Britain could emerge refashioned to take its place in the 'modern' world. The new prime minister's character, and background, grammar school education, economic expertise and scientific literacy . . . symbolized change.'[39] In a stirring speech to the pre-election Labour Party Conference at Scarborough in the Autumn of 1963 Wilson made links between socialism and the scientific revolution and stated that both could only be achieved by change:

In our plans for the future, we are re-defining and we are re-stating our
Socialism in terms of the scientific revolution . . . that revolution
cannot become a reality unless we are prepared to make far-reaching
changes in economic and social attitudes which permeate our whole
system of society. The Britain that is going to be forged in the white
heat of this revolution will be no place for restrictive practices or for
outdated methods on either side of industry . . . In the Cabinet room
and the boardroom alike those charged with the control of our affairs
must be ready to think and to speak in the language of our scientific
age.[40]

Wilson's speeches, interviews and reputation for left-wing radicalism[41]
all served to alert, and in some cases alarm, the political nation that things
would change if he became prime minister. The sub-text signalled that it
was his intention to change the secret constitution under which senior civil
servants exercised power by means of their mediating role in respect of
policy advice. Politicians operating the dignified constitution were willing
to mask the operations of real power in the efficient constitution as long
as this meant taking credit, translated as victory at the polls, for policy
successes. When the advice of the permanent government led to policy
failure and thereby electoral defeat for the transitory government, the latter
demanded better advice. The civil service would have to set its own house
in order, revitalize its policy initiatives, or politicians would seek
alternative advice outside the official machine. Harold Wilson attempted
to gain the best of both worlds: outsiders would be given a direct voice in
the conversation of government, this is turn would encourage the civil
service to be more accommodating and innovative.

The political nation by 1964 was well aware of the direction in which
the secret constitution had by now evolved. Whilst in a formal sense 'civil
servants proposed and ministers disposed' policy, the process which
preceded the presentation of the proposals placed before ministers was
geared towards compromise, so that ministers were left with little or no
choice about accepting an outcome previously agreed by officials from
those departments involved.[42] This bargaining procedure may have
produced consensus but in the process radical options seemed always to be
filtered out. The monopoly over advice claimed by senior civil servants
enabled them to control the access of experts and innovators who might be
a source of radical ideas or less mutually acceptable policies. The civil
service thus acted as a brake on policy innovation.[43]

The price of consensual policies was, by the 1960s, measured in policy
failure. In 1966, Peter Shore claimed, 'no one can doubt that poor quality
of the official advice tended to Ministers over the past decade has been

one of the major causes of our dismal national record.'[44] In economic management this failure was demonstrated by a worsening trade-off between price stability and unemployment and a continual decline in Britain's world trade position. Successful economic management had come to be regarded as crucial to electoral success and the future of British governing institutions.

The Treasury dominated not only economic policy, but also controlled the machinery of government, and therefore was also responsible for the recruitment, training and promotion of civil servants. Most high-ranking civil servants served a period in the Treasury. This enabled the Treasury to socialize the entire senior ranks and diffuse Treasury attitudes throughout Whitehall. Crossman, for instance, reflecting on the pervasive influence of the Treasury noted:

> One cannot overestimate this. All the civil servants I worked with were imbued with a prior loyalty to the Treasury and felt it necessary to spy on me and report all my doings to the Treasury . . . There was nothing I could do, no order I could give, which wasn't at once known to the Treasury, because my staff were all trained to check with the Treasury and let it know in advance what each of them was doing . . . No doubt this is explained in the case of ambitious young men and women by the fact that the Treasury is the prime source of promotion . . . But there are senior people . . . who just feel the Treasury is their natural boss; and whereas the Treasury and the head of the Civil Service are permanent, the Minister changes every three years on average.[45]

Wilson regarded these arrangements as unsatisfactory. His experience both as a civil servant during the war, and then as a cabinet minister in the post-war Attlee government, had made him realize that the only way new or radical ideas would gain access to the higher levels of the system was if the monopoly of advice exercised by the civil service in general, and Treasury attitudes and ethos in particular, could be broken. Looking back to 1963 in 1986, Wilson stated in his memoirs: 'I had now spent over twenty years in Whitehall and Westminster, and wherever possible, countering the wily and dominating ways of the Treasury. I was determined that this department should be cut down to size . . .'[46]

It was not only the efficacy of Treasury-dominated *policy* advice that Wilson regarded as unsatisfactory. Patrick Weller notes that a distinction can be drawn between policy advice and political advice:

> Advice to top decision-makers has often been categorized in ways that are analytically useful even if they are not always descriptively accurate

or precise. The most frequent distinction is between political advice and policy advice. By 'policy' is usually meant technical and professional alternatives or the outcome of 'objective' or rational analysis. 'Political' is taken to refer to consideration of the likely electoral or media consequence of a course of action.[47]

The second respect in which Wilson regarded the existing advisory system as inadequate was that it also failed to provide the right kind of *political* advice.

Civil servants, though mediating policy advice, were expected to remain neutral as to the political implications of their proposals. The prime minister's team of officials in No.10 observed strict demarcation lines between the world of public administration and the world of party politics.[48] The accepted forum for taking account of the political implications of government policy is the cabinet. Prime ministers and their cabinet colleagues, it is assumed, share a mutual interest in their political fortunes. Wilson, it seemed, regarded this arrangement as inadequate. He led a party that had been torn by internal strife throughout most of the thirteen years in opposition. He had cleverly cobbled together party unity in time for the election by avoiding stands on those policy areas which traditionally divided the left and right wings: public ownership and unilateralism, and by focusing instead upon the safe topics of science, technology and modernization.[49] His choice of cabinet had been determined partly by the previous membership of the shadow cabinet, elected by their Parliamentary colleagues, and partly by a need to unite the Bevanite and Gaitskellite wings of the party. He viewed many of his colleagues with suspicion and distrust and knew that Callaghan and Brown remained heirs apparent.[50] George Wigg claims that 'almost every senior Minister had voted against him [Wilson] in the election for the Party leadership.'[51] Marcia Williams asserts that 'nothing can rival the quality of advice given by a man or woman who has reached Cabinet level . . . Nevertheless, by its very nature, advice from someone of Cabinet rank implies certain limitations . . . Inevitably, the advice given to a Prime Minister by an individual member of his Cabinet reflects some self-interest . . .'[52] Not only was Wilson surrounded by rivals at the cabinet table they were also, with few exceptions, novices.[53] Understandably, therefore, Wilson might regard political advice arising from the cabinet as probably inadequate and possibly suspect.

These were drawbacks enough but Wilson also knew that his own power base lay within the wider electorate and prudence dictated the need to maintain direct links with this wider political constituency. Despite the formal constitutional positions of cabinet government and collective responsibility, he was aware that electoral politics placed responsibility for winning or losing elections, and, therefore, public responsibility for all aspects of the government, on the prime minister. This necessitated alternative sources of advice, sensitive to the prime minister's personal political fortunes, so that he would be better briefed to challenge civil service wisdom coming from the departments via his cabinet colleagues. Whilst still leader of the Opposition in the Spring of 1964 he had stated his intention to turn No.10 into a 'power house' of government and complained that in the period since Attlee and Churchill No.10 had become '. . . much more remote and amateurish. No.10 is far too small.'[54] No.10 was inadequate to serve a prime minister if he expected to play an interventionist role in government: '. . . no one could say that No.10 today, with a staff of less than fifty, is sufficiently well organized for the Prime Minister to know all that is going on. I think at No.10 the Prime Minister as an effective executive chairman, should be taking the initiative much more, so that he is not always just mopping up the blood when something has gone wrong.'[55]

Wilson recognized that his own political fortunes rested on his ability first to address the short-comings of the existing *policy* advisory system dominated by Treasury thinking, and secondly to address weaknesses in the *political* advisory system dominated by a cabinet composed of rivals inexperienced in the ways of Whitehall. The above short-comings of the advisory system could be expected to confront any new prime minister entering Downing Street, but Wilson suspected that his own particular problems would be exacerbated by his reputation for radicalism and self-assumed role as the bringer of enforced modernization to the corridors of power. He also anticipated that problems would arise from the political realities of a socialist government, in theory at least, confronting the conservative, and in many cases Conservative, world of officialdom and the City: permanent opposition was the fate of the Labour Party whether in or out of Office.[56]

How did Wilson intend to address these inadequacies? In what ways did he change the prime minister's advisory system? When interviewed by Norman Hunt in the Spring of 1964, Wilson voiced his misgivings about the advisory system and explained some of the ways he intended to address its apparent shortcomings.[57] Firstly Wilson explained that he envisaged changes in the machinery of government which would reflect new priorities in respect of science, technology, modernization and economic growth. To this end he planned to establish a Ministry of Technology or Science to encourage invention and innovation.[58] It was a Ministry of Production, however, that was to reflect a new kind of thinking about economic management. It was to be a ministry of vision and economic growth, promoting industrial reconstruction and modernization rather than penny counting and monetary caution. 'The Ministry of Production[59] is dividing the existing work of the Treasury, leaving the Treasury to get on with monetary jobs, taxation and the control of expenditure.'[60] The Treasury, it was argued, was preoccupied with fiscal probity and consistently gave the balance of payments priority over the expansion of the economy. Secondly, the Whitehall advisory system in general, and that of the new ministries in particular, would receive a transfusion of new ideas in the form of 'outsiders' seconded from industry, commerce, the City and academia, who would be given temporary civil service status and the same access to the policy process as senior permanent officials. Ministers were to be encouraged to appoint specialist advisers to their departments. It was expected that such specialist advisers would reinvigorate civil service attitudes and thinking and be a source of radical policy initiatives. They would be, in effect, the minister's man in the department, appointed to act as catalysts to the 'effete' bureaucrats, reminiscent of American presidential aides tasked with overseeing the execution of the president's will in the face of bureaucratic resistance.

In Britain, advice to individual departmental ministers is advice to the prime minister at one stage removed. These innovations in the ministerial advisory system would thus indirectly provide the prime minister with alternative and additional policy advice. Wilson made it clear however that these changes would be insufficient to meet the demands of the role the prime minister was now expected to play, or had assumed, in the government and in 'presidentialized' British politics in general. He therefore intended to make changes in both the Cabinet Office and in No.10. Firstly the roles of the Cabinet Secretary and that of the Cabinet Secretariat were to be more closely geared to serving the prime minister:

> They [Cabinet Secretariat] will also have to do much more in the way of briefing the Prime Minister, not only on the machinery of government and the work of any Cabinet committee, but also providing a briefing agency, so that he is right up to date and on top of the job in respect of all these important departments of state.[61]

He argued that, although such briefs would rely on departmental data, they would enable the prime minister to be informed at an earlier stage in the policy process and thereby intervene if necessary.[62]

Wilson anticipated that policy success would be achieved partly by a new emphasis on science and technology, reflected in the machinery of government changes, partly by a new economic ministry with a different ethos to that which prevailed in the Treasury, and partly by a greater use of, and direct access to, outside experts. He specified that his own briefing gap would be filled by an augmented role for the Cabinet Secretariat and a greater use of project teams, comprising outside experts and officials for policy planning. Wilson, then, made it clear he intended to break the civil service's monopoly over advice.

In the pre-election Hunt interview, Wilson replied to questions about how he intended to address the perceived problem of *policy* advice. The matter of *political* advice was not discussed. On taking office, however, he did attempt to tackle what he regarded as short-comings of the sources of political advice available to the prime minister

Wilson established the Department of Economic Affairs (DEA). This may have served to kill two birds with one stone: on the one hand the new department was specifically created to break the Treasury's monopoly over economic advice; on the other hand it was a suitable way of disposing of his two strongest rivals by appointing them to ministries designed to check one another.[63] In addition to being in receipt of economic advice arising from these two separate sources, Wilson also appointed Thomas Balogh, an Oxford economist, as a temporary civil servant, formally to the role of economic adviser to the cabinet but in fact as economic adviser to the prime minister.[64] Balogh could provide the premier with *alternative* advice untainted by officialdom[65] and free from any self-interested political advantage that might influence the judgement of Wilson's cabinet rivals.

Another ploy which may be seen as an attempt to address some of the possible shortcomings of his cabinet as a source of political advice was that of appointing George Wigg to the cabinet post of Paymaster General, in effect a minister without portfolio. Wigg was a close friend who had managed Wilson's successful campaign to secure the party leadership in 1963. Wigg had also provided Wilson with useful political ammunition to use against the Conservatives during the Profumo Affair. It was in part, at least, to prevent any similar scandals damaging the Wilson government, that Wigg was given the task of overseeing security for the prime minister. This role resulted in Wigg's colleagues regarding him as the prime ministers 'spy', monitoring cabinet rivals and reporting any suspected 'palace' revolutions.[66]

The element of Wilson's 'new' advisory system, however, which caused the greatest stir and comment was the establishment of a political office inside 10 Downing Street, headed by Mrs Marcia Williams, Wilson's private secretary. Mrs Williams was given an office in No.10 and, after much debate,[67] the title of Personal and Political Secretary. It was claimed that Macmillan's appointment of John Wyndham had set a post-war precedent for such an arrangement. Wyndham, however, was given the status of a temporary, unpaid[68] civil servant and he shared the office and work load of other members of the No.10 Private Office. Marcia Williams, on the other hand, had a separate office, a handful of assistants, no civil service status and was paid by Wilson himself. According to her own account, she was there to arrange for the political side of the prime minister's life: 'The *raison d'être* behind the establishment of a Political Office in 1964 . . . was that the Prime Minister must be seen as the Leader of his Party as well as Head of Government; and these two functions have to be catered for, separately, within the same building.'[69] Wilson recognized that the value of the kind of advice she could give required that she remain an 'outsider' separate from the civil service contingent in No.10. Otherwise she might become down-graded and/or 'house-trained', also physical proximity within No.10 was essential to ensure continued access to the prime minister, the greater part of whose time was organized, filled and effectively controlled by the civil service. Pimlott notes that

> . . . the precise nature of Marcia William's job was unspecified . . . she kept Wilson's political files, typed his speeches, paid private bills, and now increasingly did his constituency work as well. She supervised secretarial staff in the morning, and in the afternoon worked in the Prime Minister's office in the House of Commons. But these activities were merely scaffolding: her important role was to be the person who thought about Wilson's needs and cared about his well-being...[70]

The Political Office catered for the wider requirement for political advice arising from the changing role of the prime minister in the political system. It was soon supplemented by an enlarged Press Office. Wilson, in common with his predecessors since the 1930s, appointed a Press Officer, in this case an ex-*Liverpool Daily Post* journalist, Trevor Lloyd-Hughes. It was usual for such appointees to receive temporary civil service status. Lloyd-Hughes assumed this required him henceforth to remain politically neutral in the performance of his duties.[71] Wilson soon saw this as a limitation for handling the political aspects of press relations and the presentation of his government's policy to the wider public. In 1965, therefore, Gerald Kaufman, a journalist on the *New Statesman*, was appointed to the position of Parliamentary Press Liaison Officer and given an office in No.10. By 1969, Kaufman was assisted by Joe Haines, a former *Daily Mirror* journalist, who became, at first, Kaufman's deputy and eventually his replacement.

Having explored the answers to our four preliminary questions it is now possible to evaluate the constitutional implications of Wilson's innovations and to consider the extent to which they show any convergence with the American model.

According to the constitution prime ministers were not presidents: they were not individually responsible for the executive and they were not free to cast their nets widely for advice. The formal constitutional position in respect of advice to the prime minister in 1964 was that prime ministers were advised on both policy and politics by their cabinet colleagues. Policy advice forming the basis of cabinet discussions and the subsequent collectively binding decisions, was supposed to be mediated by senior civil servants. In what respects did Harold Wilson alter this pattern and what if any were the constitutional implications?

Harold Wilson attempted to break, or at least, dilute, the civil service's monopoly over policy advice on the one hand, and to undermine the cabinet's assumed prerogative over political advice, on the other. In short, Wilson constructed a new advisory system, which provided the prime minister with additional and in some respects *alternative*[72] sources of advice, which would enable him to play a more interventionist role in a presidential manner. At face value this would seem to be unconstitutional if the above formal view of the constitutional position is accepted.

The response of some senior civil servants at the time would suggest that some officials regarded Wilson's innovations as constitutionally improper. Nora Beloff, for instance, commenting on the Wilson-Hunt interview in 1964, reported that 'some prominent officials on hearing the future prime minister's plans warned that if the Prime Minister employs rival staff and gets separate briefs or, as one former Treasury official put, sets up "an Ogpu"[73] to watch over departments, he would compromise Cabinet solidarity and the responsibility of individual ministers to Parliament.'[74]

It is by no means universally accepted, however, that advice to the prime minister is circumscribed by constitutional rules. G.W.Jones, who has made a substantial contribution to the literature on the topic of prime ministerial advisers,[75] implies that there is an absence of rules in such matters. He shows that prime ministers have frequently consulted sources outside the fairly narrow formal system. He points out for instance that it was not until the 1930s, partly as a consequence of the reaction to Lloyd George's highly personalized regime, that the Private Office in No.10 was purged of its political elements. Jones notes that until the beginning of this century its composition was a mixture of personal and political appointees, and officials, and that even the latter had often entered the civil service under the patronage of a politician.[76] Between 1900 and the 1920s the career civil servants became more prominent, a trend temporarily reversed by Lloyd George who appointed 'three cronies' to the Private Office[77] and created the 'Garden Suburb'.[78] It was not until Ramsay MacDonald's premiership in the 1930s that the Private Office was completely depoliticized. Jones asserts that despite the gradual depoliticization after Lloyd George's period in office, 'Prime ministers still found it necessary to have close to them personal and political advisers who were not part of the civil service nor of the Private Office.'[79] During the Second World War Churchill introduced a much larger political element reminiscent of Lloyd George's 'Garden Suburb'. Churchill created his own team of advisers under the Oxford don, Lindemann (later Lord Cherwell), entitled the Prime Minister's Statistical Section.[80] Churchill also made use of confidential aides, or cronies, like Desmond Morton, for liaison with foreign governments in exile, and late-night drinking companions, like Lord Beaverbrook and Brenden Bracken.[81] Jones notes that in Britain '. . . there has emerged in the twentieth century a system of prime ministerial advisers and aides, very loosely structured, flexible, dependent on his personality and more adaptable to his needs . . . '[82] Referring to the changes Wilson introduced into the advisory system in the 1964–70 period, Jones comments: 'In this period attempts were made by the prime minister to counter-balance the long-established predominance of the civil service at No.10 through the introduction of a more explicitly personal and political set of advisers. Indeed, it might be said that they sought to return to the older tradition of having their personal adherents with them.'[83]

But if Jones is correct in claiming that there were ample precedents for prime ministers to construct advisory systems tailor-made to suit themselves, why did the Wilson arrangements attract so much comment and criticism and why was such criticism typically articulated in terms of constitutional proprieties having been violated?

Clearly Wilson was surrounded by a small coterie of advisers. The central figures of this group appear to have been: Gerald Kaufman, Wilson's political press officer; Peter Shore, one of Wilson's two Parliamentary Private Secretaries located in No.10.;[84] George Wigg, Paymaster General and long time close associate, and Thomas Balogh prominent left-wing Oxford economist and long time associate. Others who seemed to be 'insiders' some of the time included Richard Crossman,[85] Tony Benn[86] and then, after 1967, when Balogh and Wigg received peerages and left No.10, they seem to have been replaced at 'court' by Arnold Goodman, whom Wigg introduced to Wilson. Last, but not least, was Marcia Williams who was generally regarded as central to the group. Crossman for instance comments in 1965: 'This little group around Marcia is really quite important since she is still the most influential person in

Harold's life, far more influential I should say than Tommy Balogh, and infinitely more than me.'[87] The group came to be pejoratively labelled the 'kitchen cabinet', and Nora Beloff referred to 'the court of King Harold'.[88] Jones notes that 'journalists depicted her [Marcia Williams] as a *major domo* of the court of King Harold; the overseer of his kitchen cabinet which exercised more influence over his decisions than his ministers.'[89] Pimlott agrees that the importation of political staff into No.10 caused hostility and resistance[90] and that 'from the ensuing struggles there grew the legend of the 'Kitchen Cabinet'.'[91] But he denies that such a body ever existed, though he does concede that '. . . there was a group of advisers who were closer to Wilson . . . than many of his officials or Cabinet Ministers. Within this group . . . there was one fixture and undisputed *chef de cuisine*, Marcia Williams':[92] a 'kitchen cabinet' and court favourite by any other names. The members of this inner group did change from time to time, and some of them could, in any case, claim legitimacy beyond Harold Wilson's favour by virtue of their wider constituencies, because they were members of the cabinet (Crossman, Benn and Wigg), Members of Parliament (Shore), or could broadly be described as representative of the media and academia (Kaufman, Haines and Balogh). It was the role of Marcia Williams, the one permanent fixture in the group, however, that attracted so much adverse comment. Her sole qualification for being included rested on the fact that the prime minister seemed to trust her.[93] Whatever her formal role her contemporaries in Wilson's close circle seem generally agreed that above all Wilson valued her political judgement. Haines, for example, recalls: 'She [Marcia Williams] was then politically indispensable to the Prime Minister . . . it was abundantly clear in my early days at Downing Street that the Prime Minister depended more on her advice than any other's.'[94]

Whilst the existence of a close circle of advisers surrounding Wilson is not disputed, the extent of the influence exercised by prominent outsiders in the group is a matter of debate. Wilson's own detailed record of his 1964–70 government[95] notably makes no mention of either Williams or Balogh, and, if anything, sustains the appearance of the Whitehall model in respect of advice. There is certainly some evidence to suggest that if Wilson was 'excessively' influenced by anyone it was not by Marcia Williams, but by senior civil servants, in particular, Burke Trend who had the impeccable credentials of being Cabinet Secretary. Barbara Castle says of Trend: '. . . [he] was a power behind the throne. Pleasant and unassuming he had quickly captured Harold's confidence.'[96] Kenneth Morgan asserts: 'one of the major weaknesses in 1964-1970 was an excessive reliance on the guidance of the Treasury, the Bank of England,

and in other matters, the Foreign Office.'[97] Marcia Williams, in her own
account of life close to the prime minister, says of Harold Wilson: 'in
some ways he is a Civil Servant *manqué* . . . he was probably as much of
a civil servant as he was a Minister. . .'[98] she goes on to note that 'some
of us who were very close to him were worried it would be the civil
service who would dominate him, and I think it is fair to say that our fears
were in fact justified to some great extent through the years of the two
Labour Governments.'[99] In 1965, Alan Wakins asserted:

> He [Wilson] leans heavily upon the Cabinet Secretary, Sir Burke Trend.
> 'Prime Minister', says Sir Burke respectfully, 'I think you might do
> such-and-such'; and the Prime Minister promptly goes off and does it.
> Nor is this really surprising. Mr Wilson is himself an ex-civil servant.
> He knows the ranks, he understands the rules. . . He would not dream
> of seriously annoying the permanent officials . . .'[100]

Wilson himself gives some credence to these views. In 1967, in a second
interview with Norman Hunt, Wilson confirmed that in line with his
previously outlined plans, 'both [No.10 and the Cabinet Office] have been
strengthened'. Hunt queried whether this had catered for Wilson's being
'. . . independently briefed on matters coming before the Cabinet, so that
you could form your own independent judgement?' Wilson said that it had
and that he had '. . . underrated the extent to which the Cabinet Office
itself briefs the Prime Minister . . . the brief I get from the Cabinet
Secretary, from the Cabinet Office, is an independent brief for me.'[101]

   Marcia Williams specifically denies that she had any influence on
public policy at all. In an article written for the *Observer* in 1977 she
asserts: 'Harold Wilson knew that I had at heart the success of the Labour
Party and his own personal success. It was comfortable and secure to think
aloud to me. Not necessarily telling me about decisions he was taking or
policies he wanted to carry out, but simply going over all the political
thoughts in his mind . . .'[102] She goes on to emphasise that 'what
political advisers or any of the personal appointees in Number 10 ought to
remember is that their job is to organize the political life of the Prime
Minister and its projection. They are not in anyway involved in the
formulation of policy for which elected representatives of the party are
responsible.'[103] Caroline Moorehead suggests that 'although her [Marcia
Williams's] advice to the Prime Minister on policy matters may have been
persuasive, there is no real evidence that she acted as an ideological force.
Her views seem to have taken more the form of commonsense advice
reminding him [Wilson] of day to day realities and the line that would go
down best with his supporters.'[104] Jones asserts that, 'some of her

comments may have been incorporated into Mr Wilson's speeches, some of her assessments of personalities may have reinforced his own, but she seems not to have been influential on major issues. She was a Rhodesian 'bomber' and against American involvement in Vietnam, and if she did urge Mr Wilson to be more left-wing, many observers feel that he must frequently have overruled her.'[105]

Thomas Balogh's influence is also disputed. Although, according to Hennessy, Balogh encouraged Wilson to establish the Fulton Committee, whose report, in 1968, recommended divesting the Treasury of its control over the civil service establishment and approved the practice of ministers appointing special advisers.[106] Both Crossman's and Brown's personal accounts reveal, however, that on the crucial question of the postponement of the decision to devalue, the views of Balogh and other specialist advisers were ignored, Wilson sticking rigidly to the Bank of England and Treasury line for support of the pound, even at the cost of Labour's social policies and much trumpeted economic plan.[107] Crossman also describes Balogh's isolation and lack of access to the prime minister.[108] Gerald Kaufman claims that despite Balogh's campaign to get rid of Sir Laurence Helsby, Head of the Civil Service, 'Helsby must go!', he failed to persuade Harold Wilson to act on this advice.[109] Such views are confirmed by Marcia Williams, who describes Balogh's isolation, lack of access to Wilson and difficulties encountered with the civil service over gaining access to cabinet papers.[110] Ponting suggests that in that battle for the prime minister's favour, Balogh lost to Burke Trend. According to Ponting, early in 1967 there was a major row between Burke Trend and Balogh: '. . . the former complained to Wilson that Balogh was 'snooping', rifling through a box of papers for the prime minister and putting in dissenting comments to advice given by Trend. Wilson backed Trend and suggested to Balogh it was time for him to return to academic life.'[111]

Wilson's reputed admiration of officials, particularly Burke Trend and Michael Halls,[112] the self-effacing claims of Marcia Williams and the asserted lack of influence of Balogh, all serve to cast doubt on the extent of policy influence exercised by the 'kitchen cabinet'. If policy decisions were indeed being taken by the prime minister in consultation with a small group of *unofficial* advisers and the cabinet was subsequently placed in the position of having to bear collective responsibility for policy made elsewhere, then there would seem to be a case for saying constitutional propriety had not been observed. The prime minister was behaving in a presidential manner and had constructed an advisory system to enable him to do so.

Diary and memoir evidence about this is at best ambiguous and suffers from the drawbacks of partiality. Nevertheless, the uncodified nature of the British constitution means that what is constitutional and what is unconstitutional is decided, partly at least, by the political actors in any given period, and some of Harold Wilson's political colleagues, some officials and some sections of the media, clearly seemed to think that his advisory system failed to comply with constitutional propriety. Marcia Williams, a personal political appointee, was placed in the powerful position of being both gatekeeper and conduit. She had access to the prime minister, she had some control over the access of others and she always appeared to act as a channel of communication to and from the prime minister. Marcia Williams herself admits:

> I had long experience of knowing what the prime minister was likely to consider important and vice versa. This meant I was able to shield him from the distractions of endless petty queries or trivial decisions: it also followed that I was often used as a channel of communication by those who wanted an unofficial sounding of his state of mind, or probable reaction. It also meant I was asked to act as a go-between by those who were, quite simply, too frightened to tackle him about something themselves.[113]

This description of her role is corroborated by both Gerald Kaufman[114] and Richard Crossman.[115] Caroline Moorehead made it clear that Mrs Williams had both access and influence,[116] and supports this view by quoting a high-ranking civil servant as saying: '. . . I used to debate with her an issue I wanted to raise with the Prime Minister. I knew if I couldn't convince her I should never convince him . . . There were only four cases in four-and-a-half years when my advice rather than hers was taken.'[117] Mrs Williams in describing her own role as that of shielding the prime minister from 'distractions of endless petty queries or trivial decisions', echoes the much criticized role assumed by Sherman Adams as special assistant to President Eisenhower. Indeed, George Wigg criticized Marcia William's role on similar grounds when he noted that 'like every energetic secretary she became increasingly accustomed to taking day-to-day decisions on behalf of her employer . . . She now gradually came to take on responsibilities which I thought extended beyond those appropriate to a personal secretary and to behave towards myself, among others, as if she were a political force in her own right and a power to be reckoned with.'[118]

Marcia Williams does not deny advising the prime minister, but her claims that her advice was purely 'political' reveal that she knew what the proprieties were. Ziegler, apparently accepting her claims at face value, asserts that 'Wilson would have paid little attention to her views on the international aspects of Vietnam or devaluation, nor would she have been likely to profess them.[119] But when the question was what the average party member expected from him on such questions . . . he would listen carefully.'[120] Such claims assume that Weller's distinction between the two kinds of advice can be sustained. Weller himself notes that it may not offer an accurate or precise description of the nature of advice in practice. Advising someone which policy is likely to have the most desirable political outcome is indistinguishable from policy advice.

Both Harold Wilson and Marcia Williams seemed to think it necessary to go to considerable lengths to assert the propriety of his advisory system. They could indeed be suspected of protesting too much. Wilson's omission to mention alternative advisers in his memoirs, his repeated public reassurances that he did not intend to introduce an 'alien' system[121] and that British precedents existed for his innovations,[122] in addition to Marcia Williams's own repeated claims as to the limits of her influence and the importance of the advisory role of cabinet ministers, betray more that a hint that they knew the game.

Policy failure under the Conservatives, exemplified by continuous national economic decline, and a changing political system, which shifted the responsibility for electoral outcomes onto the prime minister prompted, Harold Wilson to seek additional and *alternative* sources of advice. This aroused a good deal of outraged constitutional noise, most of which focused upon Marcia Williams. But was Mrs Williams, as an outsider lacking a constituency beyond the prime minister's favour, simply an easy target for those wishing to express their disapproval of a premier with presidential pretensions? Was the source of constitutional fuss that Wilson was trying to presidentialize the advisory system?

The presidential model is one in which the president alone is held to be publicly responsible for the executive and is at liberty to call on wide ranging sources of advice, one of which may be the cabinet. When a president enters the White House he is accompanied by a personal entourage of assistants and advisers responsible only to himself. It is also a model in which there has been a tendency for some presidents to become isolated from traditional sources of advice and to come to rely instead on personal appointees, particularly those adept at manipulating favourable public support for the president.

Harold Wilson recognized that the electorate now expected prime ministers to bear responsibility for all aspects of government policy. This electoral fact of life implied a more interventionist premiership. Effective intervention could only be achieved by providing the prime minister with additional and new kinds of advice. Wilson was a self-confessed admirer of Kennedy's White House system:

> I think one can learn from the Kennedy experience . . . he brought into
> the White House a number of people from universities, one or two top
> scientists, top administrators. I believe we are going to need a small
> number of these in the Cabinet Secretariat . . . I would like to see our
> government doing what President Kennedy turned into a fine art, a
> project study with experts – not only Ministers – but top civil servants,
> planners within the department and also, in some cases, people brought
> in from outside.[123]

But did he attempt to construct a similar system here? Wilson reputedly
liked to consult lots of different groups. Ponting asserts that 'he was not,
as Marcia Williams and other members of the political staff complained,
swamped by Whitehall advice; neither was he, as some officials and
politicians, and hence many journalists, often alleged, the creature of the
kitchen cabinet, cut off from the wider world. Playing off one against
another, he often frustrated both; and remained his own man.'[124] Tony
Benn agrees: 'I suspect that Harold deliberately keeps all his advisers,
including me and Dick and Peter, at arms length so that he is always in
complete command . . . not wishing to be 'taken over' by anyone.'[125]
But this in itself could be construed as alien and unconstitutional, if it is
assumed that to be constitutional, advice to the prime minister must be
mediated via senior civil servants and cabinet colleagues. A preference for
consulting lots of different sources of advice and balancing one off against
another is reminiscent of the advisory strategy employed by some
American presidents, particularly FDR. Indeed, George Brown, discussing
his period as Secretary of State for Economic Affairs, complained of an
excess of sources of advice: 'Tommy Balogh had not joined the
department [DEA], but had become the Prime Minister's economic adviser
at No.10 This was another problem akin to that with the Treasury; there
was yet another separate economic advisory body in the Cabinet Office.
In fact, there were too many of us advising and counter-advising one
another.'[126] This was a criticism he reiterated when Foreign Secretary.
Discussing the failures of Wilson's 1967 Vietnam peace initiative, he
attributes part of the problem to Washington's dual foreign policy run by
the WHO and the State Department respectively and reflects that
'. . . at that time we had No.10 Downing Street trying to maintain a
private Foreign Policy in exactly the same way.'[127]

Wilson, also in a manner reminiscent of an American president, did
take some personal appointees with him to No.10, and they occupied
positions not dissimilar to those occupied by presidential aides in the White

House. Richard Neustadt distinguishes between two different kinds of presidential advisers. On the one hand there are those who provide broad, non-departmental advice on all aspects of government. This group are mainly located in the Executive Office of the President (EOP). On the other hand, there are those more intimate and personal aides located in the White House Office (WHO). He explains that 'the White House Staff would think about the man's own states and purposes, including party politics . . . '[128] Presidential aides located in the WHO act as 'eyes and ears' for the president enabling him to oversee the activities of the executive branch. Some Wilson appointees were expected to perform this kind of role. Thomas Balogh, for example, provided the prime minister with alternative economic advice, which unlike that from the Treasury or the DEA, took account of likely implications for the prime minister's personal political standing. The role of Marcia Williams also resembled that of a WHO aide in that she provided the prime minister with advice about his own political standing, and, indeed, she actually described herself as 'the eyes and ears for Harold Wilson'.[129]

In chapter three we noted that public relations are a high priority for the man in the White House. The enlargement of the No.10 press office and its more overtly political emphasis, is evidence of Wilson's recognition of the increasing importance of public relations in prime ministerial politics. Benn, for instance, grumbles in his diary, 27 November 1969, that '. . . most of the things Harold thinks about are really news management . . . '[130]

The extent of presidentialization was, however, limited. A small team composed of Balogh, Williams and Kaufman (plus clerical assistants) cannot be regarded as adequate to monitor the vast range of policy activity for which the electorate now expected the prime minister to be responsible. A reading of Crossman's diaries suggests that Balogh at least hoped that Wilson intended to emulate the White House model, but that his hopes were unfulfilled: 'Thomas told me that he has had to abandon all his great hopes of building a presidential system, so that the Prime Minister would have a real staff at No.10 enabling him to monitor the activities of his Ministers and to develop a central strategy.'[131] Wilson himself, may have simply been playing the constitutional game when, in the pre-election interview with Norman Hunt, he denied that he intended to create an advisory system that would enhance the prime minister's power or down-grade the cabinet: '. . . decisions must be the Cabinet's. It is the Prime Minister's duty to ensure that any important questions of policy . . . should be taken by the Cabinet itself.'[132] Whilst the diaries and personal records provide evidence of a disgruntled sense of exclusion of some people some of the time, they also provide evidence to suggest Wilson consulted widely among his cabinet ministers and that cabinet discussions were often protracted. These accounts present a picture of a prime minister who, though perhaps having favourites, and a penchant for intrigue, was also at pains to reach agreement with his cabinet colleagues, even if this did require a great deal of time and energy.

Was there then a tendency for the new kind of advisers in Wilson's entourage to isolate the prime minister from the traditional influence of the cabinet and civil servants? Benn, for example, is critical of the influence he thought Gerald Kaufman had over Wilson and notes in June, 1969 '. . . he [Kaufman] is completely cynical now, blown up with his own importance and feeding into Harold the most unsatisfactory ideas which make Harold think he is God Almighty and everybody else has got to fall into line.'[133] But if there was, as Benn and, to some extent, Crossman, assert, a tendency for Wilson to retreat into an inner sanctum, it was not one that had become entirely cut-off from traditional sources of advice represented by the civil service and party. Crossman himself complained of Wilson's excessive reliance on the advice of Burke Trend, the Cabinet Secretary, and the close association between Wilson and Michael Halls, his Principal Private Secretary.[134] Crossman, Wigg, Shore, Castle, Silkin and Benn were all leading party figures who were also sometime members of the inner circle. Thus whilst Wilson may indeed have tended to rely on favourites, they were not exclusively personal secretaries, creatures, or media advisers having no wider legitimacy beyond the prime minister's favour. Many of them were members of the traditional advisory constituency.

In respect of any similarities between the presidential advisory system and that constructed by Wilson it can be said that Wilson's No.10 had features that could be regarded as being the embryo of the White House Office arrangements. Wilson may not have deliberately set out to presidentialize the advisory system. On entering office in 1964 he was faced with what he perceived to be particular problems of advice, some of which were associated with the changing nature of the political system which was transforming a constitutional premiership into a presidency in the eyes of the electorate. It is hardly surprising that some of the solutions to the problems of advice this posed involved changes in the direction of the presidential model.

Perceived failure of public policy prior to Wilson's period in office led to questions being raised about the sources of policy advice. Wilson stated his dissatisfaction with the existing system and his intention to change it. Throughout his premiership Wilson's own advisory system attracted much adverse comment and questions were raised about its constitutionality. In post mortems in the wake of the 1970 election defeat for Labour, once again questions about advice, its sources and Wilson's reputed failure to observe accepted advisory and decision-making procedures, formed a central theme in explaining the perceived failure of the 1964–70 Labour governments. Kenneth Morgan, for instance, claims that what damaged Harold Wilson's record was not the intractable difficulties associated with an ailing economy, or redefining Britain's post-imperialist role in the world, nor the growing industrial unrest associated with the trade unions, not Rhodesia or Northern Ireland but that

> The real cross that Wilson has to bear was rather his highly personalized style as the Prime Minister. It focused on an intensely personal method of leadership which brought some talk of prime ministerial government, now identified with Wilson as it had been earlier with Lloyd George. . . . he himself unwisely invoked comparisons with the presidential model with talk of the 'hundred days' of Franklin Roosevelt in 1933. The existence of an entourage of advisers, formal and informal, almost courtiers, in particular the presence of Marcia Williams so close to the centre of power, further distorted the conduct of policy at No.10.[135]

It is difficult to be exact about the constitutional rules in respect of advice in Britain because of the uncodified and dual nature of the constitution. Political behaviour is usually assumed to be constitutional unless enough important people make a big enough fuss. Politicians and advisers, unofficial, and official, seek to associate themselves with policy success and disclaim any part in policy failure.[136] This, coupled with the acceptance by the political nation that secrecy is an essential attribute of government, makes it difficult to determine where decisions are made and who made them, and in turn leaves unanswered the question as to whose advice was instrumental. In the end assumptions have to be made that proximity and access to decision-makers is at least tantamount to influence in the absence of contrary evidence. This being the case, some power of influence may be attributed to Mrs Williams and members of the so called 'kitchen cabinet' during Harold Wilson's period at No.10. Such an advisory system showed some similarities to the American model and can also be said to have breached constitutional propriety in respect at least of the secret constitution under which the civil service has an assumed prerogative of advice.

The dialogue about advice, about whose advice the executive was expected to listen to before making public policy decisions, that had been conducted so publicly between King and Parliament, executive and legislature, and which had been the engine of constitutional evolution, had by the middle of the twentieth century become a dialogue conducted in private between two parts of the executive, the cabinet and the bureaucracy. When the dialogue becomes an argument conducted more or less in public, it can be taken as a signal of failure in the secret constitution, an indication, perhaps, that one side is trying to alter the existing state of things. The Wilson period can be viewed in this way. Harold Wilson can be described as having attempted to revolutionize the advisory system in a manner that appeared to be influenced at least, by the presidential model; that is, he attempted to change the secret constitution. This in turn provoked a counter-revolution among those whose positions were threatened: very senior civil servants and cabinet ministers. The counter-revolution took several forms: the isolation and thereby neutralizing of the influence and effectiveness of outsiders such as, for example, Thomas Balogh; the diversion of first the attention and energies of,[137] and eventually the killing-off of the DEA, which had been set up as a deliberate attempt to weaken the pervasiveness of the Treasury's influence in Whitehall; and the attempt to 'house-train' civil service outsiders, such as Lloyd-Hughes, and politicians, and even the prime minister himself. Advisers who proved resistant to all these ploys, like Marcia Williams, were discredited in constitutional terms and publicly vilified in personal terms.[138] The strength of such counter-revolutionary tactics go some way to explaining why Wilson's 'revolution' was to some extent a failure. However, at least some share of the 'blame' may be attributed to Wilson himself, who perhaps lacked the political nerve necessary for revolution. His own desire for credibility, both for himself and for the Labour Party,[139] rendered him vulnerable to 'subversion' by the system he had intended to alter. Maybe 'once a civil servant always a civil servant'. He was, perhaps, all too accurate when he described himself as 'house-trained'. If, therefore, as has been claimed,[140] there was a failure of advice in the Wilson period, blame for that failure cannot all be attributed to the revolution in the advisory system attempted by Wilson, since evidence suggests that advice continued to be largely dominated by traditional sources, and Wilson's can be regarded, at least in the short-run, as a revolution that failed.

Harold Wilson thought the existing advisory system was unsatisfactory and inadequate to serve the needs of a presidential premier. The changes he introduced were publicly denounced as constitutionally improper. They were changes that showed some similarities to changes in the American presidential advisory system that had developed in conjunction with the presidentialization of American politics and government, and thus provide some evidence of a 'presidentialization' process taking place in British government. Did Edward Heath continue the 'revolution' that Wilson had begun? Were the changes in the system introduced by Wilson sufficient to bring about a new equilibrium between the political and constitutional position of the prime minister or was further adjustment necessary? It is to these questions that we must now turn.

Notes

1. Wilson, Harold, 'Whitehall and Beyond: the Rt. Hon. Harold Wilson, MP Leader of the Opposition talks to Norman Hunt.', *Listener* 5 March 1964, pp. 379–81 & p. 396, p. 380.
2. Brown, Lord George, *In My Way* (Harmondsworth: Penguin, 1972) p. 161.
3. This was not the first occasion on which Brown had 'resigned' or threatened to resign. See Crossman, R.H.S., *Diaries of a Cabinet Minister Vol.1* (London: Hamish Hamilton & Jonathan Cape, 1975) p. 578 and Castle, Barbara, *The Castle Diaries* (London:Papermac, 1990) p. 75.
4. 12.15 a.m. 15 March, 1968 a Privy Council meeting was convened in order to declare the forthcoming Monday, 18 March, a bank holiday. This was itself a response to a request from the American government that the London money markets remain closed in order to avert an imminent international currency crisis. See Brown, ibid., pp. 161–73.
5. Extract from text of resignation statement. Ibid., p. 174.
6. Ibid., p. 161.
7. Ibid.
8. Ibid., p. 177.
9. In the case of America, the WHO determining policies imposed upon cabinet ministers and line departments. See above chapter three.
10. Although it is worth noting that even at the time Brown's protest was not unsupported. Whilst only Brown felt strongly enough to resign, several cabinet colleagues had gathered in Brown's office in the House of Commons on the night in question to air a common sense of grievance. They had also accompanied him to No.10 to seek a full explanation of the night's activities from the prime minister. See Benn, Tony, *Office Without Power Diaries Vol.2 1968–70* (London: Hutchinson, 1988) pp. 44–6.
11. Crossman, R.H.S., *Diaries of a Cabinet Minister* 3 Vols (London: Hamish Hamilton and Jonathan Cape, 1975,1976 & 1977); Wigg, Lord George, *George Wigg*, (London: Michael Joseph, 1972); Benn, Tony, *Diaries*, 4 Vols *Out of the Wilderness*; *Office Without Power*;

Conflicts of Interest; *Against the Tide*; (London: Hutchinson, 1987, 1988. 1989, 1992 respectively); Castle, Barbara, *The Castle Diaries* 2 Vols. (London: Weidenfeld & Nicolson, 1980).

12. Crossman, *Diaries Vol.2*, op.cit., p. 714.
13. Ibid., p. 132.
14. Crossman, *Diaries Vol.1* op.cit., p. 582.
15. Wigg, George, op.cit., p. 315. It should be noted, however, that George Wigg was not an impartial witness. Lord Goodman asserts that 'he [Wigg] had always resented Marcia Williams because of the influence she exercised over Harold Wilson and that resentment grew as his own power diminished. He was a rejected favourite who did not relish the advance of his rival.' Goodman, Arnold, *Tell Them I'm On My Way* (London: Chapmans, 1993) p. 258.
16. Ibid., p. 316
17. Benn, *Office Without Power* op.cit., p. 2.
18. Ibid., p. 34.
19. Benn, *Out of the Wilderness* op.cit., p. 334.
20. Benn, ibid., p. 345.
21. Benn, *Office Without Power* op.cit., p. 255
22. See for instance, Beloff, Nora, 'How Wilson sees Premier's job' *Observer*, I March, 1964, p. 6; 'Whitehall and Beyond: Rt. Hon. Harold Wilson, MP Leader of the Opposition talks to Norman Hunt' *Listener*, 5 March, 1964, pp. 379–81 & p. 396 (hereafter referred to as the Hunt interview); 'My Plans by Harold Wilson' interview with James Margach, *Sunday Times*, 18 October 1964, pp. 41–2, for discussion of Wilson's intentions in respect of advice.
23. See for instance Morgan, Kenneth, O., *Labour People: Leaders and Lieutenants Hardie to Kinnock* (Oxford: University Press, 1987) p. 256.
24. Pimlott, Ben, *Harold Wilson* (London: HarperCollins, 1992); Goodman, op.cit.; Ziegler, Philip, *The Authorised Life of Lord Wilson of Rievaulx* (London: Weidenfeld & Nicolson, 1993).
25. See for example, *Observer* Review 8 August, 1993, pp. 41–2; *Sunday Times Review* 12 September, 1993, pp. 1–2; *Sunday Times Book Section*, 3 October, 1993, p. 3.
26. Roy Hattersley, for example, reviewing Ziegler's 1993 Wilson biography (op.cit.) notes that Wilson consistently agonized over plots to topple his leadership. Hattersley, Roy, 'Lord of misrule?' *Sunday Times* 3 October, 1993. Ponting, a different kind of insider, asserts that Wilson was '. . . a man with a deeply insecure personality . . . his suspicion of his colleagues and his preference for covert action helped to create an atmosphere of conspiracy and mistrust in the

government.' Ponting, Clive, *Breach of Promise: Labour in Power 1964-70* (London: Hamish Hamilton, 1989) p. 402.

27. See Mackintosh, John, *The British Cabinet* (London: Metheun, 1961) and Crossman, R.H.S., 'Introduction to the English Constitution' in Bagehot, Walter, *The English Constitution* Fontana edn (London: Collins, 1963).

28. Lord Hunt of Tanworth, 'The United Kingdom' in Plowden, William, ed. *Advising the Rulers* (Oxford: Blackwell, 1987) pp. 66-70, p. 68. Formerly Sir John Hunt, Cabinet Secretary, 1973-9.

29. Williams, Marcia, *Inside Number Ten* (London: Weidenfeld & Nicolson, 1972) pp. 344-5.

30. In the introduction to volume one he states that '. . . my ambition was to write a book which fulfilled for our generation the functions of Bagehot's *English Constitution* a hundred years ago by disclosing the secret operations of government . . . ' Crossman, *Diaries Vol.1*, op.cit., p. 11.

31. In his introduction to the 1965 edition of Bagehot's work Crossman had asserted: 'in our new kind of civil service, the minister must normally be content with the role of public relations officer to his department . . . ' Crossman, R.H.S., 'Introduction' to *The English Constitution* op.cit., p. 51.

32. See Haines, Joe, *The Politics of Power* (London: Coronet Books, 1977) p. 32. See also Marcia Williams for contrasting descriptions of the reception which greeted Wilson and his entourage when they entered No.10 in 1964 and 1966. Williams, op.cit., p. 27, p. 29 and p. 99. Crossman's diary entry for 22 October 1964 also describes what it felt like to be a new minister cocooned by the departmental civil servants. Crossman, *Diaries Vol.1*, op.cit., p. 21.

33. Jones, G.W., 'The Prime Minister's Aides' in King, Anthony ed. *The British Prime Minister* 2nd edn (London: Macmillan, 1985) pp. 72-95, pp. 77-80.

34. See 'Harold Wilson: Post Experience' Harold Wilson interviewed by Norman Hunt in King, *The British Prime Minister* op.cit., pp. 93-115, p. 94.

35. See Macmillan, Harold, *Riding the Storm* (London: Macmillan, 1971) pp. 192-193.

36. Sked, Alan and Cook, Chris, *Post-War Britain: a political history* 3rd edn (Harmondsworth: Penguin, 1990) p. 201. For a detailed account of Wilson's 1964 election campaign, see Howard, Anthony and West, Richard, *The Making of the Prime Minister* (London: Cape, 1965).

37. Wigg, op.cit., p. 311.

38. Williams, Marcia, op.cit., p. 19. See also Crossman *Diaries Vol.1*, op.cit., p. 116 and Pimlott op.cit., pp. 284–5 for Wilson's own view.

39. Ramsay, R., 'Wilson and the Security Services' in Copley, R., Fielding, S. and Tiratsoo, N., eds *The Wilson Governments 1964-1970* (London: Pinter, 1993) pp. 152–161, p. 152.

40. Cit Pimlott, op.cit., p. 304.

41. Earned mainly from his close association with, and subsequent resignation in sympathy with, Nye Bevan. See Pimlott op.cit., pp. 159–64.

42. See Haines, op.cit., Chapter 2 particularly p. 16 and p. 17; Crossman, *Diaries Vol.1*,op.cit., p. 64 and p. 616; and Castle, 'Mardarin Power' *Sunday Times* 10 June, 1973, p. 17 & p. 19.

43. See Hennessy, Peter, *Whitehall* (London: Fontana, 1990) for views expressed by Shirley Williams and Sir John Nott about the civil service as a check on radicalism. p. 1 and p. xiii respectively.

44. Shore, Peter, *Entitled to Know* (London: Macgibbon & Kee, 1966) p. 12.

45. Crossman, *Diaries Vol.1*. op. cit., pp. 615–16. This view was later corroborated by Sir John Hunt (Cabinet Secretary 1973-9). Reflecting on the 1960s he notes that 'the Treasury was all powerful and thus played a strong co-ordinating role which went far beyond the 'honest broker' role . . . Senior officials genuinely, if subconsciously, felt a dual loyalty – to their own Minister and to the Treasury – when the Treasury turned over in bed the whole of Whitehall turned with it.' Hunt, Sir John, 'Cabinet Strategy and Management' (London: Royal Institute of Public Administration, 1983) pp. 90–4, p. 92.

46. Wilson, Harold, (Lord of Wilson of Rievaulx), *Memoirs 1916–1964* (London: Weidenfeld & Nicolson and Michael Joseph, 1986) p. 193.

47. Weller, Patrick, 'Types of Advice' in Plowden, *Advising the Rulers* op.cit., pp. 149–57, p. 149.

48. See for example, Marcia Williams's description of a member of the Private Office '. . . discovered physically snatching sheets of No.10 notepaper out of Gerald's [Kaufman] hands and telling him he could under no circumstances use it.' Williams, op.cit., p. 224. Kaufman was at the time a political appointee using the paper in the performance of his political duties. See also Crossman, *Diaries Vol.1* op.cit., p. 172. The principle of civil service political neutrality is also demonstrated by the withdrawal of any civil servants present from cabinet meetings if the discussion turns to party political matters. See, Castle, *Diaries* op.cit., p. 3.

49. See Walker, David, 'The First Wilson Governments, 1964–1970' in Hennessy, Peter and Seldon, Anthony, eds *Ruling Performance* (Oxford: Blackwell, 1987) pp. 186–215.
50. James Callaghan and George Brown having been the other main contenders for the party leadership, after Gaitskell's death in 1963.
51. Wigg, op.cit., p. 312.
52. Falkender, Lady Marcia, *Downing Street in Perspective* (London: Weidenfeld & Nicolson, 1983) pp. 95–6.
53. Of his cabinet only Patrick Gordon-Walker, the Foreign Secretary and James Griffith at the Welsh Office, and Wilson himself, possessed previous cabinet experience. Indeed, Wilson himself can also be said to have had only limited previous experience in that he had only held one post, that of President of the Board of Trade.
54. Hunt interview, op.cit., p. 380.
55. Ibid., p. 396.
56. A view confirmed by Marcia Williams, see, Williams, op.cit., p. 354., and Falkender, op.cit., pp. 87–9.
57. Views that were largely restated in an interview with James Margach of the Sunday Times just after the October election. 'My Plans by Harold Wilson' interview with James Margach *Sunday Times* 18 October, 1964, pp. 41–2.
58. In the event the Ministry of Technology was established but Science became an additional responsibility of Education which was rechristened Education and Science.
59. Which actually materialized as the Department of Economic Affairs.
60. Hunt interview, op.cit., p. 380.
61. Ibid., p. 381.
62. Richard Neustadt, a recognized authority on presidential power and a former Kennedy aide, asserted 'he [Wilson] means to take all decisions into his own hands. He wants not only to make ultimate decisions but to pass issues through his own mind early, sitting at the centre of a brains-trust . . . on the model, he says, of JFK . . .' Cit., Healey, Denis, *The Time of My Life* (Harmondsworth: Penguin, 1990) p. 330. Healey goes on the reflect 'this was all too true. No Prime Minister ever interfered so much in the work of his colleagues as Wilson did in the first six years. . .' Ibid.
63. See Pimlott, op.cit., p. 332.
64. See Ponting, op.cit., p. 17 and Crossman *Diaries Vol.1*, p. 92 for discussion of Balogh's appointment.
65. Balogh was, in fact, well known for his criticism of the administrative class of the civil service in general and of the inadequacy of Treasury economic advice in particular. See Balogh,

Thomas, 'The Apotheosis of the Dilettante: The Establishment of Mandarins' in Thomas, Hugh, ed. *Crisis in the Civil Service* (Tonbridge: Anthony Blond, 1968) pp. 11–52.

66. Roy Hattersley, for example, describes George Wigg as '. . . paymaster general and copper's nark'. Hattersley, Roy *Sunday Times* op.cit., p. 3. Lord Goodman notes that Wilson's anxieties were '. . . not unassisted by George Wigg, who became more and more valuable to Wilson, principally as a source of information – largely, alas, misinformation – about the behaviour of anyone in the parliamentary party.' Goodman, op.cit., p. 188.

67. See Falkender, op.cit., pp. 87–9.

68. Wyndham was a rich man and did not expect a salary. See William's op.cit., p. 356.

69. Falkender, op.cit., p. 94.

70. Pimlott, op.cit., p. 344.

71. See Williams, op. cit., p. 52.

72. Advice to the prime minister unmediated by Whitehall or members of the cabinet.

73. O.G.P.U. – Unified State Political Administration, Stalinist political police, successor to Cheka and forerunner of the K.G.B.

74. Beloff, 'How Wilson sees Premier's job' op.cit., p. 6. See also Crossman *Diaries Vol.1*, op.cit., p. 45 for an account of the hostile reaction to outside advisers during his time and the Department of Housing and Local Government.

75. 'The Prime Ministers' Advisers' *Political Studies* Vol.21, 1973 pp. 363–75; 'The Prime Ministers' Secretaries: Politicians or Administrators?'in Griffith, J.A.G., ed. *From Policy to Administration – Essays in Honour of William H. Robson* (London: George Allen & Unwin, 1976); 'The Prime Minister's Aides' in King 1985, op.cit., pp. 72–95; 'United Kingdom' in Plowden 1987, op.cit., pp. 36–66.

76. Jones, in Griffiths, op.cit., pp. 24–5.

77. John T. Davies became Principal Private Secretary aided by Frances Stevenson, Lloyd George's private secretary and mistress, and William Sutherland, who mainly managed the press and distributed honours. Jones, ibid., p. 26.

78. Hennessy describes the 'Garden Suburb' as '. . . in essence a job creation scheme for a group of Lloyd George cronies.' Hennessy, *Whitehall* op.cit., p. 66. Hennessy also notes that even before becoming prime minister and creating the Garden Suburb, whilst President of the Board of Trade, Lloyd George had surrounded himself with personal appointees, pejoratively dubbed his

'Taffiocracy'. Ibid., p. 57.

79. Jones, in Plowden, op.cit., p. 43.
80. According to Jones, its staff of mainly economists was not concerned just with the collection of statistics; it drew conclusions from them and made policy recommendations. It produced a flow of memoranda for the prime minister about papers circulated to cabinet or cabinet committees. It responded to Churchill's request for opinions and Cherwell took the initiative in rasing issues with him. Macdougall describes the unit as being: '. . . essentially personal to the prime minister; it worked continuously for him; it had some idea of what was in his mind, it knew the sort of thing he wanted to know and how he liked it presented, its loyalty was to him and no one else.' Cit. Jones, *Political Studies* op.cit., p. 370.
81. Jones, in Plowden, op.cit., p. 44.
82. Jones, in *Political Studies* op.cit. p. 365.
83. Jones, in Plowden, op.cit., p. 46.
84. The other being Harold Davies, an old Bevanite friend of Wilson's, who according to Pimlott, performed the usual PPS duties, whilst Shore an ex-policy adviser from Transport House, and newly elected MP, continued his previous role as policy adviser, while also preparing the ground for the next election. Pimlott, op.cit., p. 340.
85. Minister of Housing and Local Government 1964-6; Lord President and Leader of the House 1966-8, Secretary of State for Social Services 1968-70.
86. Postmaster General and then in 1966, Minister of Technology.
87. Crossman, *Diaries Vol.1*, op.cit. p. 363.
88. Beloff, Nora, *Transit of Britain* (London: Collins, 1973) p. 211.
89. Jones, *Political Quarterly* 1979, op.cit. p. 368.
90. See also Marcia Williams *Inside Number 10* and Falkender, *Downing Street in Perspective* op.cit., for detailed account of the personal struggle she and other members of Wilson's staff were forced to engage in.
91. Pimlott, op.cit.,p. 338.
92. Pimlott, ibid., pp. 338-9.
93. See Ziegler, op.cit., p. 119.
94. Haines, op.cit., p. 167.
95. Wilson, Harold, *The Labour Government 1964-1970: a personal record* (London: Weidenfeld & Nicolson and Michael Joseph, 1971.
96. Castle, *Diaries* op.cit., p. 3. See also Crossman, *Diaries Vol.1*, op.cit., p. 356 and *Vol.2*, op.cit., p. 51 and p. 295. Crossman also describes the close relationship between Wilson and his Principal Private Secretary, Michael Hall. See ibid., p. 880 and pp. 905-6.

97. Morgan, op.cit., p. 260. It is worth noting that Morgan goes some way to contradicting this view himself on ibid. p. 256.
98. Williams, op.cit., pp. 110–11.
99. Ibid., p. 122.
100. Wakins, Alan, 'The conservatism of Mr Wilson' *Spectator* 3 December 1965, p. 731. See also Ponting op.cit., p. 174.
101. 'Harold Wilson: Post Experience' interviewed by Norman Hunt, April 1967, in King, op.cit., p. 96.
102. Falkender, Lady Marcia, 'Eyes and Ears for Harold Wilson' *Observer* 20 February, 1977, p. 26 and p. 28, p. 26.
103. Ibid., p. 26.
104. Moorehead, Caroline, 'Profile of Lady Falkender: Part 2 'The Battle for Downing Street won, her political future is assured' *The Times* 24 July, 1974, p. 16.
105. Jones, *Political Studies*, op.cit., p. 363.
106. Hennessy, *Whitehall* op.cit., pp. 172–4.
107. See Crossman *Diaries Vol.1*, op.cit. p. 288, p. 290 and p. 305.
108. Ibid., p. 92.
109. Kaufman, Gerald, *How to be a Minister* (London: Sidgwick & Jackson, 1980) p. 81.
110. See Williams, op.cit., p. 357.
111. Ponting, op.cit., p. 178.
112. In March 1966 Michael Halls replaced Derek Mitchel as Wilson's Principal Private Secretary. Crossman noted that Halls had 'worked his way into Harold's life.' Crossman *Diaries Vol.3*, op.cit., p. 880.
113. Falkender, op.cit., p. 97.
114. Kaufman, op.cit., p. 82.
115. See for example, Crossman *Diaries Vol.2*, op.cit., p. 194 and p. 197.
116. Cit. Moorhead, Caroline, 'Profile of Lady Falkender Part 1: From a secretary's chair to a seat in the House of Lords' *The Times* 23 July, 1974, p. 18.
117. Ibid.
118. Wigg, op.cit., p. 312.
119. A somewhat naive assumption, on the part of Ziegler, given Marcia Williams's role as custodian of Wilson's political standing and given her reputation for outspokenness.
120. Ziegler, op.cit., p. 182.
121. See Hunt interview, op.cit., p. 380.
122. The past does indeed provide examples of prime ministers whose practices were not dissimilar to those of Wilson, for example, Lloyd George and Churchill. However, both these examples could, firstly,

be regarded as exceptional because they were practices resorted to in war-time, and, secondly, they too attracted adverse constitutional comment, particularly in the case of Lloyd George's 'Garden Suburb'. See Davies, Joseph, *The Prime Ministers Secretariat 1916–1920* (Newport: R.J. Johns, 1951) and Deedes, William, 'Reinforcements for No.10?' *Telegraph* 15 November, 1928, p. 14.

123. Hunt interview, op.cit., p. 381.

124. Ponting, op.cit., p. 347.

125. Benn, *Out of the Wilderness* op.cit., pp. 41–2.

126. Brown, op.cit., p. 93.

127. Ibid., p. 138 and p. 140.

128. Neustadt, Richard, E., *Presidential Power* (John Wiley & Sons, 1976), p. 49.

129. Falkender, 'Eyes and Ears of Harold Wilson' op.cit.

130. Benn, *Diaries Vol.2*, op.cit., p. 215, see also pp. 188 and 217.

131. Crossman, *Diaries Vol.1*, op.cit., p. 246. See also p. 333 and pp. 334–5.

132. Hunt interview, op.cit., p. 396.

133. Benn, *Out of the Wilderness* op.cit., p. 188. See also Benn, *Office Without Power* op.cit., p. 255 and Wigg, *George Wigg* op.cit. p. 312 and p. 315.

134. Crossman, *Diaries Vol.1*, op.cit., p. 356 and p. 582; and *Vol.3* p. 880 and pp. 905–6.

135. Morgan, *Labour People* op.cit., p. 256.

136. Tony Benn, for instance, reflecting on Harold Wilson's attitude in this respect, notes 'Harold doesn't like it to be known he has any advisers. Partly this is because he doesn't want to upset the Party Machine and partly because he likes everyone to think that all his successes are his alone.' Benn, *Out of the Wilderness* op.cit., p. 146.

137. See Crossman, *Diaries Vol.1*, op.cit. p. 247. See also Brown, op.cit., p. 104 and p. 110.

138. Crossman, for example, notes that there was a '. . . disgusting article about her [Marcia Williams] in the Evening Standard.' Crossman, *Diaries Vol.2*, op.cit., p. 201. Goodman also relates that on several occasions he was consulted by Wilson in respect of 'allegations that there was some special relationship between the Prime Minister and Mrs Williams.' He goes on to say that 'Right wing newspapers singled her out for every conceivable hostility.' Goodman, op.cit.,p. 212.

139. David Walker notes that 'the "real thing" for Wilson was to make a Labour government – *his* Labour government – acceptable in British electoral circumstances.' Walker, op.cit., p. 200.
140. See Morgan, *Labour People* op.cit., p. 256 and Goodman, op.cit., p. 264.

5 Edward Heath 1970–4: A Counter-Revolutionary?

... Heath's concentration of power obviously gives the idea ... that presidential power is slowly creeping up on No.10 with what a *Financial Times* reporter calls 'Grandmother's Footsteps'. Whenever anyone turns round to challenge him, the Prime Minister is always standing virtuously still.[1]

... perhaps Selsdon Man was always a Civil Servant at heart. . .[2]

Harold Wilson tried to bridge the gap that was developing between the political and constitutional position of the prime minister, by introducing a degree of presidentialization into the prime minister's advisory system. Edward Heath was a counter-revolutionary. Assuming Wilson's innovations to be simply the personal preferences of a premier with presidential aspirations, he tried to 'depresidentialize' the premiership and distance himself from the constitutionally dubious and controversial advisory strategies of his predecessor. He did succeed in avoiding the kind of fuss that Wilson's experiments had attracted, but controversy about advice was not entirely eliminated, and the thrust of presidentialization was not reversed.

On 17 January 1973 Edward Heath, accompanied by the Chancellor of the Exchequer, Anthony Barber, on one side, and Head of the Civil Service, Sir William Armstrong, on the other, attended a press conference in Lancaster House to announce the outlines of Stage Two of the government's statutory incomes policy. The presence of Sir William Armstrong at what could be described as a highly public political occasion was doubly symbolic. On the one hand it fuelled growing disquiet among some Conservatives that Edward Heath's abandonment of election pledges, in this instance that there would be no statutory regulation of incomes, could be attributed, partly at least, to Heath's excessive reliance on the advice of officials. David Watt in 1972 reported that 'many Conservatives in Parliament and outside it certainly suspect that the change of policy from the hard line of the lame-ducks era to the present much despised search for consensus has been engineered by soft-centred liberals in the Whitehall machine.'[3] On the other hand, it provided evidence of what appeared to be the growing politicization of one of the most senior civil servants in Whitehall. Armstrong's role in respect of statutory prices and incomes policy was particularly high profile. He was also instrumental in persuading Heath to stand firm against the miners, a stand which in retrospect can be seen to have precipitated an early general election and the subsequent defeat of the government.[4] At the time few ministers complained about Armstrong's predominance. This was apparently because many thought every prime minister needed cronies and thought it natural that Heath should choose a civil servant rather than a politician.[5] Fay and Young point out, however, that, in subsequent post mortems ministers began to recall the partnership with a 'frisson' of alarm and complained about Armstrong's influence over the direction of the government.[6] Prices and incomes policy became central to the government's fight against inflation by 1973, and, therefore, Armstrong, as Heath's special adviser in these matters became visible and appeared to be influential.

When governments begin to pursue very unpopular policies, especially if they are policies which break electoral promises, questions are raised about whom the government is listening to. On whose advice are the policies based? By 1972 the Heath government had adopted increasingly interventionist measures[7] in an attempt to stop the rising tide of unemployment and industrial unrest. Such intervention would have aroused little comment in the context of the post-war consensus which had accepted a commitment to full employment as the priority of government economic policy. It was controversial, however, in the light of the Conservative's 1970 election manifesto which had promised less interventionist policies.[8] By 1972 the government was forced into a series of 'spectacular U-turns'.[9] Even the act of policy reversal itself was a U-turn. The manifesto had claimed: 'our promises are not, like Labour's, a collection of short-lived devices . . . Nor are they a set of promises made only to be broken.'[10] After two years in office it seemed, the government had broken its promises: less intervention had become more intervention; firmness and resolve appeared to have collapsed at the first obstacle.[11]

Under the Wilson regime controversy about advice to the prime minister had centred on the constitutional implications arising from the role of unofficial advisers. Under Edward Heath controversy about advice centred on the possibly excessive influence of official advisers.[12] No one questioned the constitutionality of the source, but questions were raised about the possible constitutional implications of a supposedly politically neutral, senior civil servant behaving in a politically controversial manner. However, although the terms in which the controversies were expressed differed, the question of the presidentialization of the premiership gave them a common underlying theme. Deteriorating economic circumstances forced Heath into an increasingly interventionist, or presidential, role in the government and it was this that gave added significance to the question of 'who had the prime minister's ear?'.

Edward Heath, like Harold Wilson before him, introduced changes in the advisory system. In order to explore the constitutional implications of these changes and decide the extent to which they contributed to the process of presidentialization, it is necessary first to answer some preliminary questions. What was the constitutional position regarding advice to the prime minister when Heath entered office and what kind of advisory system-in-place did he inherit? Why did he change it? What changes did he introduce?

The formal constitutional position regarding advice to the prime minister in 1970 was much the same as it had been in 1964: prime ministers were advised in respect of both policy and politics by their cabinet colleagues. Policy advice forming the basis of cabinet discussions was still supposed to be mediated by senior civil servants. During the Wilson years there had been a slight increase in the use of special advisers who in some cases had direct access to ministers, but their overall numbers were few[13] and their impact seems to have been slight. By 1970 the DEA had been effectively emasculated by the Treasury, and, although the Labour government had accepted the recommendations of Fulton and set up a Civil Service Department to take over the establishment responsibilities of the Treasury, it was manned by civil servants previously reared in the Treasury and headed by Sir William Armstrong, a former Joint Permanent Secretary of the Treasury.[14] There had been no permanent revolutionary changes in the secret constitution.

There had also been little formal change in the advisory system within No.10. Mrs Williams headed a more structured political office than the occasional appointee of post-war predecessors, such as Macmillan's John Wyndham, and the press office had been enlarged to include political appointees, but there had been no permanent institutionalization of these changes. The new structure was developed by Wilson to meet his own needs and it could well disappear at the end of his tenure. The prime minister's staff at No.10 consisted primarily of a Private Office run by civil servants. Indeed, during the latter part of his premiership, Wilson reputedly relied predominantly on the advice of Sir Burke Trend, the Cabinet Secretary. George Wigg, Wilson's colleague and crony, and Thomas Balogh, his partisan economic adviser, had both departed No.10 for the House of Lords in 1967 and had not been replaced.

The formal structure of the prime ministerial advisory system, therefore, remained more or less unchanged, but Wilson's tactics had created a precedent which could be built upon in the future. Wilson's attempts to change the secret constitution may have met with resistance, but he had nevertheless, begun to breach the Whitehall fortress. The Fulton Report had legitimized the appointment of 'outsiders' as specialist advisers.[15] Such *alternative* advice to ministers in British government is effectively advice to the prime minister one stage removed. In addition, the territorial battles waged by Mrs Williams to establish a political office within No.10 paved the way for future political appointees and made it unlikely that they would be merely seen as one extra pair of hands in the Private Office, as seems to have been the case with John Wyndham. Mrs Williams's appointment was thought by some to breach constitutional propriety because her advisory role seemed to be without constitutional precedent. This would no longer be the case should future prime ministers wish to make similar political appointments. The same could be said about the appointments of Gerald Kaufman and Thomas Balogh.

Heath inherited an advisory system in which the civil service's former near-monopoly over policy advice had been weakened and in which the prime minister had a little more freedom to call upon *alternative* political advisers. Why then did Heath seek to introduce changes?

On the 18 June 1970 Edward Heath secured a comfortable Conservative victory[16] from the jaws of defeat, winning an election no one, not even the Conservatives themselves,[17] had expected him to win.[18] Much of the credit for the eleventh hour reversal of Tory fortunes was attributed to Heath himself. The *Economist* proclaimed: 'only one man has really won this election and that man is Mr Heath.'[19] If the Conservatives were less than confident of Heath's ability to deliver an election victory, why had they chosen him to lead them? Heath was to be the Tories' answer to Harold Wilson. Not only was Edward Heath the first elected leader of the Conservative Party,[20] he also represented a new breed of Tory MP: self-made, first-generation, professional politicians.[21] David Heasman asserts that Heath's defeat of Maudling in the Tory party leadership contest could at least in part be attributed to his modest background and the fact that '. . . he possessed the more fashionable of Mr Wilson's qualifications: humble origins, drive, ruthlessness, familiarity with the complexities of a modern economy, professional competence, dedication to efficiency and modernization.'[22]

Whilst Heath's selection as Tory leader may have been partly due to similarities that he shared with Harold Wilson, there was not much similarity in their style of leadership. Harold Wilson was a gossipy man who liked to surround himself with confidants. He continually sought reassurance and appeared to thrive on intrigue. Heath was the opposite. He was taciturn, had few close associates and for the most part kept his own counsel. George Hutchinson describes Heath as '. . . an unusually self-sufficient person. To an extent that is probably rare, he does not depend on others, even close friends . . . they are not essential to him. He is self-contained, detached, reserved.'[23]

Heath deliberately tried to distance himself from any similarities he may have had to Wilson. In his personal foreword to the Conservative election manifesto, he indicated that he intended, if he were elected, to run a very different kind of government from his Labour predecessor:

> During the last six years we have suffered not only from bad policies, but from a cheap and trivial style of government. Decisions have been dictated simply by the desire to catch tomorrow's headlines . . . Every device has been used to gain immediate publicity, and government by gimmick has become the order of the day . . . We must create a new way of running our national offices. This means sweeping away the trivialities and the gimmicks which now dominate the political scene.[24]

Sked and Cook describe how, right from the start,

> . . . the new Prime Minister made it clear that he intended his government to be substantially different from Wilson's both in style and policies. He determined to shun the publicity and personal initiatives which had characterized the previous tenure of 10 Downing Street. There was to be an end to the dramatic overnight rescue operations and the dashing new initiatives which had launched a thousand headlines but often little else.[25]

As if to demonstrate this new style he intended to adopt, when Heath arrived at 10 Downing Street on the 19 June 1970, despite the presence of the mass media, he decided not to hold a press conference but left it to his press officer to answer questions.[26]

Heath had a different political style and intended to conduct his government in a different manner to that of his predecessor. In the context of the history of the Conservative Party, the choice of Heath as leader can be regarded as a radical break with the past. This also brought a change in the approach to policy formulation. Traditionally Tory leaders had, according to Kavanagh, '. . . eschewed detailed policy-making in opposition.'[27] In contrast, Heath had used the period since the 1966 election defeat as one of intensive preparation for government.[28] This preparation process, which was in itself radical in the Tory party, culminated in the much publicized meeting of the shadow cabinet over the weekend of 31 January to 1 February, at Selsdon Park, from which emerged policies that promised a radical departure from those accepted by Heath's post-war predecessors. The Selsdon Man policies, as they came to be known, heralded a break with the post-war consensus: less state intervention in the economy; no formal prices and incomes policies; cuts in direct taxes and public spending; a shift to greater selectivity in welfare, and trade union reform, were all on the agenda[29]

Heath and his shadow cabinet had adopted a radical programme at Selsdon early in 1970. By 1970, however, senior civil servants had administered consensus policies for a quarter of a century. It seemed likely that the challenge to consensus that the Selsdon programme represented would encounter some resistance among senior policy advisers. It was to overcome this potential check on radicalism that Heath began his 'Quiet Revolution'.

Heath's 'Quiet Revolution'[30] was to be an attempt to alter the political culture both within and beyond Whitehall. Beyond Whitehall, the aim was to generate greater self-reliance within the business community and the workforce and among the citizenry at large. From Whitehall, government would aid this process by adopting less interventionist policies on the one hand, and setting an example of greater efficiency on the other. In the words of Bruce-Gardyne: 'less government and of a better quality: this was the essence of the Quiet Revolution.'[31] Heath recognized that the natural tendency of the civil service would be to thwart any proposed reduction in government programmes and resist radical initiatives. Like Wilson, he saw a need to change the secret constitution under which the civil service still exercised a near monopoly over policy advice.

What kind of changes did Heath introduce into the advisory system? Heath attempted to tackle what he perceived to be problems of the advisory system in several interconnected ways. Firstly, in accordance with his belief that opposition was a time for preparation for government, he had not only initiated an intensive policy planning exercise but he had also encouraged front bench spokesmen to specialize in the area of government they were shadowing with a view to using such specialisms in office.[32] Heath hoped that this would help to ensure that his government would be less likely to be 'blown off course' or that his ministers would be reduced to the role of salesmen for the favourite policies of civil servants. Secondly, the improvements in policy arising from such thorough preparation for office were to be complemented by a reorganization of central government. This reorganization had four elements: the restructuring of the machinery of government to create fewer, larger departments; the infusion of new ideas by recruiting outsiders to be temporary civil servants; a programme of evaluation of departmental responsibilities, and the creation of a central briefing body.

Before the election Heath made it clear that he intended to wind up the DEA and the Ministry of Technology, which he regarded as 'mere publicity stunts'.[33] They were to be reabsorbed into the Treasury and the Board of Trade respectively. He also announced his intention to create two new 'super' departments, which were intended to reduce inter-departmental friction and streamline administration. To this end the giant Department of Health and Social Security created by Wilson would be retained and in addition a Department of Environment[34] and a Department of Trade and Industry[35] would be created. This federal structure would permit a smaller cabinet, thereby making it a more effective coordinating and decision-making body.

In accordance with the recommendations of the Fulton Committee, and in line with the precedent set by Wilson, Heath also intended to encourage greater cross-fertilization of ideas for policy initiatives between outsiders and civil servants. In 1969 he put together a Businessmen's Team under Richard Meyjes from Shell, on the understanding that when the Conservative government took office a number of them would take up positions in Whitehall. It was hoped that the presence of businessmen would help to engender a new managerial ethos and a greater awareness of cost efficiency and cost benefit analysis. Heath intended to subject all departmental activities to a rigorous evaluation process, Programme Analysis and Review (PAR). Some of the businessmen recruited into Whitehall would participate in the PAR teams which would 'question the *raison d'être* for departmental activities'[36] with a view to hiving-off as much as possible to outside agencies. This process was intended to aid the streamlining of the administration to produce less, and more efficient government, in short, the 'Quiet Revolution'.

The White Paper on the Reorganization of Central Government[37] published in October 1970, which set out some of the above changes, also outlined the government's intention to create a new institution within the advisory system, a central briefing body: the Central Policy Review Staff (CPRS), soon to be known as the Think Tank. The CPRS was designed to provide periodic reviews of government strategy and to counteract the tendency of cabinet ministers towards departmentalism.

In the event the CPRS that came into being in 1971 was a small[38] multi-disciplinary body attached to the Cabinet Office. Its first director was Lord Rothschild, a scientist and chairman of Shell Research Limited. The membership comprised approximately fifty per cent 'fast stream' civil servants on secondment from Whitehall departments and fifty per cent 'outsiders' recruited from industry, the universities, the City, local government and public corporations.[39]

The CPRS, whilst under the supervision of the prime minister, was established to work for ministers collectively and it was intended that individual ministers would provide it with its assignments. From the outset its work took four forms: strategy reviews of the government's overall performance; research projects relating to areas which cut across departmental responsibilities such as those into Rolls Royce; energy; race relations; and Concorde; collective briefs intended to tackle ministers' lack of any briefing if their department had no stake in the topics on the cabinet agenda;[40] lastly, it provided a constant flow of economic advice.

Entering office armed with a set of proposed policies; maintaining greater continuity between shadow cabinet and subsequent cabinet appointments; secondment of outsiders into Whitehall and the creation of the CPRS, were all intended to improve the quality of *policy* advice available to the cabinet and so to the prime minister. These changes were expected to infuse new ideas into Whitehall and, at the same time, help to break down any resistance that might confront a government intent upon radical alternatives to post-war consensus policies. It was hoped that these new arrangements would ensure that, in contrast to its Labour predecessor, the Heath government would not be forced into ill-conceived short-term crisis management, and that policy initiative would not be ceded to the civil service.[41]

Continuing to employ Patrick Weller's analytical distinction between *policy* advice and *political* advice,[42] and having examined the changes that Heath introduced into the system of policy advice available to the cabinet and so to the prime minister, we must now consider whether Heath made important changes in the prime minister's political advisory system.

By the time Mr Wilson and his entourage left Downing Street in 1970, in addition to the prime minister's Private Office run by civil servants, there was a firmly established Political Office headed by Marcia Williams, and an enhanced, more overtly political, Press Office headed by Joe Haines. Whilst Heath retained this formal structure within No.10, he went to some length to tone down some of its controversial features. Campbell points out that 'Heath was from the very beginning determined not to surround himself with a Wilsonian 'kitchen cabinet' of cronies.'[43]

Heath demonstrated this desire to be less constitutionally controversial than his predecessor by selecting ex-civil servants to be members of his personal staff. In Campbell's view 'the clearest signal of the new tone in Downing Street was Heath's choice of a chief press officer in succession to Wilson's mouthpiece, Joe Haines. Rather than appoint a similarly sympathetic Tory journalist, he chose a career civil servant, Donald Maitland.'[44] As if to underline further this less partisan stance, Heath retained Barbara Hosking, a Wilson appointee, as Assistant Press Secretary. According to Douglas Hurd, 'he [Heath] felt that Mr Wilson had made a great mistake in turning the Press office into a political fief.'[45] Campbell describes the difference in the style of the press office that resulted from Heath's changes and claims that '. . . nothing could have better symbolized the change of government between Wilson and Heath than the contrast between Haines's *Daily Mirror* style of news management and Maitland's dapper Foreign Office style.'[46] Heath's political office was reduced to only one appointee, Douglas Hurd, who like Maitland had also been a permanent official at the Foreign Office.[47] Campbell asserts that 'the replacement of Marcia Williams by Douglas Hurd as the Prime Minister's political secretary made another piquant contrast. . . His relationship to Heath was much more that of a trusted civil servant to his Minister than the confidential friend – soundingboard, nanny and fiercely loyal protectress – that Marcia Williams was to Wilson.'[48] Hurd himself, reflects that he was a little unsure as to the specific nature of his role but that ' . . . the one point clear to me about my new duties was that I was expected to carry them out in quite a different way to Mrs Williams.'[49] He goes on to say ' . . . when I stood on the doorstep of Number Ten about teatime on 19 June 1970, I understood only that I was expected to make peace where Mrs Williams had made war.'[50] In addition to political secretary, Douglas Hurd, and the press office under Donald Maitland, Heath's only other personal staff in Downing Street were Michael Wolff, speech writer,[51] Timothy Kitson who was Heath's PPS and Geoffrey Tucker, director of publicity at Conservative Central Office, who continued to handle Heath's television appearances.

Heath's small corps of personal appointees in Downing Street indicated that, in his view, the cabinet was still the accepted forum for political advice to the prime minister. In 1978, looking back on his own arrangements, Heath stated: '. . . I think one has to be very clear about what peoples' jobs are . . . the so called political adviser at Number Ten is really the link between a Prime Minister and his Party . . . the political adviser does have the job of keeping contact with the party in the country . . . When you come to other advisers, the real advisers to the Prime Minister . . . are the colleagues who are running the Departments.'[52]

We have examined the formal constitutional position in respect of advice to the prime minister in 1970 and the nature of the advisory system Edward Heath inherited. Explanations have been offered as to why Heath found that system unsatisfactory, and the changes he introduced to correct these shortcomings have been described. We can now go on to evaluate the constitutional implications of these changes and decide whether they continued the process of presidentializing the premiership.

The formal constitutional position regarding advice to the prime minister in 1970, was much as it had been in 1964: prime ministers were advised in respect of both policy and political strategy and tactics by their cabinet colleagues. Policy advice forming the basis of cabinet discussions was supposed to be mediated by senior civil servants. It could not be claimed that Wilson's arrangements in No.10 in respect of advice, had, by 1970, achieved the status of new conventions, but they could be regarded as precedents. If Heath chose to continue such arrangements, then it might have gone some way to shifting the formal constitutional position, serving perhaps to weaken the position that the cabinet had traditionally occupied in the prime ministerial advisory system and strengthen that of personal partisan appointees of the prime minister. Did the changes introduced by Edward Heath consolidate this pattern and what, if any, were the constitutional implications of any changes?

Edward Heath did continue the process, begun by Harold Wilson, of challenging the traditional near-monopoly exercised by the civil service over policy advice. Heath also appointed personal advisers to work in No.10. Heath's advisory strategies, therefore, would appear to have implications for the constitutional conventions in respect of advice. The expectation then, is that some sort of constitutional fuss would follow. But in contrast to the Wilson years, there was little controversy about advice during Heath's period in office, he succeeded in defusing public anxiety about creeping presidentialization.

The recruitment of 'outsiders' into Whitehall potentially undermined the monopoly over advice assumed by the civil service. The appointment of irregulars by the Heath government did arouse some criticism in some instances, but the response could not be described as amounting to constitutional controversy. In October 1972, Mr John Davies, Secretary of State for Trade and Industry, appointed Mr John Cope, a former Tory candidate, to be his 'special political assistant'. When informing senior officials of Mr Cope's appointment and outlining his role, Mr Davies said:

> I have decided to appoint a special assistant to help me with the political aspects of my work, in particular as it effects the party outside Parliament . . . To enable Mr Cope to undertake his task he will need to be closely in touch with the formulation of departmental policies and decision-making. To this end he will work alongside my principal private secretary. He will attend meetings with which I am concerned, and will need to be in direct contact with officials in the department. As a working member of my private office he will have access to official papers . . . [53]

Mr William Kendall, general secretary of the Civil and Public Service Association, described the appointment of Mr Cope as being: ' . . . pregnant with constitutional implications of revolutionary kind,'[54] the criticism being that Mr Cope's was a '. . . party political appointment of quite a new kind'[55] which, according to Mr Kendall, contravened the Estacode which forbids civil servants to discuss government policies with unauthorized persons. Given that special advisers were, by 1972, no longer new in Whitehall, it is curious that Mr Cope's particular brief caused such a reaction. Klein and Lewis suggest a distinction can be drawn between special advisers brought in by specific ministers to provide general support, and experts or business men, having special skills or knowledge, attached to a department.[56] Employing this distinction, and a further qualifying distinction in relation to the source of an adviser's salary, one possible explanation of civil service disquiet about Mr Cope is that he, like Mrs Williams, was the personal appointee of a politician, paid by the party and, therefore, beyond the reach of civil service rules. Most other special advisers, by contrast, were attached to departments and given the status of temporary civil servants.

The reaction to Mr Cope's appointment was an exception. In general, the appointment of 'irregulars' by the Heath government provoked little controversy. The explanation for this may be that the real policy impact of special advisers and outside experts was in any case slight, if for no other reason than that they were few in number and their appointments temporary in nature. Although Bruce-Gardyne claims that fourteen of Mr Heath's Business Team took up temporary appointments,[57] Mr Heath himself asserts that about fourteen people from industry and the City participated in policy discussions when the Conservatives were in opposition, but only about six subsequently took up appointments in Whitehall.[58] Such a tiny contingent of outsiders aroused few fears that the prime minister was trying to create a layer of political posts in the civil service comparable to those over which an American president exercises patronage. In addition, Hutchinson, asserts that Heath intended that ' . . . the business element would be in the nature of auxiliaries rather than principals, important but never supreme.'[59] Not only were the outsiders, few in number and subordinate in position, but within eighteen months of the Conservatives taking office their numbers seem to have diminished further. In October 1972 David Watt noted that of the irregulars brought in with the government:

> . . . there are now almost none of these left in government. Mr Arthur Cockfield, the Chancellor's brilliant tax adviser remains because he caught a tide in the Revenue Department. Mr Robin Hutton

is special adviser to Sir John Eden at Posts and Telecommunications. There are also one or two businessmen in charge of new executive bodies, like Mr John Cuckney at the Property Services Administration. But the big eight-man business team has disappeared although it was originally intended that it should be replenished.'[60]

Campbell, discussing the role of special advisers during the Heath period, reflects that 'like most free-floating outsiders transplanted without adequate support into the established bureaucracy . . . they were able to make little perceptible impact.'[61] He goes on to assert 'the threat they posed to the impartiality of Whitehall was minimal . . . and as a group they quickly sank without trace.'[62]

If the impact of special advisers and/or experts attached to individual ministers or ministries was limited, and therefore caused minimal controversy, what of the new central briefing agency, the CPRS? Was the multi-disciplinary, intellectual powerhouse under the direction of Lord Rothschild, who saw himself as a 'licensed independent operator within the government machine,'[63] a source of controversy? It would seem likely that, as Dr Tessa Blackstone, a one time member of the CPRS, asserts, 'an organisation of this kind was bound to attract controversy if it did its job effectively.'[64] Arguably, however, the CPRS was relatively non-controversial.[65] Blackstone and Plowden describe the practice of civil servants 'bouncing' papers on to the cabinet agenda at the eleventh hour in order to circumvent CPRS comments[66] and assert that '. . . they [members of the CPRS] were regarded with suspicion, even resentment, by some civil servants: and they often had to do battle with the official machine if their advice was to have any effect'.[67] Bruce-Gardyne implies that Rothschild's maverick behaviour aroused the disapproval of civil service colleagues.[68] The overall impression conveyed by the fairly extensive literature examining the activities of the Think Tank,[69] however, endorses Simon James's view that 'the supreme success of the CPRS's career was its excellent relations with the civil service.'[70] Several factors account for the relative acceptance of the CPRS among both officials and politicians.

Firstly, the CPRS was only the latest in a series of prototypes that could trace their genealogy through Lloyd George's 'Garden Suburb' during the First World War; Macdonald's Economic Advisory Council of 1929; Churchill's Statistical Section during the Second World War to Attlee's Central Economic Planning Staff of 1947.[71] This ancestry perhaps encouraged Whitehall to expect the CPRS to be of a similarly transitory nature and, therefore, as representing no permanent threat to civil service dominance over the advisory system. Secondly, at least fifty per cent of CPRS members were permanent civil servants,[72] an arrangement that enabled the input of the outsiders to be monitored whilst at the same time initiating them into the ways of Whitehall. Thirdly, it was dependent on the information and cooperation of civil servants. Lord Rothschild admitted that 'the CPRS depended heavily on officials for information and advice on almost every issue with which it dealt.'[73] Whilst such a dependent relationship may have helped to reassure officials, it seems likely, at the same time, to have placed some inhibitions on the CPRS's rights of 'free speech'.[74]

Another factor which helps to explain why the CPRS provoked little controversy is that it was not an *ad hoc* arrangement of political appointees orbiting around the prime minister, but a properly constituted body whose outside members became temporary civil servants. The CPRS had impeccable parentage through the Cabinet Secretary, Burke Trend, who drafted the White Paper establishing the new briefing agency. Colin Seymour-Ure suggests that such institutionalization helps in the process of legitimizing advisory bodies.[75] Campbell agrees, he describes the CPRS as 'the most successful of Heath's Whitehall innovations' and attributes its success to '. . . its being properly constituted as a permanent entity within the official machine, set up with the support and blessing of the Cabinet Secretary.'[76]

If the above factors help to explain the acceptance of the CPRS in Whitehall, a major factor explaining its acceptance in Westminster may have been that it was not perceived to be an *alternative* advisory system serving the prime minister that might strengthen him *vis-à-vis* his cabinet. The CPRS was specifically designed to provide collective briefs to underpin the cabinet's role as a collective decision-making body, it was not intended to be a tool of an interventionist, presidential premier. Indeed, in the Commons debate on the setting up of the CPRS, Mr William Whitelaw, Leader of the House, assured the House that 'the Central Review Body will merely enable Ministers to carry out their collective responsibility better by making their decisions more soundly based.'[77] This view was endorsed by Blackstone and Plowden, who claim that the CPRS was a device intended to restore some credibility to the convention of collective responsibility.[78] Lord Rothschild rejected the idea that '. . . the introduction of the Think Tank makes Downing Street more like the White House'[79] and denied that it marked 'the beginning of a prime minister's department'.[80] Douglas Hurd also stressed that 'the CPRS . . . serves the Cabinet not the Prime Minister'.[81] The CPRS could be construed as being impeccably correct because it was designed to reinforce a long-established constitutional principle of collective decision-making. In contrast to Wilson's 'kitchen cabinet', it did not arouse anxiety in

Whitehall and Westminster that the prime minister had acquired an *alternative* advisory body that might enable him to go it alone.

If there was little by way of political or constitutional controversy about Heath's innovations in respect of *policy* advice, can the same be said of his arrangements for *political* advice inside No.10? Harold Wilson, in establishing a political office in No.10, set a precedent that was subsequently confirmed by Edward Heath. Heath, however, succeeded in his determination to avoid the kind of controversy about advice that Wilson and his entourage had aroused.

The lack of controversy surrounding Mr Hurd's role as Mr Heath's political secretary may be attributed, as indeed it is by Hurd himself, to the reduced size of the political office and the fact that he saw his duties to be restricted in scope: 'the Political Office, which was much smaller than under Mr Wilson remained responsible for liaison with the Party and for those parts of the Prime Minister's life . . . which were mainly party political.'[82] On the question of size, however, the political office under Mrs Williams rarely consisted of more than Mrs Williams herself, her assistants Brenda Drew and Susan Lewis, and secretarial support. The exception to this was that briefly before each election the staff was temporarily augmented to cope with increased political demands on the prime minister.[83] Heath's political office, though smaller at the outset was, also, like Wilson's, augmented as time went on. Hurd notes that in the autumn of 1973 ' . . . we were much strengthened by the arrival in the Political Office at Number Ten of William Waldegrave, who crossed into these stormier waters from the comparative calm of the Central Policy Review Staff.'[84] In addition, Michael Wolff, who Hurd describes as Mr Heath's 'speech writer, wise adviser and friend',[85] though nominally attached to the Office of the Lord President of the Council, in fact worked for the prime minister. In respect of job descriptions, Mrs William's claims, 'the job of a political secretary is just what it says . . . [to help] a Prime Minister . . . maintain his political support, among MPs and party workers throughout the country.'[86] This is not very different from Mr Hurd's description of his role.[87]

At face value there is little that can explain the contrast in the furore caused by Mrs William's role in No.10 and the quiet acquiescence to that of Mr Hurd. Explanations for this contrast have to be sought at a different level and may be attributed to a combination of the following factors: background; personalities; gender and precedents. Mr Hurd, an Etonian with a first class degree in history from Cambridge, followed by fourteen years in the diplomatic service, came to No.10 as one of Whitehall's own. Hurd himself, discussing the extent of his access to papers and meetings, comments that 'these arrangements would never have been possible if everyone had stood on their constitutional rights. I was probably helped by the fact that I had been a government servant myself for fourteen years, so I spoke the language.'[88] Mrs Williams's experiences prior to entering No.10, were those of a grammar school girl with a lower second in history from Queen Mary College London, followed by a shorthand-typing course and employment as a secretary, first at Transport House, and then eventually as private secretary to Harold Wilson. Marcia Williams could claim wide experience of the way the Labour Party talked and worked, but she had little experience of the codes and language of Whitehall. In a system of government by conversation, she suffered from the great handicap of speaking with the 'wrong accent'.[89] Differences in respect of personalities were twofold: firstly, as noted above, Wilson and Heath were unlike in character and this affected the behaviour of the entourage with which they chose to surround themselves. Mr Wilson needed the reassurance and support of a close group of fiercely loyal partisans. Mr Heath, on the other hand, seems to have been more self-contained and aloof. Secondly, Williams and Hurd themselves were different personalities types. Hurd, possibly because of his years at the Foreign Office, tended to employ quiet diplomacy. Jim Prior, for instance, describes Hurd as 'calm and collected' and notes that '. . . he was certainly . . . diplomatic and could resist the temptation to boil over or give way to the injudicious remark . . . '[90] Marcia Williams, on the other hand, had a quick temper and tendency to be confrontational. Joe Haines claims that 'there were many times when the smallest imagined slight by a colleague might be transformed into a major scene into which an unwilling Prime Minister was dragged to act as peacemaker.'[91] In addition, Marcia Williams went into the Downing Street office anticipating hostility from the civil service. In her own account she recalls a pre-election visit to No.10 when her reception was 'coldly polite'.[92] Suspicion, and the expectation of hostility, on both sides, may have helped to create some of the tension and controversy that surrounded the appointment of Mrs Williams. Gender was also a factor. Whilst by the 1960s the inner circles of Whitehall and Westminster were not totally male dominated, they were very near to being so. Dame Evelyn Sharp[93] and Barbara Castle,[94] were two of the very few exceptions. In the view of one of Mrs William's friends: ' . . . had she been a man no one would have had to try so hard to prove she was only a jumped up secretary'.[95] Marcia Williams herself admitted, 'my political career has been greatly complicated by the fact that I am a woman.'[96] Finally, precedent was a significant factor in explaining the contrast in the response to the appointment of Mrs Williams and Mr Hurd. Caroline Moorehead says, 'since 1964 direct political advisers have become a well established phenomenon in government. When Mr Heath came to power in 1970 he appointed Douglas Hurd as adviser . . . Lady Falkender can claim at least partly to have set the trend for them.'[97] The constitutional rules were gradually evolving.

Some of the explanations offered above to account for the less controversial nature of Heath's political office can also be extended to the press office. Both press officers appointed by Mr Heath, first Donald Maitland and then his successor, Robin Haydon, were not merely temporary civil servants, like Gerald Kaufman and Joe Haines, but civil servants who had been through the mill. Mr Heath's press officers could also be seen as having benefitted from the precedent set by the press office in the Wilson years.

There appears to have been little to provoke accusations of constitutional impropriety in Heath's advisory system either inside or outside Downing Street. The changes he introduced to the advisory system outside No.10 may at best be described as modest and limited, those introduced within No.10 could perhaps be described as reactionary in the literal sense, a return to the traditional kind of adviser. Whitehall, therefore, no longer shared a grievance with Westminster. A degree of presidentialization of the premiership was acceptable if the prime minister settled for additional advice from Whitehall in place of alternative advice from outside. But this did arouse some controversy of a different kind. Although the *changes* in the prime ministerial advisory system introduced by Heath did not provoke accusations of unconstitutionality, some of the advisory strategies employed by him did. Heath, in contrast to Wilson, was not criticized for surrounding himself with a coterie of unofficial political advisers or for nursing pretensions to a British presidency. He did, however, attract criticism for listening almost exclusively to civil servants. Hennessy notes that 'the political demonology of the new Right makes much . . . of Heath's . . . retreat from his political colleagues and into the arms of senior civil servants.'[98]

Heath had an instrinctive preference for a rational administrative approach to problem solving,[99] and according to Barber, he '. . . gave the impression of enjoying the company of officials and feeling more at home with them than with his political colleagues.'[100] Campbell suggests that mutual admiration existed between Heath and his senior officials and that the latter bestowed upon Heath the highest accolade: 'Senior Civil Servants felt that he was a heart one of them, a Permanent Secretary *manque*.' [101] Fay and Young claim that

The dominant images of Heath's time in Downing Street, which have been carried away by those who served him rarely include his Cabinet or his inner caucus of Ministers. They are of Heath surrounded by Douglas Allen (Head of the Treasury), Robert Armstrong (his principal private secretary), and William Armstrong (Head of the Civil Service). This was the Treasury mandarinate which nourished Heath's belief in lonely prime ministerial power and was fortified by a leader who seemed to share some of their contempt for the average politician.[102]

The close relationship that developed between Edward Heath and Sir William Armstrong, Head of the Civil Service, was particularly singled out for adverse comment. This latter relationship led to questions being raised, not only about Heath's lack of political advisers, but also about the dubious constitutionality of the politicization of a senior civil servant.[103] Armstrong even acquired the pejorative title of 'deputy prime minister'.[104] William Whitelaw claimed: 'he [Armstrong] became more a minister than a civil servant. He was even making political statements at our meetings'[105]

It was in 1972, when Heath decided to reverse his previous position on incomes policy, that Armstrong came to public attention. Heath chose the tripartite forum of the National Economic Development Council (NEDC) as an umbrella organization to thrash out the details, and asked Sir William Armstrong, Head of the Civil Service and ex-Joint Permanent Secretary of the Treasury, to chair the tripartite talks.[106] The result was that Armstrong became highly visible and was identified with the government's prices and incomes policy.

The pervasiveness of Armstrong's influence was not confined to incomes policy. According to Campbell, Armstrong had a major input to the 1971 Industry Act, which Campbell describes as ' . . . an attempt to construct an ambitious national industry policy behind the back of the large Department [Department of Trade and Industry] specifically created for the purpose.'[107] Campbell asserts that the Industry Act was prepared not by the Department of Trade and Industry, but by ' . . . a small hand-picked group in the Cabinet Office working closely with the Prime Minister himself. The key figure was Sir William Armstrong . . .'[108] According to Fay and Young, by 1973 'Armstrong stood closer to Heath than any other adviser'. They go on to assert that 'the relationship grew during the year, becoming what some politicians called 'the bloody duumvirate'.'[109]

Heath's desire to distance himself from the political advisory strategies of his predecessor perhaps led him too far in the opposite direction. Although Wilson, by the end of his period in office, was accused by some of relying too much on the advice of the Cabinet Secretary, Burke Trend, most of the adverse comment about Wilson's advisory system centred on the role of his 'kitchen cabinet' and the part played in it by personal appointees. Wilson was thought by some to have allowed unofficial advisers too much influence over public policy. Heath, on the other hand, was criticized for relying too much on the policy advice of his official advisers and in consequence neglecting the political dimensions of policy-making.

According to Campbell, 'the hallmark of his [Heath's] premiership was his determination to restore the dignity to the office of Prime Minister which he believed had been tarnished by Harold Wilson.'[110] Campbell also notes that 'he [Heath] was often remote and personally abrasive, but he was punctiliously correct in his observance of constitutional conventions and established procedures.'[111] This view seems to be borne out by an examination of the advisory strategies adopted by Heath. Heath kept his personal staff to a minimum and established instead the CPRS to enhance advice available to, and thereby effectiveness of, the cabinet, the traditional, and constitutionally proper, source of political and policy advice to the prime minister. Excepting the controversy surrounding the apparently partisan part played by Sir William Armstrong, Heath's advisory strategies seemed, at first sight, to serve to restore traditional constitutional practices.

Did Heath succeed in depresidentialize the premiership in respect of advice or could his advisory strategies be seen as evolving in the direction of the American model?   Did Edward Heath enter 10 Downing Street accompanied by an entourage of cronies and advance men in the manner of an American president entering the White House? If so, was there as a consequence any sign of the cabinet becoming the rubber-stamping and marketing division for policies decided by the prime minister, based on advice received from his alternative advisory system with No.10? Did the prime minister, in the manner of some American presidents, particularly those of the post-Kennedy years, tend to become isolated from traditional advisory sources by a phalanx of media advisers purporting to possess the key to the favourable opinion polls and electoral support that underpinned the enhanced powers of the chief executive?

The above examination of the advisory strategies employed   by Edward Heath when he was prime minister would suggest at first sight that these questions can be answered in the negative. Edward Heath did enter No.10 accompanied by a few personal assistants, but as was noted above in respect of his predecessor, Harold Wilson, it is doubtful that a handful of personal appointees could be construed as providing conclusive evidence for claiming that the advisory system was being presidentialized. It is also worth noting that, of Heath's six personal appointees, two, Donald Maitland the senior press officer, and Timothy Kitson, Heath's PPS, being members of the civil service and Parliament respectively, could claim legitimacy beyond the prime minister's favour by virtue of belonging to traditional advisory bodies. Such wider legitimacy could even be extended to Heath's media adviser, Geoffrey Tucker, who was an employee of the Conservative Party Central Office. Not only was the scale of the No.10 team different from that of the White House[112], but the majority of Heath's aides were not 'heroes of the campaign' in the manner of latter day White House appointees but political actors in their own right. George Hutchinson, discussing Heath's intentions in respect of personal advisory support, claims that Heath was not '. . . after a 'presidential' sort of set-up in Downing Street, with a corps of personal advisers in every major field of policy, forming a kind of private intellectual powerhouse ... '[113]

There is also little evidence to suggest that Heath's small contingent of personal appointees inside No.10 superseded or demoted the cabinet. Heath, according to Campbell, was '. . . punctilious in ensuring that major decisions were taken by the Cabinet as a whole.'[114] Kavanagh notes that, 'in spite of the U-turns, there were no resignations from the Cabinet on the grounds of policy disagreements. There were also very few leaks from the Cabinet – probably an indication of high morale and solidarity.'[115] Kavanagh contrasts the cohesive cabinet of Heath with the well-publicized divisions in the Labour cabinets of 1964–70.[116] Heath's premiership also, in contrast to that of his predecessor, did not inspire a spate of 'whistle-blowing' memoirs.[117] Accounts written by Heath's colleagues[118] upheld the principles of cabinet secrecy and collective responsibility, and may be described as personal accounts of the government's period in office rather that personal revelations of animosities or alleged constitutional improprieties. This lack of evidence to the contrary, and the fact that Heath, by creating the CPRS, appears to have demonstrated his acceptance of the traditional constitution view of the cabinet's role in the prime minister's advisory system, suggest that cabinet members did not feel excluded from either the advisory system or decision-making process.

There is also little evidence to suggest that Heath became isolated within No.10 by a phalanx of news managers. Most commentators suggest the opposite. According to Kavanagh, Heath '. . . was not very interested in the art of promoting policy and deliberately reacted against Harold Wilson's style of media management.'[119] Michael Foley describes the way that 'Heath's media advisors helped to soften his image for the 1970 election' but notes that once in Number 10, 'Heath reverted to his original posture. He shunned the press, avoided television and distanced himself in general from media attention. Heath's concern was for policy not public standing, which he regarded as a consideration confined largely to the vulgarities of the electoral process.'[120] According Campbell the presidential style of some of Heath's press conferences did give some offence to Parliamentary etiquette because he tended to use press conferences, as opposed to the floor of the House, as a forum for announcing major policy initiatives.[121] But Campbell goes on to say that Heath 'fatally neglected the skills of communication and presentation of Government policies which are an essential part of leadership.'[122] This is hardly an oversight of which a modern day American president is likely to stand accused. If indeed Heath did become isolated in No.10, it was not within a cordon of media and public relations advisers, but within a circle of civil service advisers who had little experience of, or need for, the intricacies of public relations. Indeed, even the men Heath appointed to act as senior press officers were civil servants.

According to Campbell, Heath dominated his cabinet,[123] but Campbell also claims that Heath was scrupulous about constitutional proprieties and that he ensured that all major decisions were discussed by the cabinet. Although he may have adopted presidential style press conferences, there seems to be little to support the argument that Heath's advisory strategies approximated to the American presidential model. It could even be argued that he rejected those practices of Harold Wilson that might be construed as having some similarities to the presidential model, in favour of a more traditionally British prime ministerial model. (Assuming the advisory practices of Lloyd George and Churchill to be the exceptions that prove the rule.)

Despite there being little clear evidence to substantiate the view that Heath's advisory system resembled that of an American president, there are nevertheless some ambiguities in the evidence which should not be ignored. Firstly, ostensibly Heath appears to have been scrupulously constitutional but, like Wilson, he did maintain the rudiments of an *alternative* advisory system serving the prime minister within No.10. He had a press office and a political office not greatly dissimilar in terms of size to those of Wilson. Heath also seems to have relied on the advice of a close team of people consisting of William Armstrong, Douglas Hurd, Michael Wolff, Lord Rothschild, plus a handful of senior civil servants. His cabinet appears to have been more cohesive and loyal than that of his predecessors, and, therefore, could perhaps be assumed to feel that its role was not being usurped or undermined by an alternative advisory team. This cabinet unity, however, may owe less to Heath's constitutional propriety in respect of advisory strategies and decision-making, and more to traditional Tory Party ethos, which places a premium on unity and loyalty to the leader, and to the fact that, unlike Wilson, Heath's main, or potential, rivals had been eliminated before, or shortly after, he took office.[124] (No one, at this time, predicted that Margaret Thatcher, would eventually oust Heath from the party leadership. Not only was she in her first, junior rank cabinet post, as Secretary of State for Education, she was also, after all, only a woman.)

Secondly, according to Bruce-Gardyne, '. . . even before 1970 was out it was apparent that he [Heath] was going to be the most dominant Prime Minister since the war. Mr Heath invariably insisted on the *public*[125] demonstration of departmental delegation and responsibility. Yet throughout Whitehall there was a growing awareness that the big decisions would be taken at Number Ten . . . '[126] The 1971 Industry Act would seem to qualify for the description of being a 'big decision', in that it had the effect of increasing government intervention in industry, and thereby reversing a major manifesto promise. According to Campbell, this was a decision that was taken by the advisory team at No.10. Campbell describes the covert way in which the policy was formulated by a hand-picked team under the direction of the prime minister.[127] He comments that 'it was an extraordinary undertaking, an exercise of prime ministerial power comparable to Neville Chamberlain's conduct of foreign policy in 1937–9 or Eden's handling of the Suez crisis, previously unparalleled in domestic policy except in respect of necessarily secret operations like devaluation.'[128] Campbell goes on to note that 'by proceeding in this under-cover way Heath contradicted not only the economic philosophy with which he had ostensibly come into office, but, more fundamentally, his promise of better, more honest and more open government.'[129] These views are difficult to square with claims that Heath was 'scrupulously constitutional' except in form. Such behaviour does not seem to be that of a prime minister governing in conjunction with, and on the advice of, his cabinet colleagues, but resembles a president determining policy, advised by a team of his own choosing, free from any formal constitutional restraints.

In addition, even the CPRS, though formally an agency to underpin collective cabinet government, gradually evolved into a creature of the prime minister. According to Hennessy, in the initial planning stages of the central capability unit, it had been envisaged that it would have reported to the prime minister rather than to the cabinet as a whole, but the intervention of Cabinet Secretary, Burke Trend, persuaded Heath of the difficulties that this might raise.[130] As time went on the collective nature of the Think Tank's remit became less perceptible. Blackstone and Plowden admit that the strategy briefings for the cabinet at Chequers 'fizzled out after the oil crisis of 1973–4' and note that '. . . the CPRS's relationship with the Prime Minister was always closer than with other

Ministers.'[131] Not only does the CPRS appear to have worked in practice more for the prime minister than for the cabinet, but its members also seem to have performed roles not dissimilar to that performed by presidential aides. James Fox claims that 'the think tank, with its fifteen versatile members, was conceived as a monitoring unit with antennae all over Whitehall.'[132] According to one Tory 'Heath . . . had to use 'tremendous skill' and prudence to prevent the think tank being seen . . . as a Prime Minister's Department.'[133] There was a rapport and a close working relationship between Heath and the Tank's director, Lord Rothschild.[134] Blackstone and Plowden admit that 'Heath worked closely with Rothschild and found it particularly helpful to have early warnings of problems that might arise later. But he also stressed the value of obtaining this advice *informally*[135] and maintaining the *formal* position that the CPRS worked for Ministers collectively.'[136] Rothschild had access and those having privileged access to decision-makers can be assumed to influence. Indeed, in Campbell's view 'for most of the period Rothschild was a powerfully influential voice in Downing Street, second only to Sir William Armstrong.'[137] The CPRS had the makings of an 'Executive Office' by stealth. It appeared to uphold accepted constitutional conventions in respect of the cabinet's role in the prime ministerial advisory system, but in reality it performed functions akin to those performed by the EOP in America.[138]

Behind the forms of constitutional propriety, Heath too adopted some advisory practices that could be construed as presidential. The differences between Heath and Wilson in this respect were, perhaps, more apparent that real. Heath was less conspicuously presidential. The explanation for this is fourfold. Firstly, the personalities of the two prime ministers were different. Secondly, the kind of people Heath appointed to work in Number Ten were not *parvenus* to the culture of Westminster and Whitehall, as had been the case with some of Mr Wilson's entourage, and so they ruffled fewer feathers. The controversy aroused by Mr Wilson's advisers provided on the one hand a model of what to avoid, and on the other hand helped to accustom Westminster and Whitehall to new patterns of prime ministerial advisory systems. Lastly, the press office constructed by Heath, though similar in size to that of Wilson, was very different in style, and this in turn influenced the style in which Heath's leadership was portrayed.

There is, therefore, some evidence of presidentialization of the prime ministerial advisory system under Heath. The structures of both an *alternative*[139] and a *parallel*[140] advisory network were in place but the characteristic secrecy that surrounds the giving of advice and the making of decisions in British government makes it difficult to determine the extent to which they were used. Heath may have entered office intending, and attempting, to restore the cabinet to its traditional role of advising the prime minister, but political expectations made this impossible to achieve. Edward Heath's U-turns involved not only the spectacular public reversals of economic policy, but also penetrated to a more fundamental level affecting the processes and conduct of government. Just as pressure of events had forced a radical reappraisal of pre-election promises in respect of economic policies, so experience of office brought about a realization that the traditional role assigned to the prime minister by the constitution was no longer tenable in the same way and, therefore, that the traditional advisory structure was no longer adequate. Michael Wolff asked Mr Heath what had happened to his original good intentions to stand above the battle and let his colleagues get on with their job. Mr Heath admitted that it was outside pressure rather than personal inclination that had forced him to intervene personally over Europe, over Ulster and over the pay and prices policy. 'The simple fact was that in each case those with whom the Government was negotiating insisted on dealing personally and directly with me as Prime Minister.'[141] Heath was thus forced to adopt some of the constitutionally questionable practices of his predecessor. That less controversy resulted may simply be explained by differences in personnel and personality rather than practices, and that what appeared to be controversial innovation in 1964 had become tolerated custom by 1970.

In chapter four it was suggested that when the permanent, but usually private, dialogue about advice, nowadays conducted between two parts of the executive, the cabinet and the permanent bureaucracy, becomes a public argument, as indeed it did during Wilson's premiership, it could perhaps be taken as a signal of failure in the secret constitution. The corollary of this implies that the near absence of public controversy in respect of advice to the prime minister during Heath's period in office, can be interpreted as a signal that a new settlement had been achieved in the secret constitution. Perhaps the terms of that settlement were that: a *parallel* prime ministerial advisory system is acceptable to Whitehall, an *alternative* advisory system is not.

Heath's advisory system showed signs of presidentialization and was, therefore, alien and potentially unconstitutional. By allowing the 'old' advisers to dominate the new structures, and by allowing Parliament to debate the creation of the CPRS, he avoided uniting Whitehall and Westminster in a joint hue and cry that constitutional propriety was not being observed.

It is possible to describe Wilson's attempt to change the prime ministerial advisory system as a revolution that failed. Heath too may be regarded as a revolutionary, but a revolutionary according to the 1688 cyclic view of revolution: attempting to bring about not radical change but a restoration of a better, more desirable state of affairs. In respect of the prime ministerial advisory system Heath's intention seems to have been to depresidentialize the premiership and restore the cabinet to the position it had occupied prior to Wilson's period in office. As time passed, political pressure dictated the abandonment of manifesto promises and the prime minister turned increasingly to non-cabinet advisers. In this sense Heath was a revolutionary who failed. Addressing some of the perceived weaknesses of an advisory system dominated by Whitehall mandarins was a component of Heath's Quiet Revolution. The CPRS and special advisers, however, had only a marginal impact on the civil service's monopoly over policy advice and that by the end of Heath's period in office the civil service was well on the way to recolonizing lost territory.[142] Heath did retain the structures of an alternative advisory system for the prime minister, but even in this, official or traditional kinds of advisers dominated. Both in Downing Street and Whitehall, Heath's Quiet Revolution became, in the post-1789 sense, a counter-revolution in which the civil service re-established their claim over territory threatened during Wilson's period of office. In this respect, Heath may be regarded as the quiet revolutionary who failed or the counter-revolutionary who succeeded.

Edward Heath found faults with the advisory system he inherited when he became prime minister in 1970. The changes he introduced did not lead to claims that he had failed to observe constitutional propriety. They were changes that could be described as having a closer resemblance to the prime ministerial advisory system that existed prior to Harold Wilson's period in office, than to the advisory system of an American president. Nevertheless, a closer examination of Heath's advisory strategies did reveal that he did not effect a complete reversal of the process of presidentialization that had been noted during Wilson's premiership. The skeleton of an *alternative* advisory system were retained, but those manning the structures represented a reversal to more traditional kinds of advisers. Under Heath it became a *parallel*, rather than an *alternative*, advisory system.

1974 brought the return of a Labour government under Harold Wilson. Did it also bring a return to a more overtly presidential premiership and revive the constitutional controversy about advice?

Notes

1. Fox, James, 'The brains behind the throne' *Sunday Times* (Colour Supplement) 25 March, 1973 pp. 46–57, p. 49.

2. Tebbit, Norman, *Upwardly Mobile* (London: Weidenfeld & Nicolson, 1988) p. 106.
3. Watt, David, 'Civil servants and kitchen cabinets' *Financial Times* 27 October, 1972, p. 23.
4. See Fay, Stephen and Young, Hugo, 'The Fall of Edward Heath' Pts 1 & 2, *Sunday Times* (Weekly Review) 22 & 29 February, 1976 pp. 33–4.
5. Ibid., Pt 2 29 February, 1976 p. 34.
6. Ibid.
7. For a detailed discussion of the extent of interventionist measures see Bruce-Gardyne, Jock, *Whatever Happened to the Quiet Revolution?* (London: Charles Knight, 1974) pp. 76–99 and Campbell, John, *Edward Heath: A Biography* (London: Cape, 1993) pp. 436–56.
8. The Conservative Party's election manifesto *A Better Tomorrow* had placed inflation as first priority and eschewed policies of government intervention in industry and further nationalization, promising instead some privatization and even hiving-off of government work: 'We are totally opposed to further nationalization of British industry . . . we will repeal the so-called Industrial Expansion Act which gives the government power to use taxpayer's money to buy its way into private industry' (ibid., p. 14). It had also rejected statutory wage controls:'We utterly reject the philosophy of compulsory wage controls' (Ibid., p. 6) and stated that:'Labour's compulsory wage control was a failure and we will not repeat it.'(Ibid., p. 11). *A Better Tomorrow* (London: Conservative Central Office, 1970).
9. See Kavanagh, Dennis, 'The Heath Government 1970–1974' in Hennessy, Peter and Seldon, Anthony, eds *Ruling Performance* (Oxford: Blackwell, 1987) pp. 216–40, p. 222.
10. *A Better Tomorrow,* op.cit., p. 6.
11. See Tebbit, op.cit., p. 106.
12. Though some controversy did erupt in 1972 over the appointment of Mr John Cope as Special Political Assistant to John Davies, Secretary of State for Trade and Industry. See below, this chapter, see also Routledge, Paul 'Revolutionary move by minister in creating aide attacked' *The Times* 9 October, 1972, p. 3.
13. See Crossman, R.H.S., *Inside View* (London: Cape, 1970) p. 14.
14. See Williams, Marcia, *Inside Number Ten* (London: Weidenfeld & Nicolson, 1972) p. 346.
15. Fulton Report, Cmnd. 3638 Report of the Committee on the Civil Service 1966–8, (London: HMSO, 1968) p. 106.
16. Conservatives 330; Labour 287; Liberals 6.

17. See for example Hurd, Douglas, *An End to Promises* (London: Collins, 1979) pp. 20–6.
18. Throughout the campaign, with the exception of an Opinion Research Centre (ORC) poll which foretold the correct result, the polls had predicted a Labour victory. On the Friday before polling day National Opinion Poll (NOP) was putting Labour 12.4 per cent ahead. The bookmakers were giving odds of twenty to one on Labour. For a detailed discussion of the campaign see Butler, David and Pinto-Duschinsky, Michael, *The British General Election of 1970* (London: Macmillan, 1971) and Alexander, Andrew and Watkins, Alan, *The Making of the Prime Minister, 1970* (London: Cape, 1970).
19. *Economist* 20 June, 1970, p. 9. See also, Prior, James, *A Balance of Power* (London: Hamish Hamilton, 1986) p. 65 and *The Times* 20 June, 1970, p. 11.
20. Heath's predecessors had 'emerged' as Conservative leader after a process of 'soundings' taken by the party grandees. Heath was the first leader to be chosen under an electoral system adopted in 1964.
21. See Kavanagh, op.cit., p. 216.
22. Heasman, D.J., 'The Prime Minister and the Cabinet'; in King, Anthony, ed. *The British Prime Minister* 1st edn (London: Macmillan, 1969) pp. 44–65, p. 56. See also Roth, Andrew, *Heath and the Heathmen* (London: Routledge & Kegan Paul, 1972) p. 12.
23. Hutchinson, George, *Edward Heath: a Personal and Political Biography* (London: Longman, 1970) p. 161. See also Kavanagh, op.cit., p. 218.
24. Heath, Edward, *A Better Tomorrow*, op.cit., pp. 1–2.
25. Sked, Alan and Cook, Chris, *Post-War Britain: a political history* 3rd edn (Harmondsworth: Penguin, 1990) p. 253.
26. Wood, *The Times,* op.cit., p. 1.
27. Kavanagh, op.cit., p. 221.
28. See Bruce-Gardyne, op.cit., p. 10.
29. See Kavanagh, op.cit., p. 216.
30. It was at the Conservative Party Conference in the autumn, after the election of June 1970, that Heath's plans acquired the title 'Quiet Revolution'. See Tebbit, op.cit., p. 101. However, as early as 1965 the term 'Quiet Revolution' was used in connection with Heath. On the 30 July 1965, the leader in the *Spectator* entitled comment on Heath's victory in the Tory leadership election 'Quiet Revolution'. *Spectator* 30 July, 1965, p. 139.
31. Bruce-Gardyne, op.cit., p. 7.
32. See Kavanagh, op.cit., pp. 219–20.

33. See 'When we win power: Edward Heath talks to James Margach' *Sunday Times* 3 October, 1965, pp. 11–12.
34. Incorporating the former Departments of Housing and Local Government, Public Buildings and Works, and Transport.
35. Incorporating the Department of Industry and the Board of Trade.
36. Bruce-Gardyne, op.cit., p. 14.
37. Cmnd. 4506
38. Membership fluctuated between sixteen and twenty.
39. For a full discussion of the creation of the CPRS see, James, Simon, 'The Central Policy Review Staff, 1970–1983' *Political Studies* Vol.34, 1986, pp. 423–40.
40. According to James, such briefs outlined issues for those 'unconcerned' ministers, highlighting side effects and drawbacks that the sponsoring ministers might play down and relating the proposals to the government's main objectives. James, Simon, *The British Cabinet* (London: Routledge, 1992) p. 206. In his diary entry for 19 July, 1965, Crossman attributes the sterility of cabinet discussions to the lack of such a body to brief the cabinet as a whole. Crossman, R.H.S., *Diaries of a Cabinet Minister Vol.1* (London: Hamilton & Cape, 1975) pp. 280–1.
41. See Bruce-Gardyne, op.cit., p. 164.
42. See above, chapter four.
43. Campbell, op.cit.,p. 291.
44. Ibid. p. 290.
45. Hurd, op.cit., p. 73.
46. Campbell, op.cit., p. 291. Donald Maitland, prior to taking up his position in No.10 had been a career diplomat. Maitland was replaced as Press Secretary in May 1973 by Robin Haydon, another Foreign Office man.
47. Prior to working for Mr Heath, first as Private Secretary to the Leader of the Opposition (1968-70) and then as Political Secretary to the Prime Minister, Douglas Hurd had been a member of the Diplomatic Service (1952–66) and then, in 1966, had joined the Conservative Party Research Department.
48. Campbell, op.cit., p. 291.
49. Hurd, op.cit., p. 28.
50. Ibid., p. 31.
51. Wolff was nominally a special adviser to the Lord President of the Council, but was in fact Heath's chief speech writer and political odd-job man. Campbell, op.cit., p. 489.

52. Heath, Edward and Barker, Anthony, 'Heath on Whitehall Reforms' *Parliamentary Affairs* Vol.31, No.4, Autumn 1978, pp. 363–90, p. 388.
53. Cit. Routledge, 'Revolutionary move by minister in creating aide attacked' op.cit., p. 3.
54. Ibid.
55. Ibid.
56. Klein, Rudolf and Lewis, Janet, 'Advice and Dissent in British Government: the case for Special Advisers' *Policy and Politics* Vol.6, No.1, September, 1977 pp. 1-25, p. 3.
57. Bruce-Gardyne, op.cit., p. 10.
58. Heath, op.cit., p. 369.
59. Hutchinson, op.cit., p. 183.
60. Watt, op.cit., p. 23.
61. Campbell, op.cit., p. 316.
62. Ibid., p. 325.
63. Ibid., p. 319.
64. Blackstone, Tessa, 'Ministers, Advisers and Civil Servants' Hugh Gaitskell Memorial Lecture, Nottingham University 1979, in Morgan, John, ed. *Politics and Consensus in Modern Britain: Lectures in Memory of Hugh Gaitskell* (Basingstoke, Macmillan, 1988) pp. 65–81, p. 73. Dr Blackstone was a member of the CPRS between September 1975 and August 1978. Thus whilst Dr Blackstone provides a valuable insider's view of Think Tank activities, it has to be noted that she is likely to have a vested interest in presenting the CPRS in a favourable light.
65. The Review of Overseas Representation Interim Report 1976, being a notable exception. This controversy, however, erupted after Heath had left office. For discussion of controversy, see Hennessy, Peter, 'Whitehall Hostility into Overseas Staff Inquiry' *The Times* 26 April, 1977.
66. Blackstone, Tessa and Plowden, William, *Inside the Think Tank: Advising the Cabinet 1971-1983* (London: Heineman, 1988) pp. 44–5. When considering evidence from this source it has to be borne in mind that both writers are former members of the CPRS.
67. Ibid., p. 33.
68. Bruce-Gardyne comments that an incident in September 1973 when Lord Rothschild was publicly carpeted for delivering a widely-publicized speech without first clearing it with the civil service hierarchy, was revealing '. . . not so much for the contents of the speech which provoked the public rebuke, . . . it was the fact that Lord Rothschild had given the traditional bureaucrats an opening to

put him in his place.' Bruce-Gardyne, op.cit., p. 116.

69. See for instance: Pollitt, C., 'The CPRS 1970–1974' *Public Administration* Winter 1974 pp. 375–92; Blackstone, 1979, op.cit.; Rothschild, Lord, 'A useful exercise with interest' *The Times* 2 July, 1983, p. 8; Hennessy, P., Morrison, S. and Townsend, R., 'Routine Punctuated by Orgies: the Central Policy Review Staff 1971–1983' *Strathclyde Papers on Government and Politics* No.31 (Glasgow: University of Strathclyde, 1985); James, Simon, 'The Central Policy Review Staff, 1970-1983' *Political Studies* Vol.34, 1986, pp. 423–40.

70. James, 'The Central Policy Review Staff, 1970-1983', op.cit., p. 434.

71. See Hennessy, *Whitehall*, op.cit., p. 68, p. 124 and p. 154.

72. This proportion gradually increased in favour of the bureaucracy over the life span of the CPRS. See Blackstone and Plowden, op.cit., p. 29.

73. Cit. Pollitt, op.cit., p. 379.

74. See Blackstone and Plowden, op.cit., pp. 212–13.

75. Seymour-Ure, Colin, 'Institutionalization and Informality of Advisory Systems' in Plowden *Advising the Rulers*, op.cit., pp. 175-84, p. 179.

76. Campbell, op.cit., p. 317.

77. Cit. Pollitt, op.cit., p. 376.

78. Blackstone and Plowden, op.cit., p. 23.

79. Rothschild, cit., 'Thinking about the Think Tank' *Listener* 28 December, 1972, p. 880.

80. Ibid.

81. Hurd, op.cit., p. 38.

82. Ibid., p. 32.

83. See, Williams, op.cit., p. 325 and pp. 334–5.

84. Hurd, op.cit., p. 118.

85. Ibid., p. 10 note 2.

86. Falkender, Lady Marcia, 'Eyes and ears for Harold Wilson' *Observer* 20 February, 1972, pp. 26 and 28, p. 26.

87. See above, this chapter.

88. Hurd, op.cit., pp. 34–5.

89. A handicap made worse by the fact that she was a divorcee with a complicated private life.

90. Prior, op.cit., pp. 53–4.

91. Haines, op.cit., p. 159. See also Moorehead, Caroline, 'From a secretary's chair to a seat in the House of Lords' *The Times* 23 July, 1974, p. 16.

92. Williams, *Inside Number 10* op.cit., p. 21.
93. Permanent Secretary of the Department of Housing and Local Government.
94. First as Minister for Overseas Development, then Minister of Transport and finally as Secretary of State for Employment.
95. Moorehead, Caroline, 'The battle for Downing Street won, her political future is assured' *The Times* 24 July, 1974 p. 16.
96. Falkender, 'Eyes and Ears for Harold Wilson' op.cit., p. 26.
97. Moorehead, 'The Battle for Downing Street . . . ' op.cit., p. 16.
98. Hennessy, *Whitehall* op.cit., p. 237.
99. See Kavanagh, op.cit., p. 220 and Fay and Young, pt 1 op.cit., p. 33.
100. Barber, James, *The Prime Minister Since 1945* (Oxford: Blackwell, 1991) p. 82.
101. Campbell, op.cit., p. 490.
102. Ibid., p. 33 see also p. 490.
103. See Kavanagh, op.cit., p. 221.
104. Fay and Young, 'Fall of Heath' pt 1, op.cit., p. 34.
105. Fay and Young, 'Fall of Heath' pt 2, *Sunday Times* (Review) 29 February, 1976, pp. 33-4, p. 34.
106. Pressure of work, particularly in respect of imminent EEC entry, made it difficult for the Permanent Secretary of the Treasury, the government's usual representative on NEDC, to take on the huge task of developing an incomes policy. See Heath, op.cit., p. 381.
107. Campbell, op.cit., p. 447. See also Bruce-Gardyne, op.cit., p. 162 for a discussion of Armstrong's supposed influence on the 1972 budget.
108. Campbell, op.cit., p. 446.
109. Fay and Young, 'Fall of Heath' pt 1, op.cit., p. 34.
110. Campbell, op.cit., p. 494.
111. Ibid., p. 762.
112. The contemporary WHO of Richard Nixon numbered a payroll of five hundred employees of whom forty-eight were personal presidential aides. See Schlesinger, Arthur, Jr., *The Imperial Presidency* 2nd edn (Boston: Houghton Mifflin, 1989) p. 221.
113. Hutchinson, op.cit., p. 183.
114. Campbell, op.cit., p. 485.
115. Kavanagh, op.cit., p. 232.
116. Ibid.
117. For example those of Richard Crossman, Tony Benn, Marcia Williams and to some extent Barbara Castle.

118. For example those of William Whitelaw, James Prior and Jock Bruce-Gardyne.
119. Kavanagh, op.cit., p. 220.
120. Foley, Michael, *The Rise of the British Presidency* (Manchester: University Press, 1993) p. 107.
121. Campbell, op.cit., p. 503.
122. Ibid., p. 484.
123. Ibid., p. 485.
124. Kavanagh asserts that 'Heath was a dominant leader of the Conservative Party. In opposition this had been seen in his dismissal of Edward du Cann as party chairman (1967) and Enoch Powell for his speech on immigration,(1968). As prime minister, Heath's dominance was reinforced by two events. The first was the unexpected and decisive election victory which the Conservative Party gained in 1970. . . . The second event was the death of Iain Macleod . . . thirty-one days after his appointment as Chancellor of the Exchequer. He was the finest orator in the Conservative Party and the only one in a position to challenge Heath.' Kavanagh, op.cit., pp. 218–19.
125. My italics.
126. Bruce-Gardyne, op.cit., p. 40.
127. See above, this chapter, and see also Campbell, op.cit., pp. 446–7.
128. Ibid., p. 447.
129. Ibid.
130. Hennessy, *Whitehall* op.cit., p. 212 and p. 213.
131. Blackstone and Plowden, op.cit., p. 53. See also James, *Political Studies* op.cit., p. 26. In 1972 Heath, himself, conceded that the CPRS had concentrated resources of research in his own hands. Although he denied that this had resulted in decision-making being similarly concentrated in No.10. See 'Edward Heath speaking frankly: My Style of Government' *Evening Standard* 1 June, 1972, pp. 24-5, p. 24.
132. Fox, op.cit., p. 49.
133. Ibid., p. 49.
134. See Blackstone and Plowden, op.cit., p. 54.
135. My italics.
136. Blackstone and Plowden, op.cit., p. 54.
137. Campbell, op.cit., p. 322.
138. Although no one would claim that an exact comparison could be drawn between a handful of outsiders and a few civil servants (between sixteen and twenty people in total) attached to the Cabinet Office, and the vast and elaborate two-thousand strong EOP. For a

discussion of the scale and functions of the EOP, see, McKay, David, *Power and Politics in the USA* 2nd edn (Harmondsworth: Penguin, 1994) pp. 93–129.

139. Advice to the prime minister from outside sources unmediated by members of the cabinet or civil service.
140. Advice to the prime minister directly from Whitehall unmediated by members of the cabinet.
141. Heath, cit. Wolff, Michael, 'The power of the Prime Minister: should he pick up the ball and run with it?' *The Times* 24 May, 1976, p. 14.
142. See Watt, op.cit.

6 Harold Wilson 1974–6: A Presidentializing Premier

There would this time be no 'presidential nonsense'.[1]

He was a consummate politician; and a politician has no business with principles and no business with being frank. Either would interfere with the conduct of his art, which consists not least in appearing to be principled and frank while being neither. Nevertheless Harold Wilson remains un-summarisable.[2]

In the 1970s Harold Wilson was a less presidential, but not a less presidentializing, premier than he had been in the sixties. But a combination of a more cautious approach on his part and a somewhat dispirited opposition in Whitehall, ensured that on this occasion constitutional controversy was more muted.

If it had been Edward Heath's intention to restore the cabinet to its traditional place in the prime ministerial advisory system, that intention was frustrated by events and political expectations. The central briefing agency Heath established, ostensibly to bolster the flagging institutions of a collective executive, had, by the time he left No.10, been all but transformed into an additional advisory body underpinning prime ministerial intervention. The presidentialization of the prime ministerial advisory system that had been discernible under Heath's predecessor, Harold Wilson, had not been reversed under Heath. Heath, however, was the beneficiary of changes introduced by Wilson. Wilson, by introducing alternative advisors into No.10, had prompted the civil service to respond to the prime minister's demands for more and different kinds of advice. During Heath's tenure Whitehall sought to regain its former monopoly in these matters by providing the prime minister with a *parallel* advisory system. The creation of the Central Policy Review Staff (CPRS), for which Whitehall claimed some share of the credit, can be seen as a limited concession to alternative advice. It was a concession legitimized by being preceded by Parliamentary debate, by the presence of civil servants among its members, and by the fact that it was placed under the Cabinet Secretary.

When Harold Wilson returned to office in 1974 he inherited an advisory system that provided more support for the man in No.10, but, as in 1964, it was advice which was supplied by, or mediated by, Whitehall. Did Harold Wilson still regard the prime ministerial advisory system as unsatisfactory and inadequate? Did advice once again become a political and constitutional issue during Wilson's last period in office?

Harold Wilson's return to Downing Street in March 1974 got off to an inauspicious start in respect of the politics of advice. Almost immediately, controversy erupted over Wilson's preferred advisers and associates. Wilson's name was mentioned in connection with what came to be known as the 'landsdeal affair', involving his onetime office manager, driver and golfing partner, Tony Field, brother of Wilson's Personal and Political Secretary, Marcia Williams.[3] The 'landsdeal affair' inspired much adverse press comment as to the wisdom of Wilson's choice of advisers.[4] Wilson's response to his critics was to elevate Mrs Williams to the peerage. This in turn provoked a further round of unsympathetic and unwelcome comment in the media.[5]

Two years later, after Wilson had shocked the nation with his sudden departure from office in March 1976, a further controversy arose about the supposed influence exercised by Marcia Williams, now Lady Falkender. On this occasion it was the former premier's resignation honours list that became the subject of gossip and criticism. Even before the list was published on 27 May 1976, leaks as to its contents had placed it at the centre of a great deal of media speculation and aroused much adverse comment among the political class. On the 23 May 1976 Tony Benn noted in his diary, 'the scandal of Harold Wilson's resignation honours lists is still exercising the press. The whole thing is utterly corrupt.'[6] Four days later Benn again comments, 'Harold Wilson's honours list is still the big news item today. It is unsavoury, disreputable and just told the whole Wilson story in a single episode. That he should pick inadequate, buccaneering, sharp shysters for his honours was disgusting.'[7]

It was not simply that the list reputedly contained the names of cultural lightweights, such as showbusiness tycoons Lew Grade and Bernard Delfont, and television presenter David Frost, and suspect businessmen such as Wilson's crony and raincoat manufacturer, Sir Joseph Kagan[8] and those lacking socialist credentials such as property millionaire Sir Max Rayne, Wilson's publisher, Sir George Weidenfeld, and the financier James Goldsmith,[9] that offended ideological purists and the cultural snobbery of the great and the good. It was that the list was rumoured to be the handiwork not of Wilson himself, but of Marcia Williams.[10] George Hutchinson in *The Times* squarely attributed blame for the honours list debacle not only to the prime minister but also to Lady Falkender: 'Sir Harold Wilson's retirement from office . . . has been irretrievably damaged. No honours list . . . has ever been attended by such a farce.'[11] He went on to accuse Wilson of having 'demeaned' the office of prime minister, 'embarrassed' the Crown; 'injured' the Labour Party and 'discredited' the honours system. He commented that whilst '. . . it is right that principals should accept the blame when things go wrong, Sir Harold's amanuensis and adviser (one might almost say accomplice) can hardly be exonerated. Lady Falkender has claimed too much influence and responsibility in the past to escape comment and attention now.'[12]

There lies the heart of the matter. The resignation honours list, because it failed to meet some implicit standard of cultural and political propriety, and because it exuded more than a whiff of Marcia, offered one last opportunity for the Establishment to vent its disapproval of the suspected influence of Marcia Williams, who had in the twenty years since beginning to work for Wilson in 1956, travelled from left-wing secretary to peeress of the realm, while all along being suspected of being the second most powerful person in the land during Wilson's premiership.[13]

Both Wilson and Lady Falkender denied that she had played any part in the selection of names for the honours list[14] but this did little to change the perception that the Wilson era had been more than tainted by the role of unofficial advisers in general and by Marcia Williams in particular. The resignation honours list provided a final seal of disapproval for Wilson's advisory strategies. It ensured that whatever else Wilson would be remembered for, controversy about his chosen advisers would be high on the list.

In spite of an unauspicious beginning marked by the 'landsdeal affair' and the bad taste left at the end by the honours list rumpus, in contrast to 1964–70, there was little public controversy about Harold Wilson's advisory system during his final period in office. This is somewhat surprising, since Wilson was once again innovative in respect of institutionalizing alternative advice for the prime minister, although his enthusiasm for being a presidential premier seemed somewhat dampened.

In order to evaluate the constitutional status of Harold Wilson's advisory system in the 1970s and to assess the extent to which it contributed to the presidentialization process, it is necessary firstly to answer some preliminary questions. What was the accepted constitutional position in respect of advice to the prime minister when Wilson returned to Downing Street in 1974 and what was the nature of the system he inherited? Secondly, the reasons why he regarded these arrangements as inadequate or unsatisfactory need to be explained. Thirdly, we need to examine the nature of the changes he introduced.

Rules that circumscribe advice to the executive in Britain form part of the unwritten constitution. It is, therefore, difficult to be precise as to their nature or to be exact about when they change. Public controversy about advice and/or advisers is usually taken to be an indication that previously accepted conventions have become unsatisfactory. When such controversy subsides it can be assumed to indicate that a new accommodation has been reached. Such a change appeared to have taken place in the decade between Harold Wilson's first period in office in the 1960s and his return to Downing Street in 1974. By 1974 prime ministers were still expected, as they had been in the 1960s, to rely primarily on their cabinet colleagues for both political and policy advice, advice already mediated by senior civil servants. It was now accepted, however, that prime ministers could also receive additional political advice from a few personal aides within No.10, and that a central briefing agency, the CPRS would, by incorporating a handful of 'outsiders', extend the range of policy advice to both the prime minister and the cabinet. A new settlement in the secret constitution seemed to be emerging by the end of Edward Heath's period in office: parallel sources of policy advice to the prime minister were acceptable but alternative sources, that is, advice from sources outside the official filters, were not.

If, then, the constitutional position had changed since the 1960s, how did this affect the advisory system in place? When Wilson returned to No.10 Downing Street in March 1974, he inherited an advisory system that was in some respects more presidentialized than had been the case when he first took office in 1964. Within No.10 itself, the Political Office, which had raised eyebrows and questions of constitutionality at its inception in 1964, had, by 1974, become part of the woodwork. Lady Falkender notes that 'when we went back in 1974 the whole atmosphere in Downing Street was much more relaxed and flexible. The Political Office had continued throughout Edward Heath's premiership and survived as an established fact . . . '[15] In contrast to 1964, the politicization of the Press Office also provoked little comment. According to Lady Falkender: '. . . certain posts such as that of Political Press Officer, which had caused so much argument with the Civil Service in the earlier Government [1964] were now accepted and integrated into the machinery of Number 10.'[16]

By 1974 it was becoming accepted that prime ministers needed additional support in the form of at least some political aides in No.10. There was also a perceptible shift taking place in the orientation of the Cabinet Office and the work of the Cabinet Secretary towards supporting the prime minister. Sir John Hunt, Cabinet Secretary 1973–9, noted that 'my role in advising the Prime Minister has certainly grown over the years, and over the years before me. . . . Slowly over a period of six or seven years I found I was devoting more of my time to servicing the Prime Minister in one way or another as compared with my normal duties of servicing the Cabinet.'[17]

Not only did Wilson benefit from the precedents he himself had set in the 1960s and from an improved service to the prime minister from the Cabinet Secretary, but he also inherited the CPRS created by Edward Heath. Whilst this latter was ostensibly established to serve the cabinet as a whole, in practice it was evolving into a briefing agency for the prime minister.

In 1974, in contrast to 1964, Wilson inherited a structure that went some way towards providing a parallel, and in limited respects, alternative advisory system for the prime minister, which took some account of his new responsibility for delivering parliamentary majorities. Whilst on the one hand there was an improvement in the provision of advice to the prime minister, on the other hand, Wilson made it clear that this time he intended to be less presidential and less interventionist. He would, therefore, presumably have less need for parallel or alternative advice with which to challenge and monitor advice received from cabinet colleagues. Wilson had said that, if elected, this time there would be 'no presidential nonsense'.[18] Despite the doubts of senior colleagues and advisers, to some extent Wilson was true to his word. Denis Healey, who in the 1960s had accused Wilson of being a most interventionist prime minister, admits that this time ' . . . Harold Wilson took a much more relaxed view of his responsibilities . . . he interfered much less in the work of his ministers . . .'[19] Wilson, himself, in his personal record of this period, using a football analogy, asserts:

> in the 1964 Government . . . I had to occupy almost every position on the field, goalkeeper, defence, attack I had to take the corner kicks and penalties, administer to the wounded and bring on the lemons at half-time. Now . . . I could be no more than what used to be called a deep-lying centre-half . . . concentrating on defence, initiating attacks, distributing the ball and moving up-field only for set-piece occasions.[20]

This time Wilson saw his role as being that of a member of a team, even if player-manager. That is, he saw himself in the role of a British prime minister in a collective executive, in contrast to trying to play every position like an American president.

In 1974 Wilson inherited a prime ministerial advisory system which offered greater scope for an interventionist, presidential style leadership, at a time when he claimed to have less presidential aspirations. Given the shift in constitutional conventions in respect of advice and given the proclaimed change in Wilson's own attitudes, it might be expected that, in contrast to the 1960s, this time Wilson would not feel compelled to change the advisory system. This was not the case. Whilst, in contrast to 1964, there were no pre-election interviews in which Wilson revealed his plans in respect of the advisory system, on entering office he did introduce fundamental changes designed to thwart the attempts of senior civil servants to regain their former monopoly. Although claiming to be less presidential in intention, Wilson did, nevertheless, continue the process of presidentializing the advisory system begun in the 1960s.

Why did Wilson challenge the settlement that seemed to be emerging in the secret constitution? What inadequacies did he see in the evolved system he inherited from Heath and how did he attempt to overcome them?

The secret constitution had changed little since the 1960s. By 1974, the civil service had all but regained its lost territory. The prime minister could call upon a parallel advisory system which was by definition controlled, if not entirely peopled by, civil servants. In 1964 Wilson had entered office intending to divide, and thereby rule, the Treasury. To this end the DEA had been established to challenge the Treasury's monopoly over economic policy and, in 1968, the Civil Service Department was established to weaken the pervasive influence of the Treasury over the entire culture of Whitehall. In addition Wilson had appointed Thomas Balogh to provide the government with alternative economic advice. The Treasury had mounted a successful counterrevolution against these innovations. The DEA was successfully emasculated by a process of diversion[21] and colonizati.[22] Colonization also accounts for the Civil Service Department's failure to dent the pervasiveness of Treasury attitudes and values throughout Whitehall.[23] Any influence Thomas Balogh may have hoped to exercise was frustrated by a process of isolation and discrediting.[24] Once again, Harold Wilson felt that a Labour government would find itself in office but not really in power[25] unless it could find sources of advice with which to challenge Treasury orthodoxy. Once again, also, Wilson knew he would need political advisers inside No.10 to enable him to challenge the civil service policy compromises promoted by 'captured' cabinet colleagues. Although the prime minister had inherited a 'new' advisory system, it remained largely controlled by 'old' advisers.

Members of Wilson's entourage, some of his cabinet colleagues and by implication, Wilson himself, attributed a large measure of the blame for the supposed policy failures of the 1964–70 governments to the power of the civil service to block radical initiatives.[26] Barbara Castle, a few days after the publication of the *Labour Programme 1973*, commented in the *Sunday Times*, 'Labour's programme for the next election promises vast changes in the running of the country. It presupposes . . . a revolution in Whitehall attitudes   something the last Wilson Governments never succeeded in imposing.'[27] Wilson, in retrospect, recognized that in the 1960s he had to some extent become enthraled by the mandarins, particularly Burke Trend, and he accepted that his attempts to divide and rule the Treasury had been a failure. He was determined that this would not happen again:[28] Whitehall was to be more effectively tackled. Not only did Wilson and his team believe that civil service opposition had frustrated their previous period in government, but this time they expected greater difficulties because they believed civil service power had increased in the interim. Haines asserts, 'it is the power of the civil service not least the power to prevent things being done which should be the constant concern of press and Parliament . . . its power grew alarmingly during the years of the Heath government . . . '[29]

If sources of policy advice remained suspect because of the same old Treasury dominance, what, employing once again Patrick Weller's distinction,[30] about *political* advice? In 1964 Wilson had recognized that the new electoral politics necessitated increased political support for the prime minister; he also recognized that the political interests of the man in No.10 did not necessarily coincide with those of his cabinet colleagues, who were, after all, his rivals and, in 1964, were in any case inexperienced in the ways of Whitehall. In 1974 the No.10 Political Office was accepted, even if Marcia Williams, Wilson's particular choice, was not. The enhanced role of the Press Office, and perhaps more grudgingly, its politicization, had also been recognized and accepted. What of the cabinet? Was it still seen to be an unsatisfactory forum for political advice?

All cabinets contain rivals of the prime minister, and the 1974 cabinet was no exception. This was now less of a concern for Wilson. Firstly, in 1964 Wilson himself had only been party leader for a year, the leadership contest and the campaigns of his rivals, Brown and Callaghan, were still fresh in the minds of party colleagues. In 1974 Wilson entered office as party leader of eleven years standing, having won three out of four elections. His policy record may have been shaky, but almost no one doubted that Wilson himself had delivered the election victories. Thus on the one hand his position as leader was more secure, and on the other hand he was less concerned to secure it. Wilson was aware that as leader of a minority government[31] he faced an inevitable second election.[32] He was determined that if he returned to office he would retire after serving a couple more years as prime minister.[33] Thus Wilson had less reason to be concerned about the political advice offered by rivals. In addition, in contrast to 1964, instead of being surrounded by a team of inexperienced colleagues over whose selection he had little choice, he was the leader of a much more experienced cabinet, and he had good reason for supposing it was his cabinet. Wilson himself asserts, 'in 1964 hardly a single member of the Cabinet had sat in a previous Cabinet' whilst in 1974 '. . . the Cabinet was richer in previous experience than perhaps any incoming Government this century. Fourteen members had sat in the outgoing 1970 Cabinet.'[34] He also points out that

> in making these appointments I was in a much happier position than in 1964. An incoming Labour Prime Minister must have regard to the membership of the Parliamentary Committee of the previous Parliament . . . On this occasion the PLP had elected the very ones I would have chosen, indeed I voted for them in the secret ballot. This was very different from the 1963–4 Shadow Cabinet. I had voted for only a minority of them and only a minority had voted for me.[35]

Given improved political support within No.10, given the changed relationship that existed between Wilson and his cabinet, and given his proclaimed more modest ambitions, what did Wilson perceive to be shortcomings of the political advisory system?

Wilson's political agenda was one not necessarily shared by all of his cabinet colleagues. Whilst in opposition Wilson had been much criticized for his conduct of government in the 1960s, in particular for his preference for pragmatism over manifesto and party programme. This time Wilson claimed he intended to be 'keeper of the manifesto', a manifesto which committed Labour to a more radical interventionist programme.[36] But according to Martin Holmes, 'Mr Wilson never had his heart in the industrial strategy originally worked out by the NEC in opposition, and backed to the hilt by Tony Benn.'[37] Wilson's position was made worse by the Social Contract, a bargain between Labour and the trade unions, under which the unions were to deliver industrial peace and wage restraint in exchange for the social wage.[38] The public expenditure commitments implied by both the interventionist manifesto and the Social Contract were difficult to reconcile with the economic conditions that Labour inherited in 1974.[39] In addition to being tied to a left wing manifesto and being obliged to placate the more militant industrial wing of the party, Wilson also faced the very real possibility that the party would split over the issue of continued membership of the Common Market. Whilst the cabinet was composed of experienced politicians, they were not the united band of optimists (and rivals) that had surrounded him in 1964. The divisions between left and right had widened, and this, coupled with the precarious Parliamentary position, and with the economic problems, gave Wilson reason to believe that the political advisory system would be unsatisfactory. He would need independent political advice, to enable him to challenge that offered by cabinet colleagues, if he was to stand any chance of balancing the expectations of party whilst simultaneously convincing the City, the Establishment and international financiers that their economy was safe in his hands. Wilson needed independent political support and advice to fulfil his constant and remaining political ambition: to make Labour the party of government.[40]

The 'second coming' was accompanied by none of the razzmatazz or optimism of the first. This time there was no 'white heat' of technology to be a universal panacea, no anticipated, or promised, reversal of economic decline. It was no longer accepted, if indeed it ever had been, that science linked to managerialism was the real future of socialism. This time there was no blueprint setting out how the persisting shortcomings of the advisory system would be tackled. Nevertheless, despite, or perhaps because of, the difficult political and economic situation in which Wilson found himself, he returned to office in 1974 determined to tackle the inadequacies of an advisory system dominated by the Treasury mandarins. What changes in the prime ministerial advisory system did Wilson introduce?

Patrick Weller's analytical distinction between policy and political advice provides a less useful framework for examining Wilson's advisory strategies in the 1970s. The Policy Unit, Wilson's major innovation in 1974, was created to provide *partisan policy* advice to the prime minister, and, therefore, blurs the distinction. On this occasion, therefore, advisory support first within and then beyond No.10 will provide the framework for analysis.

In the 1960s Harold Wilson's attempts to provide himself with alternative political advice had exposed him to accusations of behaving unconstitutionally and had met with frustration, if not outright obstruction, from the official machine. The unprecedented role assumed by Mrs Williams in No.10, in particular, had aroused much adverse comment, as to a lesser extent had the appointment of Gerald Kaufman as Parliamentary and Political Press Liaison Officer. One reason why both these posts seemed to have aroused disquiet was that the occupants were not paid from the official coffers,[41] and so they remained beyond the reach of the civil service rules of the game. However, even economic adviser Thomas Balogh, who was appointed as a temporary civil servant, whilst exposed to less direct criticism was, nevertheless, successfully neutralized by being granted only limited access to both the prime minister and to relevant documents.[42]

On his return to Downing Street in March 1974, Wilson was determined not to repeat these earlier mistakes. Mrs Williams, still in the personal employment of Wilson, reestablished his Political Office, but was now the beneficiary of precedents set by herself and consolidated by Douglas Hurd. Joe Haines, who had served as Gerald Kaufman's deputy in 1969, and continued in Wilson's employment as his press adviser during the opposition years, returned this time as a temporary civil servant combining the posts of Press Officer and Parliamentary Press Liaison Officer. This represented a politicization of the Press Office and a rejection of the accepted convention in the 1960s that the Press Officer, as a temporary civil servant, should aspire to political neutrality. Whilst both the above appointments and those of their accompanying assistants are a testament to the growing politicization and personalization of the support provided for the prime minister within No.10, the creation of the Policy Unit can be described as a major leap forward in this respect.

In March 1974 Harold Wilson established a prime minister's Policy Unit in the form of a small team of partisan policy advisers under the leadership of Dr Bernard Donoughue. Donoughue, a Senior Lecturer in Politics at the London School of Economic, had served Wilson as a political adviser during the February election campaign.[43] According to the Downing Street press release, the new Policy Unit would '. . . assist in the development of a whole range of policies contained in the Government's programme, especially those arising in the short and medium term.'[44] Jones describes the Policy Unit as 'a major step in strengthening the assistance available to the Prime Minister', and notes that '. . . for the first time in British peacetime history a Prime Minister had decided to establish a systematically organised personal bureau.'[45] Wilson himself said of the Policy Unit,

> I have set up a special Policy Unit in my own office. This team, which I have deliberately kept small, is made up of people with expert knowledge of the fields of economics, industrial and social policy. They advise me directly on the immediate decisions to be made, whether in Cabinet or elsewhere and on longer term issues and developments . . . the purpose of this Policy Unit is not only to bring in experts to extend the range of policy options from which the Government and in particular the Prime Minister . . . has to choose. The Policy Unit was set up, and its members were selected to provide a team with strong political commitment to advise on, propose and

pursue policies to further the Government's political goals.[46]

If Wilson created the Policy Unit to formalize the role of political advisers to the prime minister in Downing Street, what change, if any, did he introduce into the advisory system beyond the confines of No.10? What was the fate of the CPRS? What measures, if any, did he introduce this time to combat the dominance of the Treasury?

The intention behind the Policy Unit was not that it would be an isolated body operating within Downing Street, but that it would be linked with a network of political advisers throughout Whitehall.[47] When last in office, Labour ministers had complained of their isolation within their ministries.[48] This sense of isolation was increased by ministers' awareness that their senior civil service advisers were themselves part of a network that linked Permanent Secretaries and Private Office staff throughout Whitehall.[49] This time in accordance with the recommendations of the Fulton Report, and in accordance with the *ad hoc* arrangements of the previous Labour government and the Conservatives under Heath, Wilson allowed ministers to appoint political advisers. Wilson asserts that 'the incoming Labour Government in 1974 regularized the position [of ministerial appointees] by treating them as a special category of "political adviser".'[50] He goes on to note that approximately thirty such appointments were made. The intention was that a network of political advisers would provide an alternative colonial advisory system mitigating ministerial isolation and counteracting the tendency for ministers to 'go native'. This would enable the prime minister to receive less departmentally biased advice from his cabinet colleagues and act as an early warning system against civil service 'bouncing'.[51]

What about the CPRS? Contrary to expectation, Harold Wilson did not it. The official explanation for its retention, despite its newly created 'rival', was that the 'Policy Unit was concerned with short-term, and the CPRS with the medium and longer-term.'[52] Whilst the CPRS received a reprieve it suffered from several weaknesses that resulted in it playing a less prominent role under the new government. Firstly, the civil service colonization process to which it was subject by the end of Edward Heath's period in office was accelerated by Wilson himself. In October 1974, Wilson appointed Sir Kenneth Berrill, formerly Chief Economic Adviser to the Treasury, to be the new director of the CPRS. According to Blackstone and Plowden, '. . . when Harold Wilson had to appoint a successor [to Lord Rothschild] he had so completely accepted that this was a Civil Service post that he had no candidate of his own to propose and gratefully confirmed the civil service nomination of Sir Kenneth Berrill.'[53] The second weakness of the CPRS was that, it no longer had the ear of the prime minister.[54] Lastly,[55] the location of the CPRS in the Cabinet Office worked to its disadvantage; it had proximity to neither individual cabinet ministers nor to the prime minister. It therefore suffered from the great weakness of limited access to decision-makers. The CPRS survived but it had lost the place in the 'inner circle' that it had occupied during the Heath-Rothschild period. Wilson the politician, sought partisan advisers who offered not only expertise but political sympathy and political *nous*.

What measures, if any, did Wilson introduce this time to check the Treasury knights? In some respects Wilson's answer was to try more of the same, once again appointing alternative advisers. Nicholas Kaldor returned to the Treasury as special adviser to Chancellor of the Exchequer, Denis Healey. Thomas Balogh, now a member of the House of Lords, became Minister of State for Energy. Harold Lever, as Chancellor of the Duchy of Lancaster, assumed the role previously undertaken by Balogh, and became a sort of roving economic adviser and prime ministerial assistant, described by Peter Jenkins as 'Minister to the Prime Minister'.[56] Alternative economic advice this time was a major function of the Policy Unit,[57] and unlike the ill-fated DEA it was not peopled by Treasury progeny, and its location inside No.10 guaranteed its access to the most powerful decision-maker.

What was the constitutional status of these changes Harold Wilson introduced into the prime ministerial advisory system and to what extent did they contribute to the process of presidentialization? By 1974, the accepted constitutional position in respect of advice to the prime minister was that prime ministers were still expected to rely on the political and policy advice of their cabinet colleagues, who in turn were supposed to rely on the advice of civil servants. Prime ministers were not expected to cast their nets widely for advice in the manner of an American president, but there had been some concessions to their need for additional sources of advice. It was now accepted that prime ministers could also receive additional political support from personal aides within No.10 and that a central briefing agency, the CPRS, which included a few outsiders, would extend the range of policy advice available to both the cabinet and the prime minister. Although the Heath government had continued the special advisers experiment begun by Wilson in the 1960s, it had not achieved clear constitutional acceptance, especially if advisers were neither experts in a particular field nor on the official payroll. The emerging constitutional settlement seemed to be that *parallel* sources of advice to the prime minister were acceptable, but *alternative* sources, that is advice not filtered through the official channels, were not.

In 1974, Harold Wilson, attempted for a second time to tackle what he perceived to be weaknesses of an advisory system dominated by the Treasury and the inadequacy of political support for a prime minister who, in electoral terms, now bore presidential responsibilities. In doing so he challenged the emerging settlement in the secret constitution. The introduction of a network of special political advisers and the establishment of the No.10 Policy Unit, were a clear attempt to construct an alternative advisory system. Outsiders were placed at the heart of government, both within No.10 itself and in the Private Offices of cabinet ministers. They were granted access to official documents, committees and top decision-makers. The shroud of secrecy surrounding the inner workings of government means that the extent of the outsiders' influence can never be precisely determined. Proximity and access suggest that these irregulars may be assumed to have exercised influence. There is, therefore, a *prima facie* case for describing Wilson's innovations as unconstitutional.

However, because the rules governing advice are at the heart of the unwritten constitution, determining the constitutionality of prime ministerial advisory strategies is largely dependent upon assessing their acceptability to other important, contemporary political actors. In the 1960s Wilson's advisory strategies could be described as unconstitutional because they aroused a great deal of public fuss. In the 1970s this was not the case.

This is not to claim that there were no objections raised or questions asked about the role of alternative advisers.[58] Joe Haines and Bernard Donoughue, as the 'court favourites',[59] inevitably attracted some criticism. The autocratic manner in which Haines performed his duties as Press Officer aroused adverse comment among his colleagues in Whitehall, and provoked former colleagues in the Westminister lobby to dub him the 'Anti-Press Officer'.[60] Tony Benn was suspicious about the nature of Bernard Donoughue's role. Benn noted that his own personal political adviser, Frances Morrell, got the impression that 'Bernard Donoughue really saw his main role as spying on Ministers.'[61] By 1975 Benn complained that 'Bernard Donoughue is power mad and he just wants to establish a dominant position for himself in Whitehall.'[62] Donoughue rebutted these charges, asserting, 'Tony Benn was over sensitive. Ministers were personal friends . . . sometimes we might "spy" *for* ministers and would alert them to what was going on in their departments.'[63] Benn was something of a special case. The champion of the left, he made no secret of the fact that he distrusted (with good cause) Wilson's intentions in respect of the manifesto. Barbara Castle in her detailed account of life in the 1974 government makes only a passing reference to meeting Donoughue,[64] and claims that she never found '...

either the CPRS or Donoughue's unit had any noticeable effect on the decisions we took.'[65]   Denis Healey admits that initially he had some misgivings about the role of Harold Lever:

> Wilson had an independent source of information about economic and financial matters, Harold Lever. . . At first I resented Harold's [Lever's] privileged access to the Prime Minister, and his tendency to second-guess my decisions without having any responsibility for carrying them out. When I felt more at ease in my job [as Chancellor of the Exchequer] I found his understanding of the financial market invaluable, and I normally accepted about one out of four of his suggestions a high average for an external consultant.'[66]

This time there was no twentieth century Bagehot like Crossman to provide an analytical appraisal of the new advisory machinery. Neither were there any spectacular resignations attributed to Wilson's advisory strategies as had been claimed in George Brown's case.

Not only was there little disquiet expressed by Wilson's political colleagues, but there was also little overt resentment from officials. When describing his new Policy Unit to the Commonwealth Heads of Government in May 1975, Wilson claimed: '. . . most regular senior civil servants who might have been expected to be wary of the idea [of the Policy Unit] have openly welcomed the experiment and are cooperating to make it a success.'[67]

Several explanations may be offered to account for the contrast in the way political actors reacted to the changes introduced by Wilson this time. Firstly, the Policy Unit, unlike Wilson's attempts to import political appointees into No.10 in 1964, was a properly constituted body with credentials traceable to Fulton.[68] Secondly, its members became temporary civil servants, and, although political appointees whose contracts would expire when Wilson left office, they were nevertheless on the official payroll and, in principle at least, part of the official machine. Thirdly, Donoughue, aware of the problems of access that had blunted the potential effectiveness of Thomas Balogh, agreed formal arrangements about access to the prime minister, to documents, departmental officials and cabinet committees, with the Cabinet Secretary.[69]

There was some public controversy about special advisers. This primarily centred on questions about conflicts between the principle of political neutrality attached to their civil service status, and the political privileges they were seeking in order to stand as Labour candidates in the October election.[70] In general, however, Whitehall appeared to be more reconciled to the presence of irregulars. The special advisers were able to claim Fulton credentials and were on the official payroll as temporary civil servants, and experience of handling special advisers over the previous decade helped to diminish any threat Whitehall may have felt in the past. These were perhaps sufficient reasons to explain why the special adviser network aroused so small a constitutional fuss. A further reason is that a network never quite materialized in any formal way to rival that of the mandarins or to become an influential alternative advisory system. Although informal contacts between some special advisers did exist, there was no connecting structure linking them with each other or with the Policy Unit at the centre. The irregulars remained isolated political appointees loyal to their individual ministers. They did not in any sense become the prime minister's troubleshooters within the departments, 'riding herd' on the bureaucracy in the manner of presidential appointees in Washington.

The reasons suggested above help to account for the comparative lack of public controversy in Whitehall and Westminster over Wilson's alternative advisory system. Three further explanations can be offered to account for the apparent readiness of his cabinet colleagues to accept the new arrangements. Firstly, being permitted personal political advisers themselves may have helped to reconcile political colleagues to the prime minister's Policy Unit. Secondly, true to his word, Wilson was less interventionist. Donoughue asserts that 'probably Mr Wilson could have dominated his colleagues a little more in 1974–6 had he so chosen, but he was anxious not to repeat the "presidential" experience of 1964 . . . thus it was that Wilson chaired the Cabinet rather than leading and dominating it.'[71]   There was the notable exception of Tony Benn, who could legitimately claim that the prime minister was interventionist in his particular area of responsibility. Whilst Benn's complaints should not be dismissed, he did constitute a special case.[72] Lastly, this time there was no conspicuous 'kitchen cabinet'. Although Donoughue, Haines and Williams were each assumed to exercise great influence over the prime minister, if a 'kitchen cabinet' still existed it was now camouflaged by the Policy Unit. This trio, though close to the prime minister, were divided amongst themselves and thus less visible as a group. In addition, Marcia Williams was less often present to act as gatekeeper and to generally ruffle feathers within No.10.[73]

If institutionalization of the Policy Unit and the regularization of the role of special advisers helped to avoid public controversy about Wilson's alternative advisory system, did it also prevent private resistance and resentment in the corridors of power? Were the changes in the public constitution accepted in the secret constitution? Did the Treasury concede ground in respect of its control of economic management, the front line in the struggle for power between the elected wing and the permanent wing of the government.[74]

Robert Chesshyre, describing Wilson's innovations and predicting Whitehall's likely response, asserted, 'the Civil Service is too urbane to declare immediate open warfare, but tough battles can be expected... '[75] Undoubtedly behind closed doors a power struggle over economic policy was waged. Donoughue and Haines provide detailed accounts of the attempt by the Treasury to panic Wilson into adopting a statutory pay policy during the economic crisis of 1975, despite Wilson's publicly stated rejections of such measures.[76] According to their accounts, the Policy Unit, and in particular, Donoughue in partnership with Haines, succeeded in their eleventh hour bid to persuade Wilson to adhere to his publicly stated pledges.[77] This outcome, according to Haines, provoked the Treasury to seek revenge by attempting to restrict Donoughue's access to ministerial papers.[78]

According to the above accounts the interventions of the Policy Unit in economic policy were resented and resisted by the Treasury. The individual meddling of Harold Lever aroused a similar response. Haines claims, 'Treasury officials resented the interference of Harold Lever and the fact that the prime minister boasted that Lever was his own personal "think tank".'[79] Haines describes the way that the Treasury sought to undermine Lever, and says that '. . . no Minister, not even Tony Benn, had more complaints laid against him to the prime minister than were laid by the Treasury against the Duchy of Lancaster.'[80]

Despite its efforts to combat the influence of alternative advisers, the Treasury this time seems to have been less successful. Lever, for example, legitimized by being an MP and member of the cabinet, was placed in a less vulnerable position than Thomas Balogh had been, and was, therefore, better able to resist attempts to undermine and discredit him. According to Bernard Donoughue,

> The traditional approach of keeping economic policy tight within the Treasury and then 'bouncing' it through Ministers was undermined from 1975 onwards by the existence of special policy advisers who worked to Cabinet Ministers and especially to the Prime Minister. That had been one of Harold Wilson's objectives in 1974 when introducing a more comprehensive system of special advisers into Whitehall, namely to provide alternative economic policy options to those conventionally proposed by the Treasury.[81]

Such failure may owe less to any design of Wilson's than to the fact that this time there was less need to divide and rule the Treasury because it was already divided and, therefore, easier to rule. If the 'Treasury line' had ever existed, by the 1970s it no longer did. Failure of economic policy that had been serious during the 1960s had become critical by the 1970s. The Treasury was dividing along the lines of un-reconstructed Keynesians headed by Sir Douglas Wass, the Permanent Secretary, and monetarist hawks like Derek Mitchell.[82]

Not only was the Treasury itself divided; it also had to contend with another usurper on the economic policy terrain in the shape of Sir John Hunt, the Cabinet Secretary. According to Donoughue, 'Sir John Hunt appeared not over impressed by the way the Treasury was being run and he directed his attention increasingly toward the economic policy field.'[83] Donoughue claims that the CPRS '. . . often assisted the Cabinet Secretary in this policy role . . . ' and that 'such Whitehall imperialism led the Cabinet Office at this time into several battles with the Treasury . . .'[84] Tony Benn asserts that '. . . it [the CPRS] has in practice become a powerful lobby for the Cabinet Secretary himself, to whom it is responsible.'[85] Haines describes the way that 'the growing strength of the Cabinet Office under Sir John caused tension to develop between it and the Treasury.'[86] He suggests that 'the Cabinet Office may yet fulfil the function which Harold Wilson conceived for the Department of Economic Affairs in 1964: to be an alternative source of power to the Treasury.'[87] Lord Hunt himself accepted that the above views were at least 'half-truths', although he rejects that he pushed particular policies: 'what I was able to do was to make sure the Prime Minister knew of the different kinds of arguments going on within the Treasury and what was the Bank of England view.'[88] He did not deny that he worked closely with Sir Kenneth Berrill, exlaining that Berrill, as a former Economic Adviser to the Treasury, had insider access to Treasury views.[89]

If a divided Treasury, the Cabinet Secretary aided by the CPRS, the Policy Unit and Harold Lever were not enough contenders in the struggle for control over economic policy, there was yet another group of players in the field. This period was the high summer of trade union influence. The Labour Party's election victory, if it can be so described, was publicly attributed partly to the electorate's belief, or perhaps hope, that Labour could work with the unions, as Heath had seemingly failed to do. The Social Contract formed the basis of a trade union and Labour Party understanding which served to integrate the unions into economic policy formation. In effect, some union leaders, Jack Jones of the Transport and General Workers Union in particular, were involved in devising pay restraint policies and thereafter expected to deliver grassroots cooperation. As early as June 1975 Benn notes, 'I think Harold Wilson, Michael Foot and Jack Jones run the country.'[90] Holmes claims that 'the incomes policy U-turn introduced in July 1975 was evidence of a Wilson-Jones axis which presented the Cabinet with a *fait accompli.*'[91] Weakened by divisions within and confronted by a plurality of 'outside' contenders, the Treasury was faced with finding its way through the thicket in its efforts to retain control over economic policy.

Innovations in the advisory system introduced by Wilson in 1974 challenged both the secret and the public constitution. The Policy Unit and the special advisers working to ministers constituted an alternative, as distinct from a parallel, advisory network (or the rudiments of one), breaching understandings of the secret constitution which held that the mandarins' voices should dominate in discussion about policy. The Policy Unit also, by providing the prime minister with an alternative source of political advice breached the public constitution under which the cabinet was assumed to be the forum of political advice to the prime minister. This time Wilson avoided accusations that he had violated constitutional propriety by institutionalizing his alternative advisory body. In effect, he unilaterally changed the constitution by citing the Fulton report and issuing a Downing Street press statement.[92] Why was he able to get away with it without arousing a public hue and cry of both official and political voices? It was partly because institutionalization itself lent legitimacy to the system,[93] partly because he faced a dispirited and divided opposition in Whitehall and in the cabinet, and partly that he himself was less energetically interventionist. He now had the means to be more presidential but lacked the will to use it.

To what extent then did the changes introduced by Harold Wilson, in 1974, continue to presidentialize the premiership in respect of advice? Did he enter No.10 accompanied by a team of personal aides, whose loyalty was to himself rather than to the institution, who would not only provide alternative advice to enable him to be interventionist, but would also progress-chase his policies through the government machine, warn him of impending crises, and generally act as guardians of his political interests? Did he, in short, create a WHO within No.10? Was the cabinet relegated to the role of being just one among many sources of advice that the prime minister could call upon, if he so wished? Is there any evidence to suggest that Wilson became the prey of those skilled in news management or that he allowed members of a personal entourage to man the barricades against traditional advisers, leaving him isolated within No.10, a captive of his creatures as had been noted in the Nixon model of the presidential advisory system?

Despite the fact that this time Wilson denied he had any presidential aspirations, he could, nevertheless, be accused of having provided himself with an advisory system which would enable him to be more interventionist in the presidential manner. In America the Reorganization Act of 1939, which permitted the establishment of the WHO as part of the EOP, was a measure which legitimized presidential 'kitchen cabinets'.[94] The establishment of the Prime Minister's Policy Unit in 1974 had a similar result in Britain. In the 1960s, Wilson's informal attempt to provide himself with personal political support to meet the prime minister's increased political responsibilities, exposed him to claims that he had constructed a 'kitchen cabinet' and had failed to observe constitutional propriety in respect of advice. When he returned to office in 1974 he rectified his earlier error, and legitimized his advisers, by opting for a more formal arrangement.

The Policy Unit, a team of eight personal political appointees, whilst much smaller in scale than the approximately fifty strong team of presidential aides nowadays, was not greatly different in size from FDR's team of eleven presidential assistants.[95] It provided the prime minister with a means of monitoring the way in which his cabinet colleagues carried out their duties. By providing alternative advice it enabled the prime minister to challenge departmental advice mediated by cabinet colleagues, and enabled him to intervene when he deemed it necessary. Robert Chesshyre says that in setting up the Policy Unit,

> . . . Mr Wilson will have strengthened his personal hand in relation to his departmental ministers, having in future alternative guidance on which to judge conflicting claims. . . While individual departmental ministers have their armies of civil servants, the Prime Minister has been rather short on advice. With the creation of Dr Donoughue's unit, the Prime Minister at last has someone with towel and sponge in his own corner.[96]

Simon James agrees that it was the role of the Policy Unit to question ' . . . what departments proposed or failed to propose, and to alert the Prime Minister to dangers and omissions in departmental policies and give him the ammunition to argue back effectively.'[97] According to Donoughue, one of the major variables which determine the extent of prime ministerial intervention is the scale and competence of the advisory services at his disposal.[98] He claims 'the most important contribution of the Policy Unit . . . was that it increased the prime minister's capacity for effective intervention in other Ministers' policy areas, for which more than mere personal willpower and the status of Downing Street is required.'[99]

Some parallels can be drawn between the institutional developments that took place in the American presidency in the 1930s and those taking place in Downing Street in the 1960s and 1970s. The CPRS created by Heath, and the increased orientation of the Cabinet Office towards serving the prime minister, can be said to parallel the development of the EOP. Similarly, the Policy Unit in conjunction with the Political and Press Offices at No.10, can be said to parallel the kind of support an American president receives from the WHO. Indeed, Harold Wilson described the proposed Policy Unit as his 'eyes and ears'[100] a clear echo of Sorensen's description of the role of political aides in Kennedy's White House Office.

Not only was there a discernable presidentialization of formal advisory support for the prime minister, but presidentialization was also discernable in the greater use of *ad hoc* advisory bodies under the prime minister's supervision. Proposals to reform the constitution, in the shape of a manifesto commitment on devolution for Scotland and Wales, and the question of continued membership of the Common Market, were high on the political agenda during this period. Both these issues, although the responsibilities of designated ministers,[101] remained under the prime minister's eye by being placed under the auspices of the Cabinet Office.[102] Wilson also took the unprecedented step of appointing an adviser on constitutional questions. Lord Crowther-Hunt, a former member of the Fulton Committee, and personal friend, acquired his title along with a desk in the Cabinet Office.[103]

The prime minister, instead of being at the head of the traditional advisory system in which policy advice arising from the civil service, and political advice arising from party and Parliament, were filtered via cabinet colleagues, was now at the hub of the central executive territory[104] orbited by a plurality of advisory bodies, only one of which was the cabinet. The prime minister was coming to resemble an American president at liberty to tap a very wide range of advisory sources. A combination of factors like, a tiny Parliamentary majority, a more or less permanent economic crisis, and a prime minister lacking the energy and enthusiasm for being interventionist, suggest that it would be premature to consign the cabinet to the 'outer circle' of influence occupied by its American counterpart. Bernard Donoughue describes Harold Wilson as '. . . a natural Treasury man, skilfully slipping items through Cabinet',[105] but he says that 'all major decisions (except those concerning highly sensitive discussions on monetary intentions or defence technology) were fully debated in the Cabinet room.'[106] He also claims that 'Cabinet government was certainly alive and kicking in the 1970s . . . '[107] Donoughue's views of course must be treated with some caution. He was, after all, chief alternative adviser, and, therefore, might be expected to have a vested interest trying to head-off any suggestion that his role, and that of the Policy Unit, might breach constitutional propriety. However, a reading of Barbara Castle's diaries, and even those of Tony Benn, the cabinet maverick, would suggest that the cabinet could at least still claim to be 'first among un-equals'.

The American model not only showed that it was acceptable for the president to cast his net widely for advice, but it also revealed that increased presidential power rested on public support and that this had made it obligatory for presidents to pay increasing attention to public relations. Harold Wilson's recognition of the importance of media relations and the increased politicization of the press office, has already been noted. In 1975 this trend was taken a stage further. According to Marcia Williams, in conjunction with the counter-inflationary measures launched in 1975, a Counter Inflation Unit (CIU) was set up under the control of the prime minister, although reporting in fact to Press Officer, Joe Haines. It consisted of

> . . . a small think-tank physically sited in the Cabinet Office, but with a watching brief over every Whitehall department. The CIU's work was partly policy and partly propaganda: it aimed to discover the economic weak spots both within the Government and outside, work out how they could best be plugged and present both the need for this and the method chosen in the best and most encouraging light to all concerned.[108]

Mrs Williams notes that the CIU was manned by Sydney Jacobson, former Editor-in-Chief of the *Daily Mirror*, and Geoffrey Goodman, another *Mirror* man. She goes on to describe the advisory role of members of the *Daily Mirror* board: 'the *Daily Mirror* has (almost) always supported Labour editorially, but perhaps not everyone knows what a key role the paper played, in terms of the active involvement of its personnel rather than column-inches of newsprint, in Labour Party politics; in particular, from 1974 onwards.'[109] According to Mrs Williams,

> *Mirror* dinners, or luncheons, were frequently held at Number 10, attended by members of the *Mirror* Board. . . . Their advice would be sought, soundings taken, opinions given, help promised. It was therefore a natural progression that the CIU should be put in the charge of Lord Jacobson and Geoffrey Goodman . . . with access to the Prime Minister to give and receive advice: always channelled efficiently . . . through Joe Haines.[110]

Donoughue dismisses the idea that the CIU had any policy making role and claims that it had very little contact with the prime minister. He asserts that '. . . it was basically a unit for marketing pay policy' and that '. . . although it did a good job, after about six months it was closed down.'[111]	Although the CIU had only a brief existence, its creation is a testament to the importance placed on public relations and the recognition that policy had to be marketed.

The increasing importance of media relations was also reflected in the dominant role assumed by Wilson's news manager, Joe Haines. Donoughue claims that Haines's role in No.10 '. . . went further than just dealing with the media. He possessed remarkable political insight and judgment and for most of the 197476 period he was effectively the Prime Minister's main political adviser.'[112] Haines's dominance was a source of some discontent. Tony Benn, for example, lays some of the blame for his own poor relationship with the prime minister at Haines's door.[113] Pimlott suggests that, 'Haines's fierce protectiveness towards his master made him unpopular among ministers and in the lobby.'[114] Joe Haines's particular style may have ruffled some feathers, but he was neither gatekeeper nor sole adviser to the prime minister. It would be inaccurate, therefore, to describe Wilson as being cut off by public relations officers and media advisers.

Some convergence was discernible between the American presidential model as exemplified by FDR and the advisory strategies of Harold Wilson. However, despite the increasingly high priority given to media relations and policy-marketing, there is little to suggest that Wilson had either become a captive of public relations advisers, or that he had become a creature of his creatures, in the manner of Richard Nixon. The Policy Unit did provide the prime minister with a small team of personal political advisers. Its members were, however, selected by Bernard Donoughue, their appointments being confirmed by the prime minister. They were chosen not only for their political sympathies but also for their expertise. It was not a job creation scheme for cronies. Its members were not merely Wilson's creatures or heroes of the campaign. Wilson liked to surround himself with favourites and seemed to thrive on the gossip and intrigue they fed him, but according to Mackintosh: 'it is hard, after careful study to see any specific actions of the Wilson premiership that owed more to his entourage than to him. He was his own man and they fulfilled his needs.'[115] Pimlott agrees with this view: 'in this administration, even more than in the last, Wilson was happiest when he felt that advice was reaching him from different angles.'[116] Harold Wilson might, therefore, be described as an FDR in No.10 but not as a Richard Nixon.

On the 16 March 1976, just after his sixtieth birthday, Harold Wilson announced his imminent retirement, to take effect as soon as the Labour

Party could elect his successor. The sudden departure from office of this consummate politician launched a flood of media speculation as to the real reasons that lay behind his decision, as opposed to his proclaimed reason that he had reached retirement age and decided it was time for him to go. In Donoughue's view, Wilson was simply suffering from *déjà vu.*[117]

By way of an epitaph on Wilson's leadership, Tony Benn wrote the following: 'he [Harold Wilson] hasn't inspired any affection, he's just done his job like a Civil Service Prime Minister for years, fudged every issue, dodged every difficulty, but kept us in power, kept us together,[118] ground out the administrative decisions.'[119] These sentiments are echoed by Philip Whitehead, who described Wilson as an 'unfrightening Pooter of politics', and reflecting on his premiership noted:

> Times of contraction do not produce an enthusiasm for radical experiment, but Wilson was happy enough with that. He produced no innovations, apart from his Downing Street Policy Unit, left every stone unturned in the barren fields of constitutional practice. By the time of his retirement there was not a permanent secretary in Whitehall to whom he would have given a moment of unease.[120]

It is possible to argue, however, that Wilson was not a civil servants' prime minister and that in some respects he did arouse much unease in Whitehall. Wilson recognized that the prime minister had become presidential in relation to his party and the electorate, but remained constitutionally a prime minister. To effect a reconciliation between the expectations and powers of the office he attempted an informal presidentialization of the advisory system in the 1960s. The civil service felt sufficiently threatened by these innovations to mount a counterrevolution under the banner of constitutional propriety. They all but achieved their objective under Heath. In 1974 Wilson mounted his own counter offensive. This time he was more successful. This success was partly achieved because, on the one hand, he formalized, and thereby legitimized, his alternative advisory structure. On the other hand, he was the beneficiary of a crisis in confidence in the civil service in the wake of the economic policy failures that marked the decade, and which, temporarily at least, rendered civil service opposition less effective.

The duly constituted nature of both the Policy Unit and the positions of special advisers placed the alternative advisory system beyond the reach of public comment in respect of constitutional propriety, but this did not completely reconcile senior policy advisers to these innovations. Thus to some extent, the 'landsdeal affair', but more especially the peccadillos of the resignation honours list, provided the required excuses for a public expression of private hostility to Wilson's advisory strategies.

   Heath, possibly more by accident than design, aided and abetted by the mandarins in the Cabinet Office and the Civil Service Department, constructed a parallel advisory system for the prime minister. It had some resemblance to the kind of support provided by the EOP to an American president. Wilson by intention,[121] and in the face of Whitehall resistance, but aided by economic circumstances that divided and demoralized the opposition within, created an alternative advisory system. It was composed of advisers loyal to the man in No.10, and thus resembled the kind of support an American president receives from the WHO.

James Callaghan became the new tenant of No.10 Downing Street after Wilson's surprise retirement. It is to Callaghan's advisory strategies that we must now turn our attention. Did the arrival of a new premier bring an end to the controversy about advice that had been one of the hallmarks of the Wilson years? Did Callaghan advance the presidentialization process that was discernible under his two predecessors?

Notes

1.   Harold Wilson, cit. Donoughue, Bernard, *Prime Minister. The Conduct of Policy under Harold Wilson and James Callaghan* (London: Cape, 1978) p. 47.

2.   Powell, Enoch J., *The Times* 4 October, 1993, p. 35.

3.   See Childs, David, *Britain Since 1945* 2nd edn (London: Routledge, 1986) p. 249. For Marcia Williams's account of the 'landsdeal affair' see Falkender, Lady Marcia, *Downing Street in Perspective* (London: Weidenfeld & Nicolson, 1983) pp. 134–42.

4.   See for instance Jenkins, Peter, 'Heat in the Kitchen' *Guardian* 5 April, 1974, p. 12, and Watkins, Alan, 'Cronies and kitchen cabinets' *Sunday Times* 7 April, 1974, p. 9.

5.   See for example Moorehead, Caroline, two part profile of Lady Falkender *The Times* 23 and 24 July 1974, p18 and p16 respectively. For Marcia Williams's views see Falkender op.cit., pp150-1. It is worth noting that Wilson could cite both recent and more distant precedent for his decision to ennoble Mrs Williams. Harold Macmillan had expressed his gratitude to his Political Secretary, John Wyndham by creating him Lord Egremont, and Disraeli had ennobled his Personal Secretary, Montague Corrier, who became Lord Wroughton.

6.   Benn, Tony, *Against the Tide, Diaries 1973-76* (London: Arrow Books edn 1990) p. 570.

7.   Ibid., p. 571.
8.   In 1978 Lord Kagan fled to Israel after a warrant had been issued for his arrest for tax and currency offenses. Childs, op.cit., p. 262.
9.   Benn for example, claims that '. . . this list was subject to a great deal of cross-party criticism for bringing the honours system into disrepute as a result of doubts as to the propriety of some of those rewarded including a number of capitalist entrepreneurs.' Benn, *Against the Tide* op.cit., p. 570. According to Haines, Goldsmith, for example, was a known contributor to Tory party funds. Haines, Joe, *The Politics of Power* (London: Coronet, 1977) p. 155. Haines also asserts that Goldsmith had offered Marcia Williams a directorship of one of his enterprises. Haines implies that a link existed between this and Goldsmith's inclusion on the honours list. Ibid., p. 156.
10. See Goodman, Arnold, 'The Power and the Vain Glory' *Observer* (Review) 8 August, 1993, pp. 41–2. See also Pimlott, who notes that from the outset '. . . it was widely rumoured that Marcia – whose own ennoblement still rankled in many quarters – was the real architect of the list.' Pimlott, Ben, *Harold Wilson* (London: HarperCollins, 1993) p. 688.
11. Hutchinson, George, 'After the fiasco of Sir Harold's list, can the honours system now survive?' *The Times* 29 May, 1976, p. 14.
12. Ibid.
13. A *curriculum vitae* reminiscent of that of the first Duke of Buckingham. (See above, chapter two). Although it is important to note that in Lady Falkender's case, despite the inevitable gossip to the contrary, there is no evidence that any sexual relationship existed between favourite and patron. See for example, Haines, op.cit., pp. 159–60, and Goodman, *Observer* op.cit., p. 41.
14. Wilson, according to Lord Goodman, claimed the list was his own and blamed criticism on anti-semitism within the Establishment. See Goodman, *Observer* op.cit., p. 41. See also Pimlott, op.cit., pp. 688–9. Lady Falkender wrote a strong disclaimer to *The Times* in which she emphasised that the 'Resignation Honours List was Sir Harold Wilson's and his alone.' See *The Times* 31 May, 1976, p. 9.
15. Falkender, op.cit., pp. 88–9.
16. Ibid., p. 89.
17. Cit. Hennessy, Peter, *Whitehall* (London: Fontana, 1990) p. 255.
18. Cit Donoughue, op.cit., p. 47.
19. Healey, Denis, *The Time of My Life* (London: Penguin, 1990) p. 388.

20. Wilson, Harold, *Final Term: the Labour Government 1974–1976* (London: Weidenfeld & Nicolson and Michael Joseph, 1979) p. 17.

21. Peter Jenkins reflects that '. . . the DEA was permitted to draw lines on graph paper, but the Treasury still controlled the allocation of resources. Consequently the DEA became not so much a rival centre of real economic power as a lobby for economic growth within the government.' Jenkins, Peter, *The Battle for Downing Street* (London: Charles Knight, 1970) p. 3.

22. Sir Douglas Wass, Permanent Secretary to the Treasury 1974–9, doubted the Treasury ever felt threatened by the DEA. 'I'm not sure that the Treasury ever vulgarly saw the DEA as a rival . . . The Treasury did . . . export some of its most able people to the DEA . . . not something it would have done if it had really feared the DEA.' Wass, Sir Douglas cit. Hennessy, *Whitehall* op.cit., p. 187. This may have been the real reason why the Treasury did not regard the DEA as a threat to its monopoly. The DEA was not peopled by outsiders but by Treasury progeny.

23. See Williams, op.cit., p. 346. For a full account, see Kellner, Peter and Crowther-Hunt, Lord, *The Civil Servants: An Inquiry into Britain's Ruling Class* (London: Macdonald & Jane, 1980), particularly 'How Armstrong Defeated Fulton', pp. 59–76.

24. Both Balogh and fellow 'outsider', Professor Nicholas Kaldor, who was appointed adviser to the Chancellor of the Exchequer, were frequently pilloried in the press as 'the Hungarian twins' in an attempt to highlight their outsider status and cast doubt on their credentials. See, Williams, Marcia, *Inside Number 10* (London: Weidenfeld & Nicolson, 1972) p. 52.

25. Impotence expressed in the title of the second volume of Tony Benn's diaries, *Office Without Power* (London: Hutchinson, 1988).

26. See Williams, op.cit., p. 344.

27. Castle, Barbara, 'Mandarin Power' *Sunday Times* 10 June, 1973, pp. 17 and 19.

28. Haines, op.cit., p. 198.

29. Haines, op.cit., p. 38. This view is endorsed by Kellner and Crowther-Hunt, op.cit.

30. See above, chapter four.

31. Industrial unrest had prompted Heath to call the election of February 1974 on the question of Who Governs Britain? The electorate gave no clear answer. The result was inconclusive. Labour emerged the single largest party in Parliament and had four seats more than the Tories, but lacked an overall majority. (Labour 301; Conservatives 297; Liberals 14; Ulster Unionists 11; SNP 7; Plaid Cymru 2;

others 3). See Whitehead, Philip, 'The Labour Governments, 1974–9' in Hennessy, Peter and Seldon, Anthony, eds *Ruling Performance* (Oxford: Blackwell, 1987) pp. 241–74, p. 242. At first there was even some question as to whether Wilson would be asked to form a government at all. Heath initially tried, unsuccessfully, to cobble together an agreement with the Liberals and it was not until Monday 4 March that he conceded defeat and Harold Wilson returned to Downing Street.

32. The second election which took place on the 10 October 1974, brought Wilson only a slightly improved Parliamentary position. Labour secured an overall majority of only three. (Labour 319; Conservatives 277; Liberals 13; SNP 11; Plaid Cymru 3; others 1).
33. See Falkender, op.cit., p. 3 and Donoughue, op.cit., pp. 86–7.
34. Wilson, *Final Term* op.cit., p. 16 and p. 17.
35. Ibid.,p. 12.
36. See Coates, David, *Labour in Power? A Study of the Labour Government 1974-1979* (London: Longman, 1980) pp. 6–7. The manifesto was based on *Labour's Programme 1973*. It committed Labour to extensive public ownership and a new Industry Act (in the hands of Tony Benn, Secretary of State for Industry) designed to provide the next Labour government with all the industrial power it would need to meet its economic objectives. See also *Labour's Programme 1973*, p. 17.
37. Holmes, Martin, *The Labour Government, 1974–79* (London: Macmillan, 1985) p. 41.
38. To include the abolition of Heath's 1971 Industrial Relations Act; legislation to strengthen the position of unions and workers *vis-a-vis* employers; subsidies on some basic items of food; a rent freeze and general increases in pension and welfare benefits.
39. In 1964 Labour had inherited economic problems associated with a determination to support an over-valued pound and a balance of payments deficit of £800 million. This time the legacy was worse. The miners' strike had reduced industry to a three-day week; inflation was running at 19 per cent and rising; (it rose to 28 per cent by December, 1974) unemployment exceeded one million and the balance of payments deficit of £4000 million dwarfed that of 1964.
40. See Walker, David, 'The First Wilson Governments, 1964–70' in Hennessy and Seldon *Ruling Performance* op.cit., pp. 186–215, p. 200.
41. Mrs Williams's was paid by Harold Wilson himself, whilst Gerald Kaufman was paid by Transport House.

42. See Williams, op.cit., p. 357.
43. In addition to Donoughue, the Policy Unit consisted of seven appointees chosen by him, taking account of expertise and political sympathy. See Donoughue, op.cit., p. 21 and Jones, G.W., 'Harold Wilson's policy-makers' *Spectator* 6 July, 1974 pp. 12–13.
44. Cit. Donoughue, op.cit., p. 21.
45. Jones, 'Harold Wilson's policy-makers', op.cit., p. 12.
46. Wilson, Harold, *The Governance of Britain* (London: Weidenfeld & Nicolson and Michael Joseph, 1976) p. 204.
47. Ibid., p. 204.
48. See for example, Crossman, R.H.S., *The Diaries of a Cabinet Minister Vol.1*, (London: Hamish Hamilton & Cape, 1975) P. 21.
49. Barbara Castle claims that '. . . civil servants have the best spying organization I have ever known. I used to leave Cabinet meetings, perhaps after a departmental battle. I would ring my Private Secretary or walk into my Private Office, three minutes later. I'd say 'We've won.' "Oh yes I know, Minister," my secretary would reply. All round the village before the Minister got home . . . The official net is terrific, the political net is non-existent.' Castle, 'Mandarin Power' op.cit., p. 17.
50. Wilson, *Governance of Britain* op.cit., p. 98.
51. According to Donoughue the Policy Unit and special advisers were intended to get information about what the departments were planning. They would then be able to alert the prime minister and a response could be prepared. Civil servants would thus not be able to 'bounce' policies through at short notice. Lord Donoughue, interview, 19 May, 1994.
52. Blackstone, Tessa and Plowden, William, *Inside the Think Tank: Advising the Cabinet 1971–83* (London: Heinemann, 1988) p. 66. They go on to suggest that a further reason for keeping the CPRS was that the Policy Unit '. . . because of its small size . . . lacked the capacity to do large scale pieces of work or produce long reports.' Ibid. A further significant difference between these two bodies, however, which Blackstone and Plowden omit to mention, is that whilst the CPRS advice was supposedly politically neutral, that of the Policy Unit was intentionally partisan. See Wilson, *The Governance of Britain* op.cit., p. 204.
53. Blackstone and Plowden, op.cit., p. 31.
54. Simon James notes that 'Mr Wilson appreciated the theory behind the CPRS but two general elections and deepening economic troubles sapped his interest in the long-term'. [His intended resignation may also explain this attitude.] He held only two cabinet

strategy reviews and from 1975 onwards used the Staff increasingly as a 'fire brigade'. James, Simon, 'The Central Policy Review Staff' *Political Studies* Vol.36, 1986 pp. 423–40, p. 433.

55. A further important weakness of the CPRS, though less significant in respect of the prime ministerial advisory system was that some senior Labour politicians saw it as a Heath creature and therefore regarded its advice as suspect. Tony Benn, for example, complained that 'Sir Kenneth Berrill introduced the paper exactly as if he were a Minister, so we have now found a way of getting Tories into the Government regardless of whether or not they win an Election.' Benn, *Against the Tide* op.cit., p. 279, see also p. 497.

56. Cit. Pimlott, op.cit., p. 619.

57. See Donoughue, op.cit., p. 21.

58. See for example, Chesshyre, Robert, 'Wilson's new outsiders worry Whitehall' *Observer* 24 March, 1974, p. 4.

59. Marcia Williams complained, ' . . . now it's Haines who's the official man and Bernard Donoughue . . . I have good personal relations with Harold but I'm shut out completely.' Cit. Benn, *Against the Tide* op.cit., p. 427. Pimlott confirms the view that this time '. . . politics among the No.10 courtiers increasingly revolved around [a] Donoughue-Haines alliance against Marcia'. Pimlott, op.cit., p. 621.

60. Aitken, Ian, 'Mr Haines's real scandal' *Guardian* 14 February, 1977, p. 10. See also Benn, *Against the Tide* op.cit., p. 191.

61. Ibid., p. 120.

62. Ibid., p. 454.

63. Lord Donoughue, interview, op.cit.

64. Castle, Barbara, *The Castle Diaries 1974–1976* (London: Weidenfeld & Nicolson, 1980) p. 440.

65. Ibid., p. 437.

66. Healey, op.cit. pp. 388–9.

67. Wilson, *The Governance of Britain* op.cit., p. 99.

68. Hennessy describes the founding of the Policy Unit as '. . . a conscious implementation of the Fulton recommendations for Planning Units.' Hennessy, *Whitehall* op.cit., p. 203. Although the Unit's focus on short to medium term policy advice makes its links with 'planning units' somewhat tenuous.

69. See Donoughue, op.cit.,pp. 22–3. Lord Hunt confirmed the view that the Policy Unit was accepted because Donoughue, in contrast to Balogh in 1964, had set out to work with the Civil Service. Although Lord Hunt emphasised that this was not to imply that 'the Civil Service successfully "nobbled" Bernard Donoughue.' He

claimed that Donoughue '. . . managed to work with the departments but fully retained his independent, and often dissenting view.' Lord Hunt of Tanworth, formerly Sir John Hunt, Cabinet Secretary 1973–9, interview 28 April, 1994 and follow-up correspondence 5 May, 1994.

70. See for example, 'Boys in the back room' Leading article, *Guardian* 29 June, 1974.

71. Donoughue, op.cit., p. 5. See also Healey, op.cit., p. 388.

72. Benn as Secretary of State for Industry was responsible for transforming the radical industrial strategies of the manifesto into the Industry Act. Wilson, less committed to this interventionist policy than Benn, and anxious to reassure the City and the CBI, in the event insisted that the Cabinet Office redrafted the proposals under his own supervision. See Whitehead, op.cit., pp. 246–7.

73. Mrs Williams remained Harold Wilson's Personal and Political Secretary but Albert Murray, a former junior minister who had lost his seat in the 1970 election, was given responsibility for the day-to-day running of the prime minister's political office.

74. Haines, op.cit., p. 26.

75. Chesshyre, op.cit., p. 10.

76. See Donoughue, op.cit., pp. 66–78 and Haines, op.cit., pp. 45–66.

77. See Haines, op.cit., p. 60. It is important to note that Marcia Williams disputes Haines's account of these events. See Falkender, Lady Marcia, 'Eyes and ears for Harold Wilson' *Observer* (Review) 20 February, 1922, p. 26 and p. 28, p. 26.

78. See Haines, op.cit., pp. 62–3.

79. Ibid., p. 29.

80. Ibid.

81. Donoughue, op.cit., p. 72.

82. See Benn, *Against the Tide* op.cit., p. 652. By 1976, Denis Healey also complained that Mitchell seemed to be pursuing his own preferred economic policy during the IMF negotiation that autumn. Healey asserts that 'In the British Cabinet, at first only Roy Jenkins and Edmund Dell were prepared to support any cuts at all. Inside the Treasury there was a group, mainly surrounding Derek Mitchell, who wanted very large cuts indeed; some press stories suggested that they were briefing the IMF against me.' Healey, op.cit., p. 430.

83. Donoughue, op.cit., p. 76.

84. Ibid., p. 77. See also pp. 28–9 for further comments on the policy making role of the Cabinet Office and the resentment this caused among some ministers.

85. Benn, Tony, 'Manifestos and Mandarins' in *Policy and Practice: the experience of government* (London: RIPA, 1980) pp. 57–78, p. 71.
86. Haines, op.cit., p. 17.
87. Ibid. Haines reflects that 'The danger then would be that the Cabinet Office would become too powerful. There were signs of that in the 1974–6 period. The Office not only co-ordinated policy at the highest level, which is its function, but showed strong desires to originate it.' Ibid.
88. Hunt, interview, op.cit.
89. According to Hennessy et al Berrill also confirmed that the Cabinet Secretary and himself had closely liaised over economic policy at this time. See Hennessy, Peter, et al 'Routine Punctuated by Orgies: the Central Policy Review Staff 1970–1983' Strathclyde Papers on Government No.31. (Strathclyde: University, 1985) p. 54.
90. Benn, *Against the Tide* op.cit., p. 106. See also Hennessy ibid., pp. 413 and 445.
91. Holmes, op.cit., p. 177.
92. Although technically Wilson legitimated the Policy Unit by reference to Fulton, the process of creation itself could perhaps have been expected to arouse some comment. Whilst the creation of the CPRS was preceded by a White Paper and debate in Parliament the Policy Unit came into being by means of a Downing Street press release and an internal memorandum. See Donoughue, op.cit., p. 21–2.
93. See Seymour-Ure, op.cit., pp. 175–84.
94. Alan Parker asserts that '. . . the presence of a Kitchen Cabinet can be detected in every administration since Jackson. What the provision of a White House Office, perhaps inadvertently did, was to give many of these unofficial assistants recognizable government positions.' Parker, Alan, *The Organization of the American Presidency 1933-1972: the Politics of Advice* (unpublished doctoral thesis, University of Nottingham, 1976) p. 15.
95. Such comparisons can only be approximate. Exact figures for the numbers employed in either the WHO or No.10 are difficult to calculate. Firstly, the numbers are constantly changing, and secondly, different writers take different categories of staff into account. The number of personal presidential assistants in the WHO rose from about eleven in FDR's day to about forty-eight during Nixon's incumbency. The overall figure for those on the WHO payroll, however, currently stands at around five hundred. During Harold Wilson's premiership in the 1970s, prime ministerial aides, including members of the Policy Unit, Political Office and Press

Office, numbered approximately sixteen, but the overall figure for those working in No.10, including civil servants, political aides, typists and messengers was nearer to eighty. See Jones, G.W., 'The Prime Minister's Aides' in King, Anthony, ed. *The British Prime Minister* 2nd edn (London: Macmillan, 1985) p. 75.

96. Chesshyre, op.cit., p. 10.
97. James, Simon, *British Cabinet Government* (London: Routledge, 1992), p. 228.
98. Donoughue, op.cit., p. 6.
99. Ibid., p. 24.
100. Ibid., p. 20.
101. Edward Short, Leader of the House was responsible for overseeing Devolution, whilst Roy Hattersley, Minister of State at the Foreign and Commonwealth Office was responsible for Common Market negotiations.
102. See Wilson, *The Governance of Britain* op.cit., pp. 95–6.
103. See Mather, Ian, 'Wilson's crisis shooter' *Observer* 17 March, 1974, p. 5.
104. See Madgwick, Peter, 'Prime Ministerial Power Revisited' *Social Studies Review* May 1986, pp. 28–35, pp. 31–2.
105. Donoughue, op.cit., p. 88.
106. Ibid., p. 34.
107. Ibid., p. 191.
108. Ibid., p. 186.
109. Ibid.
110. Ibid., pp. 186–7.
111. Lord Donoughue, interview 19 May, 1994.
112. Donoughue, op.cit., p. 25.
113. Benn, *Against the Tide* op.cit., pp. 307–8.
114. Pimlott, op.cit., p. 622. See also Aitken, op.cit.
115. Mackintosh, John P., 'Harold Wilson' in *British Prime Ministers in the Twentieth Century Vol.II Churchill to Callaghan* (London: Weidenfeld & Nicolson, 1978) p. 211.
116. Pimlott, op.cit., p. 620.
117. Donoughue, op.cit., p. 11, see also, pp. 86–7.
118. No mean feat.
119. Benn, *Against the Tide* op.cit., p. 543.
120. Whitehead, op.cit., pp. 254–5.
121. It is difficult to imagine Wilson's constitutional changes were accidental or subconscious given the views he expressed in the Hunt interview in 1964 and in view of the fact he wrote on constitutional matters. See Wilson, *The Governance of Britain* op.cit.

7   James Callaghan 1976–9: A Caretaker

> Callaghan was neither a villain nor an easy-going, relaxed chapel-goer. Rather he was an experienced politician with a considerable love of power . . .[1]

Under James Callaghan the presidentialization of the premiership marked time. A degree of depresidentialization in public was balanced by an extension of presidentialization in private. The inclusion of, and collaboration of, key political actors ensured that constitutional controversy about advice was all but avoided.

In 1966 Richard Neustadt said that 'it would be possible to enlarge the Private Office and reorient the Cabinet Office in such way, really, as to presidentialize the system.'[2] By 1976 this had largely happened. Although the Private Office itself had changed little during the previous twelve years, the extent and nature of advisory provision within No.10 had significantly altered. The prime minister was now no longer solely dependent on the advice of a handful of 'high-flyers' on loan from Whitehall, but could also call upon a team of personal political advisers in the No.10 Press Office, the Political Office and the Policy Unit. The same period witnessed the reorientation of the Cabinet Office towards serving the prime minister. Not only had the Cabinet Secretary become *de facto* permanent secretary to the prime minister,[3] but there were also several advisory bodies[4] working primarily for the prime minister located within the Cabinet Office. By 1976 the evolving prime ministerial advisory system showed clear signs of presidentialization. Prime ministers were now supported by an advisory network resembling in structure, though smaller in scale, that of an American president. The kind of support loyal to the institution, provided by the Executive Office of the President (EOP) in America, was being provided by the parallel advisory system under the auspices of the Cabinet Office. The kind of loyal personal support given to the president by the White House Office (WHO), was being provided by the political appointees within No.10.

Prime ministers were thus becoming better equipped to challenge the advice filtered from the departments of Whitehall via ministers in the cabinet and were acquiring the institutional and advisory means to act in an interventionist manner reminiscent of an American president. At the same time the traditional prime ministerial advisory body and collective executive, the cabinet, was becoming more like its American counterpart:

a forum for discussion and endorsement of policy decisions reached elsewhere.

Harold Wilson had actively encouraged these developments in an attempt to reconcile the gap between the limited view of the prime minister's power and position accepted by the constitution and the almost unlimited political responsibilities forced upon him by international relations, the media and the electorate. Edward Heath had attempted to conduct his premiership according to the traditional constitutional model but his intentions were frustrated by events and the imperatives of presidentialized electoral politics. Did James Callaghan, like Wilson, enthusiastically advance the presidentialization of the advisory system, or was he like Heath, forced to accept presidentialization as an outcome of the changing political system?

It is important to note that of necessity a study of Callaghan has to be based on a limited range of sources. Although much has been written about the politics and the advisory strategies of both Callaghan's predecessor and his successor, little has been written about his own. Callaghan's sudden entry to No.10 in the wake of Harold Wilson's unexpected departure, preceded not by a general election, but only by a Labour Party leadership contest,[5] and his relatively brief period in office, seems to have caught both media commentators and academics by surprise. Few of Callaghan's colleagues have contributed to the sources for this period. Tony Benn's diaries[6] do provide a wealth of detailed discussion, but they cannot be regarded as an impartial source of reference because Benn himself remained an almost lone voice in the cabinet promoting his Alternative Economic Strategy. Richard Crossman was now dead, and Callaghan had decided against reappointing Barbara Castle to his cabinet. Therefore the kind of cross-referencing of diary evidence, possible in respect of Wilson, is no longer available. Nor were there any revelations about advisory strategies in resignation speeches of the George Brown kind. Callaghan's aides have also been notably silent. He appointed Tom McNally to head his Political Office and Tom McCaffrey to be his Press Secretary, neither of whom wrote either a record of life in Downing Street in the vein of those written by Marcia Williams[7] and Douglas Hurd.[8] Nor were there to be sensational 'kiss and tell' memoirs of the kind written by Joe Haines.[9] Callaghan's own memoirs reveal little. Philip Whitehead, noting that the 1974–9 government has not enjoyed the close attention given to its successor (or for that matter the previous Labour government 1964–70), dismisses James Callaghan's account as 'bland and discreet.'[10]

This shortage of material on the Callaghan period extends even to the genre of satire and political gossip. *Private Eye* drew a blank when it tried to unearth gossip or intrigue about Callaghan.[11] Brian Redhead suggests that 'the student of James Callaghan must, of necessity, bury himself [or presumably *herself*] in newspaper cuttings and copies of Hansard.'[12] These sources, however, yield little about aides or advisory strategies.

In contrast to both Heath and Wilson, Callaghan introduced no publicly visible changes in the advisory system on the lines of the CPRS or the Policy Unit; neither were there any rumours or complaints that Callaghan resorted to a 'kitchen cabinet'. Callaghan's advisory strategies, therefore, attracted little analysis or comment in the media or Parliament. Nor did they become the subject of academic study. Unlike Wilson, Callaghan wrote nothing on the lines of *The Governance of Britain*,[13] which did at least provide some clues as to Wilson's views of the prime minister's need for advice and the reasons underlying some of his own innovations.

The number of academic studies of Callaghan's period in office are relatively limited. Bernard Donoughue, whom Callaghan reappointed to head the Policy Unit, in his book *Prime Minister*,[14] does provide some insights into Callaghan's advisory strategies and draws informed contrasts between the techniques employed by Wilson and Callaghan for managing their colleagues. Kellner's and Hitchins's study, *Callaghan: the Road to Number Ten*, is, as the title implies, an account of Callaghan's rise to the top and, as it was published in 1976, gives no clues as to his advisory strategies while in office. Most of the remaining press commentary and academic analysis concentrates primarily on the trials and tribulations faced by the Callaghan government, discussion mainly focusing on the 1976 International Monetary Fund (IMF) loan; Callaghan's precarious Parliamentary position; the Lib/Lab pact; and the eventual demise of the government after the 'Winter of Discontent'.

This study would be incomplete if James Callaghan's advisory strategies were omitted. In view of the sparsity of the sources, however, any conclusions drawn must at be regarded as very tentative.

James Callaghan's handling of the IMF loan crisis in the Autumn of 1976[15] is cited as a classic example of the conduct of orthodox cabinet government.[16] Callaghan referred the IMF loan negotiations to no fewer than twenty-six meetings of the full cabinet. Economic policy underpins all other aspects of government, and, therefore, the forum in which economic policy is decided can be described as the centre of power. It would seem, therefore, that during the premiership of James Callaghan the cabinet was restored to its traditional place in the advisory system and that the collective executive was alive and well. A closer examination of Callaghan's advisory strategies, after the cabinet's agreement had been gained in respect of the IMF loan terms, suggests this not to be the case.

On the 5 April 1976, James Callaghan was elected leader of the Labour Party and simultaneously became prime minister.[17] According to Peter Jenkins, Callaghan '. . . took over during what was still rip-roaring inflation. Sir Harold had suddenly bequeathed him a desperately weak economy and a divided party. By-elections rocked his government that summer and pared away its slender majority. His first Autumn brought a frightful Sterling crisis and a crisis in his Cabinet as the IMF moved in.'[18] What sources of advice and support were available to the prime minister to help him tackle this unwelcome political and economic legacy?

The constitutional position in respect of advice to the prime minister had changed during the two years Wilson had held office. When Wilson entered Downing Street in March 1974, a new constitutional settlement was emerging. Members of the permanent government, senior policy advisers in Whitehall, now accepted that prime ministers needed more advice, but they were reluctant to accept that it should by-pass the official filter. *Parallel* advisory bodies, manned or controlled by civil servants, were permissable, even if they short-circuited the traditional prime ministerial advisory body, the cabinet. *Alternative* advisers, advisers who were not members of the permanent civil service, were not acceptable, or were at best suspect, especially if they enjoyed direct access to the prime minister. An exception to this rule was the No.10 Political Office, which, although lacking whole-hearted official approval, had by 1974, in the wake of Douglas Hurd's occupancy, gained grudging acceptance. Such acceptance was on the understanding that its activities were confined to party political matters. In 1964 Wilson had defied precedent by establishing a Political Office in No.10. In 1974, once again, he challenged accepted constitutional norms by creating the Policy Unit: a small team of alternative advisers having direct access to the prime minister. During the two years Wilson was in office the Policy Unit appeared to have exercised considerable influence on policy[19] but at the same time aroused relatively little public controversy.

By the time James Callaghan became prime minister the Policy Unit had gained public acceptance, even if some private reservations still existed in the corridors of power. By 1976 the constitutional position in respect of advice to the prime minister was that parallel advisory bodies were accepted, alternative advisers were still regarded with suspicion, but not open hostility as had been the case in the 1960s.

If this was the constitutional position in respect of advice when Callaghan entered Downing Street, what did it imply in terms of advisers and advisory bodies serving the prime minister? First, even if perhaps no longer foremost, there was the traditional prime ministerial advisory body, the cabinet. This remained the forum of policy advice arising from the civil service. The Cabinet Secretary and the Cabinet Office, including under its umbrella the special units and the CPRS, and the No.10 Private Office, now constituted the prime minister's parallel advisory network. The Policy Unit, the No.10 Political Office and the Press Office constituted the prime minister's alternative advisory network.

Did Callaghan regard this advisory system that he inherited as inadequate or unsatisfactory? If so, how did he address any perceived weaknesses?

James Callaghan's rather sudden promotion to the premiership precluded speculation by him about such matters. On 5 April, in an acceptance speech to the Parliamentary Labour Party (PLP), Callaghan declared: '. . . I want no cliques. There will be no insiders or outsiders.'[20] On entering office, as might be expected, he did introduce some changes, but they were fairly limited in scope. Out of a cabinet of twenty-three, Callaghan replaced only five of Wilson's appointees with his own candidates. Sixteen ministers remained in the posts in which Wilson had placed them.[21] Within No.10, according to Marcia Williams, '. . . roughly the system then designed continued when James Callaghan took over . . .'[22] Although the structure was retained, some changes of personnel were inevitable. Tom McNally, a former Transport House researcher who had served as adviser to Callaghan in the Foreign Office, accompanied him to No.10 to take up Mrs Williams's former position as head of the Political Office.[23] Tom McCaffrey, a permanent civil servant and former press officer at the Home Office when Callaghan had been Home Secretary, and who had been permitted to move to the Foreign Office after the 1974 election, became No.10 Press Officer in place of Joe Haines. Members of the Policy Unit were reappointed *en bloc*, including Bernard Donoughue to the position of senior policy adviser. Referring to the Policy Unit, Callaghan said, 'this was one of Harold Wilson's effective creations which I was happy to inherit. It was staffed by specialists from outside the civil service more overtly political than the Think Tank. It provided me with systematic policy analysis . . . [and] I was in a stronger position to challenge Departmental proposals . . . '[24] Beyond Downing Street, the CPRS was also retained and initially experienced something of a revival.[25] Callaghan admits that he found its advice useful on several occasions.[26]

That Callaghan made only modest changes in the advisory system he inherited from Wilson can be taken as an indication that he found it to be satisfactory. Indeed, reflecting on the advisory system in his memoirs, Callaghan notes that

. . . from time to time there is discussion about the need for a formal Prime Minister's Department . . . such talk frequently overlooks the instruments he already has. He is able to provide himself with his own sources of information, he can send up a trial balloon or fire a sighting shot across a Ministerial bow without directly involving his own authority or publicly undermining that of the Minister; and he has the necessary facilities to take a decisive hand in policy-making at any moment he chooses to intervene.[27]

By retaining the advisory structures created by his predecessors did Callaghan help to transform precedent into new constitutional conventions in respect of advice? Was a degree of presidentialization of the prime minister's advisory system now becoming an accepted constitutional norm? What was the constitutional status of Callaghan's advisory system? Once again in order to answer these questions, it is necessary first to ask: did Callaghan's advisory strategies attract criticism from important contemporary political actors and did they become a matter of public controversy and debate?

A negative answer could be given to both these questions. The status of special advisers remained suspect: was an American spoils system being introduced by stealth? In 1978 there were some murmurings when Callaghan decided to waive the five year time-limit rule on the temporary appointments of the special advisers.[28] The announcement was described as having important 'political and constitutional implications' and was predicted to cause 'widespread concern in Whitehall'.[29] It was claimed that it had introduced a 'new concept into British Government', creating a new type of civil servant appointed directly by ministerial patronage.[30] That is about all the evidence there is available to suggest that contemporary political actors found anything to complain about.

Callaghan's advisory strategies did not become a matter of public debate. His relationship with Whitehall was good. Philip Whitehead notes that 'He [Callaghan] knew the key permanent secretaries throughout Whitehall, trusted them and was trusted by them. The relationship was entirely free from the mutual suspicion and ignorance with which an incoming Labour Prime Minister and top mandarins usually regarded each other.'[31] There is a similar story to tell in respect of his cabinet colleagues. Callaghan avoided favouritism and succeeded at least in creating the impression that his was a government without cliques. According to Kellner and Hitchins, writing in 1976, 'some leading Labour politicians even find Callaghan's style of leadership a refreshing improvement. Where Wilson was considered shifty . . . Callaghan is seen by his colleagues as straightforward.'[32] Peter Jenkins also notes that 'instinctively, as well as quite deliberately he made his Prime Ministership in every way the opposite of Wilson's.'[33] Redhead asserts that whilst Callaghan '. . . took to No.10 for his private staff two old friends . . . there was no question of creating a private office that would be a 'kitchen cabinet' competing with Whitehall and becoming a centre of gossip and intrigue.'[34] Callaghan claims that '. . . the Labour Cabinet of 1976 to 1979 would stand comparison with most as a good-tempered body, with a minimum of personal backbiting, very little malicious leaking and a strong feeling of solidarity.'[35] Even Tony Benn, who clashed with Callaghan over specific policies and who felt particularly aggrieved at the activities of Berrill and the CPRS,[36] seemed to respect Callaghan's authority and straightforwardness.[37]

On this occasion, however, the absence of controversy about advice may not be a reliable indication of the constitutional status of Callaghan's advisory strategies. The above comments suggest that Callaghan eschewed the kind of secrecy and intrigue associated with Harold Wilson and that the IMF loan period had restored the cabinet to its collective decision-making and advisory role. But it can be argued that the reverse is true. Callaghan did introduce an innovation into the advisory system, the Economic Seminar, but, in contrast to changes introduced by Wilson, it was really secret and remained so until after the end of Callaghan's period in office. Callaghan's innovation therefore attracted no comment in the media and aroused no constitutional controversy.

Around the time of the IMF loan negotiations in the Autumn of 1976, Callaghan established an Economic Seminar which undermined the role of the cabinet in that most fundamental field, economic policy. Callaghan explains that when he was appointed shadow chancellor he felt the need to supplement his limited formal education in economics. To this end, Anthony Crosland had arranged for him to meet with '. . . a distinguished group of economists at Oxford . . . every fortnight to discuss the economic problems that a Labour Government would face.'[38] This arrangement can be seen as a prototype for Callaghan's Economic Seminar. The Economic Seminar was a 'mixed' committee, containing ministers and officials[39] under the chairmanship of the prime minister. It met regularly throughout the period 1977 to 1979 in order to discuss the major decisions on interest rates and sterling.[40]

It was said Wilson never trusted the Treasury because he had never worked in it, whilst Callaghan never trusted it because he had.[41] The Economic Seminar was regarded as Callaghan's strategy for dealing with Treasury power. Denis Healey notes that '. . . he [Callaghan] remained distrustful both of the Treasury, the Civil Service and the Bank of England throughout his time at No.10 . . . partly for this reason, in 1977 he set up an informal 'seminar' to discuss interest rates and exchange rates.'[42] Kenneth Morgan claims that 'institutionally, his [Callaghan's] "economic seminar" in Downing Street . . . was a remarkable, covert attempt, through Harold Lever and others, to shackle the Treasury's ancient ascendancy in determining financial policy.'[43] Peter Hennessy agrees with this view and notes that 'when Callaghan institutionalized his [Lever's] role as a one-man counter-Treasury task force inside his highly secret economic seminar . . . Harold Lever's influence on policy was probably greater than that ever achieved by the Department of Economic Affairs.'[44] Lord Hunt commenting on the role of the Economic Seminar, suggested that '. . . it met the demand for in-depth briefing on monetary matters of a Prime Minister who had previously been Chancellor of the Exchequer . . . in Harold Lever it included a clever maverick who could test the conventional wisdom of the Treasury and the Bank of England.'[45] Lord Donoughue described the Economic Seminar as a response to the changing economic policy climate,

> By the mid 1970s we were running into monetary economics and there was no advisory system geared to that. Our fate was being decided by monetarism but there was no forum for discussion. The Bank of England and the Treasury dealt with monetary policy. The Economic Seminar was a way of including No.10 in the monetary discussion.[46]

The Economic Seminar may be regarded as an attempt by the transitory government to impose its will on the permanent government, but it was also an instrument which brought about an erosion of the cabinet's traditional position in collective decision making and policy advice. Although, as noted above, Callaghan consulted the cabinet conscientiously during the IMF loan crisis, its role in economic policy was soon to be usurped by the Economic Seminar. According to Peter Hennessy, 'after the IMF had departed, Callaghan institutionalized part of this power-sharing. The Cabinet's salad days as the key economic forum were past. But the Treasury's did not return. Instead the key discussions on exchange rate policy, interest rates and monetary policy were moved into a group Callaghan camouflaged beneath the innocuous title of the 'Economic Seminar'.'[47] In a similar vein Philip Whitehead notes that '. . . key market-related issues were discussed in a tight group called the Economic Seminar . . . Ministers whose responsibilities were influenced by the level of interest rates (housing for example) knew nothing of all this . . . The Prime Minister who had so scrupulously observed the conventions of collective responsibility in the IMF debates was now extending the power of Downing Street.'[48]

Lord Hunt and Lord Donoughue, former members of the Economic Seminar, deliberately play down its decision-making role. Lord Hunt says that '. . . it was primarily concerned with longer term strategy issues rather than particular decisions coming before the cabinet'.[49] Lord Donoughue claims that the Economic Seminar was only a forum for discussion: 'it did not take decisions.'[50] He did admit, however, that its wide ranging discussions prepared the way for final decisions. The Economic Seminar can, therefore, be regarded as unconstitutional in as far as it usurped the power of the collective executive in the key area of deciding economic policy. This had become the province of the chief executive, the prime minister, and an assortment of advisers, only two of whom were members of the cabinet. If the seminar did not in fact, as a body, take the final decisions, its discussions made the nature of such decisions a foregone conclusion.[51]

If the past was anything to go by plainly the Economic Seminar would have raised questions about the constitutionality of advice, accusations about creeping presidentialization, why did it not arouse disquiet or controversy? This can partly be explained by Callaghan's constitutionalist strategy of placating political colleagues by encouraging the exhaustive IMF discussions in the cabinet. Callaghan claims, 'it was my practice that Ministers should have the fullest opportunity to state their views and argue for them in any important matter that it fell to the Cabinet to decide.'[52] Denis Healey confirms this to be the case, noting that Callaghan '. . . would allow his colleagues to exhaust themselves in argument before forcing a decision. During the IMF he often did both.'[53] Edmund Dell, Secretary of State for Trade (1976–8), dismissed this as a purely tactical ploy on the part of the prime minister. Reflecting on the numerous 'IMF' cabinets, Dell says, 'in retrospect, it is quite clear that this public spectacle of a Cabinet in travail was a farce . . . Either the Cabinet would have to concede substantially to Denis Healey's proposals or it would collapse . . . the Prime Minister's dilemma was purely tactical.'[54] A more significant explanation for the absence of controversy is that most members of the cabinet remained in blissful ignorance that a new economic forum had usurped them. According to Peter Hennessy, 'probably the first the majority of the Callaghan Cabinet heard of the Economic Seminar was when it was 'blown' after they had left office.'[55]

During Callaghan's period in office, therefore, the constitutional position of the prime minister's alternative advisory system, particularly the Policy Unit, ceased to be an issue. Economic policy, that front line in the power struggle between the elected government and the bureaucracy, had become the effective monopoly of the Economic Seminar. This was a forum in which alternative advisers had a voice but it was also a forum in which the weight of numbers was on the side of Whitehall.[56] Once again, the civil service had found an instrument to monitor any influence that might be exercised by alternative advisers. By the inclusion of Sir Douglas Wass, the Permanent Secretary of the Treasury, and Sir John Hunt, the Cabinet Secretary, who himself remained a key player in the formulation of economic policy, Callaghan achieved the acquiescence and silence of Whitehall.

According to Bernard Donoughue, Callaghan's methods were, '. . . quite different from those of Harold Wilson. For one thing he was more open with Cabinet colleagues, putting the economic problems starkly before them and encouraging full discussion . . .'[57] This, however, may have been little more than a willingness on the part of Callaghan to play the constitutional game. He may indeed have encouraged full discussion in his cabinets but his reputation for openness with his colleagues is difficult to reconcile with the creation of the Economic Seminar.

Secrecy, however, is the hallmark of the English constitution. Callaghan's apparent secretiveness therefore should not perhaps be regarded as conspiratorial or sinister. In removing key areas of decision-making from public view[58] Callaghan was merely upholding a tradition legitimized by Bagehot. Bagehot's secret constitution was, however, an open secret known to insiders. Callaghan's Economic Seminar was not. It formed part of a *secret* secret constitution. Like the *Secret* Treaty of Dover, it could not arouse controversy, and therefore did not form part of the constitutional discourse, until later when its existence was revealed.[59]

To what extent, then, did the advisory strategies of James Callaghan show convergence with the American presidential model? Callaghan inherited an advisory system that was becoming presidentialized in structure when he entered Downing Street. The parallel advisory system, composed of the Cabinet Office headed by the Cabinet Secretary, the CPRS and the No.10 Private Office, performed advisory functions reminiscent of the EOP. The No.10 Policy Unit, the Press Office and the Political Office provided the kind of personal political advice and support presidents receive from the WHO. Did Callaghan's advisory strategies advance this presidentialization process that was already discernible?

In some respects Callaghan did advance the presidentialization process. The traditional advisory system of the British prime minister can be described as an hierarchical model according to which prime ministers were expected to receive both political and policy advice from their cabinet colleagues, who in turn were supposed to rely on the advice of departmental civil servants (see appendix). The American presidential model, on the other hand, can be described as being more like a wheel (see appendix) with the president as the hub legitimately seeking advice from a plurality of sources. Callaghan's Economic Seminar was an additional advisory body in the increasingly diverse advisory system that had been evolving since 1964. By 1979 there were, therefore, a number of advisory bodies orbiting round the prime minister, (including the Policy Unit; CPRS; Cabinet Office; No.10 Private Office; Political Office; Press Office, numerous cabinet committees, the Economic Seminar and the cabinet itself), in a pattern similar to that found around the American president, only one of which was the cabinet. Whilst the advice of individual cabinet ministers still counted,[60] the role of the cabinet as a collective decision-making and advisory body continued to decline.

In other respects Callaghan reversed the presidentialization process. He did not enter Downing Street accompanied by a personal team of aides and advisers. Only one personal political adviser, Tom McNally, and one personal private secretary, Ruth Sharpe, entered Downing Street with Callaghan. Tom McCaffrey was seconded to No.10 to take up the position of Press Officer. In contrast to Joe Haines, who had been in Harold Wilson's personal employment as press spokesman before he became Downing Street Press Officer, McCaffrey was already a member of the permanent civil service. In addition, whilst Callaghan retained the Policy Unit, which had been created by Wilson to provide a team of policy advisers sensitive to the political needs of the prime minister, he did not substitute his own appointees for those of his predecessor, as would be expected of a new incumbent in the White House.

Callaghan could, therefore, be described as a caretaker in respect of the presidentialization of the advisory system. He moved it one stage further towards presidentialization by creating the Economic Seminar, but one stage back by depersonalizing the advisory support within No.10.

Did Callaghan seek advice from a plurality of competing sources in the manner of Franklin Roosevelt and John Kennedy, or did he become isolated by cronies, creatures and public relations experts in a manner reminiscent of Richard Nixon? As noted above, Callaghan introduced few personal appointees to No.10. He did not surround himself with cronies and favourites, nor did he rely on the advice of a 'kitchen cabinet'. Callaghan's Press Officer, Tom McCaffrey, in contrast to his predecessor Joe Haines, was not a focus of gossip and intrigue. Anthony Holden says of McCaffrey, '. . . a Prime Minister's Press Secretary less like Joe Haines would be hard to imagine.'[61] Donoughue says that 'Tom McCaffrey, was more the civil servant, keeping a lower profile and not attempting to have the same political or policy influence with Mr Callaghan, as Joe Haines had enjoyed with Mr Wilson.'[62] Tony Benn reports a conversation with Dick Maibon in which the latter complained that Callaghan '. . . has this idea that he is God – he is so dictatorial. He's got to go . . . He no longer talks to any of his friends, only Tom McCaffrey.'[63] Benn, however, remained the cabinet maverick, and in the absence of supporting evidence this would seem to be an isolated complaint. There is little evidence, therefore, to support the view that Callaghan became isolated by cronies, creatures or public relations experts. Blackstone and Plowden note that Callaghan claimed, '. . . he found it helpful to have a variety of views from different sources. He liked to hear all the arguments, to establish the facts and then to decide what to do.'[64]

On 28 March 1979 the premiership of James Callaghan was brought to an end by a vote of no confidence in the House of Commons. During his period in office Callaghan had made only modest changes in a prime ministerial advisory system that already showed signs of becoming presidentialized. Whilst his advisory system had not been the subject of public debate or aroused constitutional controversy, it was presidential. In his memoirs Callaghan notes, somewhat naively for a former Chancellor, that 'it was not my intention when I became Prime Minister to over-involve myself in economic policy . . . I found, as I suppose other Prime Ministers have done, that economic problems obtrude at every street corner.'[65] Possibly by default then, in a manner reminiscent of Edward Heath, Callaghan found that the traditional roles assigned by the constitution to prime minister and cabinet were untenable. Political reality dictates that the prime minister must be interventionist in the departmental responsibilities of his cabinet colleagues, especially in the field of economics, particularly when faced with a period of almost permanent crisis. The Economic Seminar became the vehicle for prime ministerial intervention in all crucial economic discussions and decisions. At the same time, it served to erode further the traditional constitutional position of the cabinet. By 1979 a pattern was beginning to emerge of a prime minister at the centre of a plurality of advisory bodies taking decision with shifting groups of colleagues and advisers, for which the cabinet still bore public collective responsibility but in which, despite exhaustive discussion, it had little real collective force.

In the period since 1964 there were clear indications that, at least in respect of advice, the premiership was becoming presidentialized. Wilson, in contrast to his successors, enthusiastically advanced this process, and this helps to explain why his advisory strategies provoked a great deal of constitutional controversy. Traditional prime ministerial advisers in the cabinet and Whitehall feared that they would lose out in the competition for the prime minister's ear. The prime minister, advised by 'outsiders', would be able to rule alone. The Heath years and the Callaghan years were periods of consolidation when some of the 'dangers' of the presidentializing thrust of Wilson had been neutralized, at least as far as Whitehall was concerned. The election of Margaret Thatcher in 1979 once again raised questions about the constitutionality of advice and about the degree to which the premiership was becoming presidentialized.

Notes

1. Holmes, Martin, *The Labour Governments 1974–79* (London: Macmillan, 1985) p. 79.
2. Neustadt, Richard E., '10 Downing Street: interview by Henry Brandon' in King, Anthony, ed. *The British Prime Minister* 1st edn (London: Macmillan, 1969) pp. 119–30, p. 126.
3. Callaghan himself notes, 'the conventional role of the Cabinet Office is to serve all members of the Cabinet but if the Prime Minister chooses, as nearly all of them do, to work closely with the Secretary to the Cabinet, then it becomes an instrument to serve him above all others.' Callaghan, James, *Time and Chance* (London: Collins, 1987) p. 407.
4. For example, the Central Policy Review Staff (CPRS); units for co-ordinating European Community policy and devolution issues; and a small team working for the Duchy of Lancaster, Harold Lever, in his capacity as 'roving financial and industrial adviser'. See Hennessy, Peter, *Whitehall* (London: Fontana, 1990) p. 243.
5. For details see, Kellner, Peter and Hitchins, Christopher, *Callaghan: the Road to Number Ten* (London: Cassell, 1976) pp. 168–74.
6. Benn, Tony, *Against the Tide Diaries 1973–76* (London: Arrow Books, 1990) and *Conflicts of Interest Diaries 1877–1980* (London: Arrow Books, 1991).
7. Williams, Marcia, *Inside Number 10* (London: Weidenfeld & Nicolson, 1972. Falkender, Lady Marcia, *Downing Street in Perspective* (London: Weidenfeld & Nicolson, 1983).
8. Hurd, Douglas, *An End to Promises* (London: Collins, 1979).
9. Haines, Joe, *The Politics of Power* (London: Coronet Books, 1978).
10. Whitehead, Philip, 'The Labour Governments 1974–1979' in Hennessy, Peter and Seldon, Anthony, eds *Ruling Performance* (Oxford: Blackwell, 1987) pp. 241–75, p. 241.
11. Holmes, op.cit., p. 79.

12. Redhead, Brian, 'James Callaghan' in Mackintosh, John P. ed. *British Prime Ministers in the Twentieth Century Vol.II Churchill to Callaghan* (London: Weidenfeld & Nicolson, 1978) pp. 216–39, p. 239.

13. Wilson, Harold, *The Governance of Britain* (London: Weidenfeld & Nicolson and Michael Joseph, 1976).

14. Donoughue, Bernard, *Prime Minister The conduct of policy under Harold Wilson and James Callaghan* (London: Cape, 1987).

15. Between October and December 1976, Britain was plunged into the deepest financial crisis since the 1930s. Just six months after becoming prime minister Callaghan and the Chancellor of the Exchequer, Denis Healey, were obliged to go cap in hand to the IMF to secure a loan in an effort to 'stem the haemorrhage of financial capital from the City'. Protracted negotiations followed in which the IMF insisted on wide ranging cuts in public expenditure was a prerequisite for loan facilities. This was a hard pill to swallow for a Labour government elected on a programme committing them to large scale public expenditure, and which had already reluctantly been forced to accept several previous rounds of public expenditure cuts. See Hodgson, Geoff, *Labour at the Crossroads* (Oxford: Martin Robertson, 1981) pp. 111–15.

16. See Hennessy, *Whitehall* op.cit., p. 259.

17. Whitehead reflects that Callaghan, '. . . an elementary schoolboy . . . had seen off five Oxford men to capture the leadership.' Whitehad, op.cit., p. 255. However, whilst his formal education may have been limited he could claim to be one of the most experienced prime ministers this century in terms of Whitehall and Westminister. Callaghan had held all three of the great offices of state.

18. Jenkins, Peter, 'Epitaph for a Prime Minister' *Guardian* 30 March, 1979, p. 17.

19. See Donoughue, op.cit. and Haines, op.cit. It is important to note that the extent of influence exercised by any one input into policy formation is inevitably speculative, inviting claims and counter-claims.

20. Cit. Kellner and Hitchins, op.cit., p. 172.

21. See Benn, *Against the Tide* op.cit., pp. 718–20.

22. Falkender, *Downing Street in Perspective* op.cit., p. 100.

23. According to Jones, McNally was appointed not as political secretary, as Mrs Williams had been, but as political adviser. Jones also notes that in contrast to Mrs Williams, McNally was appointed as a temporary civil servant and paid from public funds. The salaries of

his four assistants, however, were met from Party sources. Jones, G.W., 'The United Kingdom' in Plowden, William, ed. *Advising the Rulers* (Oxford: Blackwell, 1987) pp. 36–66, p. 53. Callaghan however claims that the Political Office was '. . . made up entirely of non-civil servants . . . and paid for by funds that the Prime Minister [had] to find for himself.' Callaghan, op.cit., p. 406.

24. Callaghan, op.cit., p. 404.
25. See Blackstone, Tessa and Plowden, William, *Inside the Think Tank* (London Heinemann, 1988) p. 56.
26. See Callaghan, op.cit., p. 404.
27. Ibid., p. 408.
28. The five year temporary civil service status of special advisers appointed by Labour in March 1974 was due to expire March 1979. Including that of Bernard Donoughue.
29. See Norton-Taylor, Richard, 'Callaghan shields advisers' *Guardian* 2 August, 1976, p. 1.
30. Ibid.
31. Whitehead, op.cit., pp. 255–6.
32. Kellner and Hitchins, op.cit., p. 180.
33. Jenkins, op.cit., p. 17.
34. Redhead, op.cit., p. 231.
35. Callaghan, op.cit., p. 444.
36. See Benn, *Conflicts of Interest* op.cit., p. 257 and p. 260.
37. See Benn, *Against the Tide* op.cit., p. 566, pp. 596–7 and pp. 600–1.
38. Callaghan, op.cit., p. 400.
39. Denis Healey, Chancellor of the Exchequer; Harold Lever, Chancellor of the Duchy of Lancaster; Sir Gordon Richardson, Governor of the Bank of England; Kit McMahon, deputy governor; Sir Douglas Wass, and Ken Couzens of the Treasury; Sir John Hunt, Cabinet Secretary; Sir Kenneth Berrill, CPRS; Ken Stowe, Callaghan's Principal Private Secretary; Tim Lankest of the No.10 Private Office and Bernard Donoughue, Policy Unit. See Donoughue, Bernard, 'The Conduct of Economic Policy 1974-79' in King, Anthony, ed. *The British Prime Minister* (London: Macmillan, 1982) pp. 47–71, pp. 69–70.
40. Donoughue, *Prime Minister* op.cit., p. 101.
41. See Willetts, David, 'The Prime Minister's Policy Unit' *Public Administration* Vol.6 Winter 1987, pp. 443–54, p. 444.
42. Healey, op.cit., p. 450.
43. Morgan, Kenneth O., *Labour People: leaders and lieutenants Hardie to Kinnock* (Oxford: University Press, 1987) p. 275.
44. Hennessy, *Whitehall* op.cit., p. 244.

45. Hunt, Lord Hunt of Tanworth, formerly Sir John Hunt, Cabinet Secretary, letter 5 May, 1994.
46. Lord Donoughue, interview 19 May, 1994.
47. Hennessy, *Whitehall* op.cit., p. 260.
48. Whitehead, op.cit., p. 250.
49. Hunt, letter op.cit.
50. Donoughue, interview op.cit.
51. Ibid.
52. Callaghan, op.cit., p. 558.
53. Healey, op.cit., p. 448.
54. See, Dell, Edmund, 'Collective Responsibility: fact, fiction or facade?' in *Policy and Practice* (London: RIPA, 1980) pp. 27–48, pp. 31–2.
55. Hennessy, *Whitehall* op.cit., p. 260.
56. See Hennessy, 'The Quality of Cabinet Government' *Political Studies* Vol. 6, 1985, pp. 15–45, p. 33.
57. Donoughue, *Prime Minister* op.cit., p. 88.
58. See Whitehead op.cit., p. 259.
59. The Treaty of Dover 1670, which tied England and France into an alliance against Holland, included secret clauses under which Charles II undertook to declare his conversion to Catholicism. The secret clauses did not cause a fuss until their existence was leaked around 1678, when it was rumoured that there was a popish plot to depose Charles and make his Catholic brother James king in his place.
60. For example, Chancellor of the Duchy of Lancaster, Harold Lever and Chancellor of the Exchequer, Denis Healey. Callaghan describes the close partnership that existed between himself and his Chancellor, Denis Healey. Callaghan, op.cit., pp. 414–5.
61. Holden, Anthony, 'After Marcia and Joe' *Sunday Times* 27 February, 1977, p. 32.
62. Donoughue, *Prime Minister* op.cit., p. 25.
63. Benn, *Against the Tide* op.cit., p. 416.
64. Blackstone and Plowden, op.cit., p. 56.
65. Callaghan, op.cit., p. 399.

8 Margaret Thatcher 1979–90: An Outsider

> Like many of her people, Thatcher was an outsider. Her generation did not accept women as equal to men. She had not been in a good regiment. . . . She had studied chemistry: not one of the right subjects . . . she would probably never have been invited to chair a Royal Commission. . . . She went through three of the traditional leaders' institutions of Britain – Oxford, the Bar and Parliament – and they left hardly a mark on her.[1]

> Margaret was . . . not willing to take the advice of the 'great and the good', whom she knew would dearly liked to have sacked her in 1979.[2]

Margaret Thatcher's entry to No.10 introduced a renewed period of turbulence in the history of advice politics. Philosophically a free-marketeer, her enthusiasm for competition extended to her advisory strategies. As a consequence, controversy about advice was an enduring theme of her eleven years in office and claims that she was presidentializing the premiership became commonplace.

Questions about advice that had been raised during Harold Wilson's first period in office (1964–70) had been all but resolved by the time James Callaghan left office in 1979. Whilst a degree of presidentialization of the advisory system had continued in the intervening years, the process had been spasmodic, more discreet and partially aided and abetted by some key civil servants, and had, therefore, aroused little public debate. In contrast to the accepted position when Wilson first entered office in 1964, the prime minister was now served by a plurality of advisers and advisory bodies. The absence of public controversy about advice suggests that a new accommodation had been reached within the secret constitution: No.10 had almost become the 'power house' desired by Wilson, but most of the levers were still pulled by or available to civil servants. The arrival of Mrs Thatcher in Downing Street changed all this.

Nigel Lawson blamed his sudden departure from the chancellorship in October 1989 on Mrs Thatcher's failure to observe the constitutional proprieties of cabinet government, particularly in respect of advice.[3] Mrs

Thatcher's champions have cast doubt on Mr Lawson's claims, suggesting that constitutional principle had been invoked to mask personal political expediency.[4] In Hugo Young's view, 'Walters supplied Lawson with the ideal pretext . . . [giving] him the occasion for a dignified exit, which even cast him as something of a hero . . .'[5] Mr Lawson's motives can only remain a matter for conjecture. It might indeed be possible to discount the constitutional implications of the chancellor's resignation had it been an isolated incident in an uncontroversial premiership, but this was not the case. Lawson was not the first of Mrs Thatcher's ministers to question her stewardship or the first to express doubt about the constitutional legitimacy of her preferred advisory strategies.

On 9 January 1986 Michael Heseltine spectacularly resigned from his post as Minister of Defence. Storming out of a cabinet meeting, Heseltine announced his resignation to the media corps in Downing Street. He did not send the prime minister the customary resignation letter but instead delivered a detailed statement on television in which he implied that Mrs Thatcher had used her power over the agenda to conspire against him. He claimed there had been a 'deliberate attempt to avoid discussion in Cabinet'.[6] Heseltine's dramatic exit gave rise to much debate about Mrs Thatcher's *modus operandi*. The manner of Heseltine's departure, and his complaints were bad enough, but the matter did not end there. The furore prompted a further ministerial resignation, that of the Trade and Industry Secretary, Leon Brittan. Ostensibly Brittan resigned on a matter of individual responsibility.[7] It was soon revealed, however, that his departure may have been an act of sacrifice to protect the prime minister herself, or as Brittan was later to claim, her press secretary, Bernard Ingham, from the damaging implications that the leaks and cover-ups might hold for No.10. The conflict leading to these resignations was a dispute over the future of the Westland helicopter company, between Michael Heseltine at Defence and Leon Brittan at Trade and Industry, in which Mrs Thatcher sided with the latter, but as Bill Jones points out, 'the real issue . . . quickly became the alleged impropriety of Mrs Thatcher's conduct. It emerged that her personal staff had been involved with DTI officials in authoritizing the leak of a highly confidential letter . . . which undermined Heseltine's position.'[8] If Mr Brittan was responsible for the actions of his staff, was not the prime minister similarly responsible for the activities of her personal staff, and if not, who was? Robert Harris describes Westminster as '. . . fizzing with rumours that the Prime Minister herself would be brought down, Nixon-style, by her knowledge of her subordinate's wrong doing.'[9]

Alan Walters then was not the only one of Mrs Thatcher's advisers to attract gossip and criticism. Bernard Ingham, in the high profile post of

Downing Street Press Secretary, had already become the target of a great deal of adverse comment. Questions were raised about the overtly political manner in which this supposedly impartial civil servant performed his duties and about the extent of the influence he was suspected of having over the prime minister. Robert Harris, for example, provides a catalogue of accusations and protestations of former ministers who felt aggrieved at being 'rottweilered' by Ingham and who suspected that he had been implicated in their demise.[10]

Walters and Ingham were the most conspicuous and among the most frequently criticized prime ministerial aides, but they were not the only ones whose roles were questioned. Controversy erupted in 1983 when Mrs Thatcher appointed Anthony Parsons, a former diplomat, to be her personal foreign affairs adviser. Parsons's appointment was portrayed in the quality press as 'a setback to one of Whitehall's proudest departments'.[11] In 1984 the appointment of David Young, former chairman of the Manpower Services Commission, to the post of Downing Street chief of staff, disconcerted some of Mrs Thatcher's colleagues and inspired a wave of speculation about the 'privatization' of Downing Street and the possibility that Mrs Thatcher was about to establish a Prime Minister's Department. After the Westland affair, a close and almost exclusive relationship that developed between the prime minister and her Private Secretary for foreign affairs, Charles Powell, became a source of discontent and gossip. From time to time rumour and speculation also stirred about some of the more shadowy figures thought to be influencing the prime minister. *World in Action*, for instance, tried to make David Hart, a millionaire property dealer, farmer, and self-professed adviser to the prime minister, the subject of a documentary. A good deal of general speculation and academic interest was also aroused concerning the extent of the influence exercised by various unofficial right-wing policy think tanks[12] which boasted a direct line to the prime minister.

Controversy about advice, advisers, and the implications they had for cabinet government, that had characterized Mrs Thatcher's period in office contributed to her demise.[13] On 1 November 1990 Sir Geoffrey Howe, Leader of the House of Commons and Deputy Prime Minister, tendered his resignation and in doing so delivered what turned out to be the *coup de grace* to Margaret Thatcher's long 'reign' in Downing Street. Howe attributed his resignation to substantial policy differences that existed between himself and Mrs Thatcher about Europe, but he also made damaging attacks on her leadership and expressed deep misgivings about her conduct of cabinet government.[14] Echoing Michael Heseltine, Howe implied that the prime minister was pursuing a policy which had not been legitimized by a process of discussion and persuasion in cabinet. He said that cabinet government called for 'mutual respect and restraint in pursuit of a common cause'[15] which, he clearly implied, was absent in the Mrs Thatcher's administration. Public policy was no longer an agreed outcome of deliberations conducted in private within the executive branch, but an argument conducted in public between a prime minister advised and supported by her own team, and members of her cabinet, the collective executive, advised by the permanent government in Whitehall.[16]

Questions about Mrs Thatcher's conduct of government and the role of, and constitutional status of, her personal advisers were not confined merely to Whitehall gossip and the complaints of former ministers and displaced favourites. Such questions formed part of a wider public debate during and after Mrs Thatcher's period in office.[17] Mrs Thatcher succeeded in reviving questions about the presidentialization of British government and in placing the British constitution back on the public and academic agenda.

Did Mrs Thatcher resort to constitutionally questionable advisory strategies that served to further presidentialize the premiership? Before this question can be answered some preliminary questions must first be addressed. What was the accepted constitutional position in respect of advice to the executive when Mrs Thatcher became prime minister and what kind of advisory system was in place? Why did she regarded these arrangements as inadequate or unsatisfactory? What changes did she introduce?

What then was the constitutional position in respect of advice to the prime minister when Mrs Thatcher took office? James Callaghan, in contrast to his predecessor, Harold Wilson, cannot be regarded as a constitutional innovator. His brief premiership, dogged by economic crises and the political headaches associated with managing a minority government, had left little time for tinkering with the advisory system. The Economic Seminar was the only change of any significance introduced by Callaghan. This was a change dictated more by a gradual shift towards monetarism than a conscious attempt by the prime minister to presidentialize the advisory system. The constitutional position in respect of advice had changed little during the Callaghan years. The civil service recognized that prime ministers required more advice and was determined to provide it from within Whitehall or to monitor as closely as possible any outside sources. The prime minister's Policy Unit established by Harold Wilson in 1974 was gaining acceptance partly because formal agreement had been reached between its head and the Cabinet Secretary about access to the prime minister himself and to documents and to other parts of the system. It was not perceived to be composed of mavericks intent upon undermining Whitehall, but as a concession in the direction of institutionalized political support. Its members were temporary civil servants, not, perhaps, socialized into Whitehall's culture but bound, at least, by its rules. The constitutional position, therefore, in respect of advice to prime ministers in 1979 was that they were no longer expected to receive all advice through the cabinet filter. Prime ministers were no longer at the top of an advisory pyramid underpinned first by the cabinet, then by Whitehall, and, below Whitehall, by various experts and outside advisers whose advice was mediated by Whitehall. Instead there was a growing recognition that the prime minister was at the centre of an advisory network of which the cabinet formed only one component. Other components included bodies such as the Political Office, the Policy Unit, the Economic Seminar, and the Central Policy Review Staff (CPRS). The inclusion of outsiders in these bodies allowed for some alternative advice but at the same time the presence of permanent civil servants enabled Whitehall to monitor it. The prime minister could, therefore, call on an expanding network of *parallel* advice but *alternative* advice remained suspect.

What advisory-system-in-place did Mrs Thatcher inherit upon entering No.10 in 1979? The cabinet remained the traditional, even if no longer the only, official source of policy and political advice to the prime minister. Cabinet ministers continued to perform the dual role of filtering policy advice arising from the departments of Whitehall and of mediating the political support of back-benchers in Westminster. The cabinet's position, however, was becoming more problematical in both these respects. A parallel prime ministerial advisory system was evolving composed of the Cabinet Secretary and the Cabinet Office, including under its auspices a variety of special units, the CPRS, the Economic Seminar and the No.10 Private Office. This provided the prime minister with advice dominated by Whitehall sources but not by departmental vested interests. The rudiments of an alternative advisory system, composed of the Policy Unit, the Political Office and to some extent the Press Office, provided the prime minister with advice which was sensitive to the prime minister's personal political fortunes.

Mrs Thatcher inherited a larger and more diverse advisory system than had been Harold Wilson's experience in 1964. Why did she regard this advisory system as inadequate and unsatisfactory? What were its shortcomings and what did she do about them?

Mrs Thatcher was an outsider and a radical, two major handicaps in a system of government that relies for its smooth operation on the easy intercourse between those sharing backgrounds and club membership, and which makes a virtue out of moderation and consensus. This made it likely that unless the system changed her, she would have to change the system.

In terms of her party, her class, past Whitehall and ministerial experience and her gender, Margaret Thatcher was an outsider. Ranelagh notes that '. . . she had no attachments to the traditional political bases. She was not close to the Established church, to organic Toryism, to the Civil Service, the Crown, the City, the House of Commons or the House of Lords.'[18] She shared a similar class and educational background with both Harold Wilson and Edward Heath, but she did not share their need to be accepted by the ruling elite. She had neither awe for the patrician grandees of the Tory party nor reverence for the philosopher kings of the civil service. Both Wilson and Heath had in their time been described as civil servants *manqués*, and Callaghan was noted for his easy compatibility with the mandarins of Whitehall. This could not be said of Mrs Thatcher.[19] In contrast to her three predecessors, Mrs Thatcher had never been a civil servant and had only limited ministerial experience prior to becoming prime minister.[20] She was clearly self-conscious of her outsider status:

> Of course in the eyes of the 'wet' Tory establishment I was not only a woman, but 'that woman', someone not just a different sex, but of a different class, a person with an alarming conviction that the values and virtues of middle England should be brought to bear on the problems which the establishment consensus had created. I offended on many counts.[21]

Mrs Thatcher represented those who were suspicious of the establishment. She entered office a worthy citizen from the provinces sent to the capital to oversee the way 'her' people's taxes were being spent.[22]

Not only was Mrs Thatcher in so many respects an outsider, she was also a radical. Hers was a radicalism not so much of policies but of attitudes and values.[23] She was elected to office in a period that was witnessing the disintegration of the post-war consensus, promising a set of policies not greatly dissimilar to Heath's Selsdon programme, but in contrast to Heath, she claimed that she was a conviction politician. She was convinced not only of the correctness of her policies but was determined upon their realization. She believed that the political initiatives of the early 1970s, of the government of which she had been a member, had been correct and that failure to carry them through was attributable to political faint-heartedness, reinforced by the doubts and persuasions of a Whitehall grown fat on Keynes.

Mrs Thatcher was a conviction politician in a system of government that prized detachment, caution and compromise. Young notes that 'there was a genuine clash of cultures, between a political leadership fired by an almost Cromwellian impatience with the status quo, and the mandarin world of Whitehall in which scepticism and rumination were more highly rated habits of mind than zeal or blind conviction.'[24] She was also a doctrinaire leader of a party which throughout its history had usually fought shy of doctrine. She inherited an advisory system dominated on the one hand by effete bureaucrats and on the other by Tory wets.

In order to examine in detail what Mrs Thatcher saw as the shortcomings of the advisory system that she inherited, Weller's distinction between policy and political advice will once again be employed, although, as noted in chapter six above, the increasing complexity of the prime ministerial advisory system makes this distinction difficult to sustain. It does, however, provide a framework for analyzing a network of advisers and advisory bodies that in reality defy categorization.

Despite greater tolerance of the presence of a few irregulars offering alternative advice, Whitehall had succeeded in maintaining its near monopoly over policy advice to the prime minister. What did Mrs Thatcher perceive to be the weaknesses of Whitehall as a source of policy advice? She saw Whitehall as being peopled by consensus seekers having a vested interest in big government.[25]

In 1964 Harold Wilson had entered office determined to revolutionize the attitudes of Whitehall. He identified the Treasury as his main opponent. By means of its control of the purse strings on the one hand and of the civil service establishment on the other, the Treasury was able to ensure its preferred virtues of good housekeeping penetrated to all the corners of Whitehall and would, it was assumed, thereby successfully resist expensive radical initiatives favoured by a party of the left. Wilson attempted to combat the Treasury's influence by introducing structural change. He established the Department of Economic Affairs (DEA) to be a competitor of the Treasury in the field of economic policy and the Civil Service Department (CSD) to weaken the Treasury's influence on Whitehall's culture. In the short term it appeared Wilson's revolution had failed. The Treasury succeeded in killing off the DEA and in neutralizing any potential threat to its cultural hegemony posed by the CSD, by ensuring that Treasury men dominated its higher echelons. By the late 1970s, many on the right, including Mrs Thatcher herself, began to suspect that Wilson's had been a successful revolution. Whitehall was now dominated by those believing that the nation's problems could be solved by ever increasing public expenditure. By the 1970s senior civil servants had known only the policies of the post-war consensus. Keynesians not only held the highest positions in the spending ministries, but had colonized the Treasury.[26] Whilst Wilson's attempts, via Fulton, to improve planning and management in the civil service had been successfully smothered by Whitehall, he had nevertheless succeeded in exploiting the now entrenched Keynesian orthodoxy towards more collectivist ends. This gave rise to claims by the new right that the middle ground of the post-war consensus had gradually been shifted to the left. Mrs Thatcher, then, needed to reverse the Wilsonian revolution in respect of policy advice if she was to stand any chance of realizing her radical agenda of pursuing a tight money economic policy and rolling back the state.

Policy advice from Whitehall was suspect. What about advice arising from the traditional source of policy and political advice to the prime minister, the cabinet? Mrs Thatcher in 1979 was placed in a similar position to that of Harold Wilson in 1964 *vis-a-vis* her cabinet. Few of her cabinet could be regarded as 'one of us'[27] and few could be described as Mrs Thatcher's personal choices. Mrs Thatcher's early cabinet was dominated not only by potential rivals but rivals from the 'wet' paternalist or One Nation wing of her party, therefore, making their political advice doubly suspect. In addition, most of her cabinet colleagues were likely to have their views reinforced by Keynesian civil servants in the departments they headed. This cast further doubt on the reliability of cabinet advice.

How did Mrs Thatcher tackle these weaknesses of her advisory system? Mrs Thatcher's limited experience of the civil service had made her doubtful of the virtues of Whitehall, but she did not, in contrast to Wilson in 1964, reveal many clues as to the nature of any reforms she intended to introduce. When leader of the Opposition she had consulted a variety of right wing think tanks, therefore some increase in the input of alternative advisers may have been expected, but few in 1979 could have anticipated the imminent launch of Mrs Thatcher's cultural revolution. In Young's view, 'no government has been elected whose leader was as deeply seized as this one of the need to overturn the power and presumption of the continuing government of the civil service: to challenge its orthodoxies, cut down its size, reject its assumptions, which were seen as corrosively infected by social democracy and teach it a lesson in political control.'[28]

In contrast to Harold Wilson, Mrs Thatcher did not necessarily regard the Treasury as her *bête noire*. She recognized that in the Treasury there might be some potential allies in her battle against Keynesian orthodoxy. She wanted to reduce public expenditure and revive the virtues of prudent housekeeping that had once characterized the Treasury's predominance. She sought, therefore, to reinforce the Treasury's hegemony over the spending ministries, whilst at the same time exploiting to her advantage the divisions between monetarists and Keynesians, that now existed in the

Treasury, by a process of promoting the former.[29]

Reviving the habit of prudent housekeeping would not alone suffice to achieve the revolution Mrs Thatcher desired. She also needed to counteract the traditional attitudes of caution, moderation and consensus-seeking compromise that dominated Whitehall culture. She employed a variety of means to this end.

On entering office in 1979 Mrs Thatcher gave the first signal of the impending revolution when she chose her alternative advisers. She appointed Sir John Hoskyns, a successful businessman and an outspoken critic of the ways and wisdom of Whitehall,[30] to head her Downing Street Policy Unit. Hoskyns quickly confirmed civil service suspicions when he identified 'deprivileging the civil service' as a priority to be considered by the new government.[31] A further signal of Mrs Thatcher's intentions was the appointment of another outsider, Sir Derek Rayner of Marks and Spencer, to head a new Efficiency Unit to be located in the Cabinet Office. The cosy Keynesian fiefdoms of the civil service were to be exposed to the rigours of private sector management and to be reformed, abolished or privatized if found wanting. Peter Hennessy describes Rayner's unit as literally an 'anti-CSD in 1979–1981'.[32] The changes sponsored by the Efficiency Unit were to be reinforced by a gradual process of preferment of civil servants displaying 'can do' attitudes over those steeped in caution and doubt. Mrs Thatcher admits to taking a close interest in senior appointments in the Civil Service '. . . because they could affect the morale and efficiency of whole departments.'[33]

In 1981, a five month long civil service strike provided Mrs Thatcher with an excuse to abolish the CSD, a relic of Wilson's 1960s revolution. Headed by Sir Ian Bancroft, whom Young describes as '. . . out of inclination and duty alike, . . . a custodian of the Whitehall culture and the public service tradition.'[34] The CSD was seen to be the propagator of the very values and attitudes Mrs Thatcher was trying to eradicate. Bancroft was persuaded to take early retirement and the work formerly performed by his department was redistributed.

Mrs Thatcher also set out to remove some functions from the sphere of the bureaucracy altogether. As part of her policy of rolling back the state she wanted to encourage not only the hiving-off of some segments of departmental activity but also a widespread policy of privatization, reversing some of the nationalization programme of the 1945 Labour Government. This policy would serve simultaneously to reduce both the size of civil service empires and numbers of civil servants.

It is no surprise that, given Mrs Thatcher's preference for private over public provision, she paid little heed to civil service sensitivities in respect of alternative advisers. Although she did not regard the Treasury in quite the same light as Harold Wilson had, she was nevertheless suspicious of all things bureaucratic and knew Sir Douglas Wass was not 'one of us'. She feared that once the economic recession really began to bite, the Keynesians would find willing collaborators among cabinet 'wets' and would attempt to force her to make a U-turn as Heath had done in 1972. Partly in order to counteract such possibilities, she appointed Professor Alan Walters, a long-standing monetarist and enthusiast for the free market, to be her personal economic adviser.[35] Walter's role was to provide really alternative economic advice that would enable Mrs Thatcher and her small band of true believers in the cabinet to challenge the orthodoxies still peddled by the spending ministries and by some in the Treasury.

Alan Walters was specifically appointed to be an alternative adviser but he was not the only source of alternative policy advice to the prime minister. Mrs Thatcher continued to maintain close links with the various right wing think tanks that had helped to shape her policy agenda whilst she had been leader of the opposition. Such links included the appointment of some former think tank members to positions on her Downing Street staff.[36] She also sought the advice of a shifting group of individuals such as David Hart and Alfred Sherman.[37] In 1984 she launched what appeared to be another broadside at the civil service's prerogative of advice by appointing David Young to be Downing Street Chief of Staff.

Mrs Thatcher, then, attempted to tackle what she regarded as weaknesses in the policy advisory system, by on the one hand, resorting to a variety of different tactics aimed at revolutionizing attitudes and values of the civil service, in order to effect changes both in the kind of policy advice from this source and in Whitehall's response to radical initiatives from outside. On the other hand, she chose to ignore Whitehall's traditional sensitivities about alternative advisers and consulted whoever she thought might be useful to her cause. How did she tackle the shortcomings of the cabinet?

By the time Mrs Thatcher left Downing Street in 1990 she was said to be isolated in Number 10 relying almost exclusively on the advice of her personal staff.[38] This had not always been the case. On entering office in 1979, Mrs Thatcher had, in common with her predecessors, ritualistically expressed an intention to rely on the advice of her cabinet. The *Economist* reported that she '. . . explicitly rejected a kitchen cabinet of advisers on the ostensibly sound basis that they led to divisions in previous governments. Cabinet ministers were her advisers . . . she would not have a Downing Street cabal.'[39]

These intentions appeared to be reflected, initially at least, in the advisory arrangements within No.10. She did not introduce any formal change in the structure, nor did she enter Downing Street accompanied by a large team of personal appointees. Whilst Mrs Thatcher retained the Policy Unit, she reduced it in size, from ten under her predecessor, to just two outsiders, Sir John Hoskyns, its director, assisted by Norman Strauss, on secondment from Unilever, and including in it for the first time, a civil servant.[40] In contrast to both Wilson and Callaghan, Mrs Thatcher had little interest in personalizing or politicizing the Press Office. She was dissatisfied with the way her first Press Secretary, Henry James, performed his duties, but when she decided to replace him, her choice, Bernard Ingham, was not known to her personally and was in any case a permanent civil servant.[41] Mrs Thatcher maintained the No.10 Political Office and established a new position by appointing David Wolfson, a former businessman from Great Universal Stores and secretary to the Conservative shadow cabinet, to be chief of staff. Although Wolfson did not become a temporary civil servant (he was in fact unpaid), his appointment was not controversial.[42] Wolfson was assisted by Mrs Thatcher's Political Secretary, Richard Ryder, a former *Daily Telegraph* journalist.

Mrs Thatcher seemed to have little inclination for a 'kitchen cabinet', but this did not, even in the short-run, lead to a revival of classic cabinet government. Instead the shortcomings of her 'wet' colleagues led to the emergence of a two-tier cabinet. John Vincent claims that 'neither in 1975 nor in 1979 did she [Thatcher] reconstruct the front bench in her own image. In 1975 it was enough to isolate Heath, while in 1979 she seized the Treasury, leaving the Tories to have the rest as they chose.'[43] Mrs Thatcher admits that '. . . the hardest battles would be fought on the ground of economic policy, so I made sure the key economic ministries would be true believers in our economic strategy.'[44]

Once Mrs Thatcher felt sufficiently confident of her own position, she would be able to replace some of her 'wetter' colleagues with some of her own supporters, and, if she was successful in her cultural revolution in Whitehall, this would in the long term tackle some of the weaknesses of the cabinet as a forum of policy advice. In the short term she resorted to personal intervention to oversee the implementation of her agenda. In 1984 Francis Pym[45] complained, 'the Prime Minister . . . would ideally like to run the major Departments herself and tries her best to do so – not just in terms of overall policy but in strategic detail.'[46] Pym went on to note that the only thing stopping Mrs Thatcher from running the government almost single-handed was the limited extent of her personal advisory sources.

By 1981 Mrs Thatcher began the gradual process of 'drying out' the cabinet whilst at the same time augmenting her personal advisory support system to overcome the handicap noted by Pym. In 1982, in the wake of the Falklands War, she decided that not only was Treasury advice suspect, but she could no longer rely on the advice of the Foreign Office either. To remedy this she appointed Sir Anthony Parsons, a former diplomat and ambassador to the United Nations, to be her personal adviser on foreign affairs. In addition, Roger Jackling, a civil servant from the Department of Defence, was seconded to No.10 to advise the prime minister on defence matters. Also in 1982, Ferdinand Mount, a journalist and former member of the Conservative Party Research Department, replaced Sir John Hoskyns as head of the newly enlarged Policy Unit.

The abolition of the CPRS in 1983 contributed to this process of gradually shifting the advisory system in the prime minister's favour. On becoming prime minister in 1979, Mrs Thatcher had retained the CPRS, replacing Sir Kenneth Berrill, who was due to retire, with her own appointee, Sir Robin Ibbs.[47] Immediately after the 1983 election she decided to abolish it and transfer some of its former members to the staff of her Policy Unit.[48] This was a decision that aroused a good deal of public controversy and was construed by some to be a further step in the direction of presidentialization: the personal advisory body of the prime minister was being strengthened at the expense of the collective briefing agency for the cabinet.[49] The official explanation for the abolition of the CPRS was that it was redundant. The departments now had expanded policy units for long-term planning; the Cabinet Secretariat's role had expanded to included collective briefing and the prime minister had a Policy Unit. Mrs Thatcher's own explanation is that the CPRS had become a freelance 'Ministry of Bright Ideas' out of touch with the government's philosophy.[50] Hennessy reflects that whatever the official rationale, an important explanation for these changes lay in the nature of the advisory bodies themselves, '. . . the acutest and most important difference between the CPRS and the Policy Unit is that the Policy Unit was hers to its last paperclip. There was no question of it serving other Cabinet ministers or some notion of the wider interest.'[51]

Gradually during her long period in Downing Street Mrs Thatcher developed an advisory system which provided greater personal support for the prime minister, facilitating her intervention in most major aspects of government activity. As she strengthened her personal team, informal groups, composed of the prime minister and her advisors and the sponsoring departmental minister and his, became the forum for public policy decisions. The role of the more formal cabinet committees, and the cabinet itself, in the discussion and policy decision-making process, declined.[52] The cabinet was becoming the 'dignified' facade masking an 'efficient' government of ad hoc groups around the prime minister.

We have examined the formal constitutional position in respect of advice to the executive when Mrs Thatcher became prime minister and the nature of the advisory system she inherited. We have explored some of the reasons why she found that system unsatisfactory, and described the nature of the advisory system she evolved to address these weaknesses. What then was the constitutional status of Mrs Thatcher's advisory system and how presidential was it?

Mrs Thatcher's advisory strategies certainly provoked the kind of public controversy that would suggest constitutional change was afoot and was being resisted. But was the change such that it continued the presidentialization of the premiership in respect of advice?

It was noted above that by 1979 the constitutional rules about advice had evolved, to the extent that the prime ministerial advisory system inherited by Mrs Thatcher already showed signs of presidentialization. The traditional British hierarchical model (see appendix), according to which prime ministers were expected to receive both political and policy advice from their cabinet colleagues, who in turn were supposed to rely on the advice of departmental civil servants, was giving way to something resembling a wheel model (see appendix) associated with the American presidential advisory system, according to which it was accepted that the president at the centre would be advised by a plurality of sources. By 1979 the prime minister could be described as being at the centre of an increasingly diverse advisory system. The distinction between alternative and parallel advisory systems, between insiders and outsiders, and any clear distinction between policy and political advice were breaking down. Many advisers and advisory bodies now blurred all the lines of demarcation: the CPRS and the Economic Seminar were hybrids which included in their membership insiders and outsiders; the Policy Unit provided *political* policy advice. The cabinet had become only one spoke of the wheel. The advice of individual members of the cabinet still counted, but the role of cabinet as collective decision-making and advisory body was declining. Mrs Thatcher continued this process. Like an American president she seemed to regard it as her right to trawl widely for advice. But the amount of constitutional fuss this stirred up during her tenure signalled that prime ministers still lacked presidential freedoms in these matters.

The American constitution places executive responsibility clearly in the hands of the president. The cabinet exists to advise him if he wishes to consult it. Its members are his agents and have no share in his constitutional responsibilities. Despite the changes that have taken place in the British political system, noted in chapter two above, which have meant that in the eyes of the British electorate government has increasingly come to be perceived as being the responsibility of one person, the prime minister, the public constitutional position remains that government is the responsibility of a collective executive, the cabinet. In Britain, in contrast to America, all executive power is vested by Act of Parliament in individual departmental ministers. Whatever his or her personal influence, the prime minister has no formal executive power to override other ministers. To which of these models did Mrs Thatcher arrangements most closely conform?

Mrs Thatcher certainly seemed to regard it as her right to intervene in all major aspects of government activity and to seek advice from any sources she chose in order to do so. This attracted a good deal of criticism and comment. She was accused of behaving presidentially and of failing to observe the conventions of cabinet government. Peter Jenkins, for instance, said of Mrs Thatcher's advisory system: 'her outsider mentality led her to regard government as a personal conspiracy against her. Her technique was to conspire against it. This she did by bringing in outsiders, by dealing directly with officials who took her fancy, by operating a network of trusties, strategically placed in the departments'[53] Anthony Sampson reflecting on Mrs Thatcher's premiership noted that 'Number Ten became much more like a permanent court, with viziers and courtiers. The government was looking still more like an elective dictatorship . . . and close to some kind of presidential system . . . '[54] In 1984 the *Economist* claimed that 'full cabinet is regarded with little greater respect than Parliament. Cabinet committees are withering on the bough . . . A quite different hierarchy of influence is established from the classic one of the ministers in cabinet responsible to Parliament. The new hierarchy is responsible to Downing Street, fount of patronage and custodian of the government's public appeal.'[55] Kenneth Harris notes that Mrs Thatcher's colleagues 'soon came to realize that she did not see the role of the Cabinet as her predecessors had seen it. To her, Cabinet members were her agents; they were there not to influence or inform Government policy, but to execute it. She saw her Cabinet more as an American president sees his.'[56] This is a view borne out in the comments of Francis Pym, who complained,

> I do not object to questioning the received wisdom or to encouraging a thorough argument about it, and no one can object to having a well-informed Prime Minister. But I object to a system that deliberately pits Downing Street against individual Departments, breeds resentment amongst Ministers and Civil Servants and turns the Prime Minister into a President.[57]

Pym goes on to say, 'I do not like the growing tendency of Ministers (and indeed Civil Servants) to be accountable to Downing Street, and only accountable to Parliament as agents of the Prime Minister.'[58] Norman St John-Stevas,[59] one of the first casualties of Mrs Thatcher's 'drying out' process, claimed: 'there is no doubt that as regards the Cabinet the most commanding Prime Minister of modern times has been the present incumbent, Mrs Thatcher. Convinced of both her own rectitude and ability, she has tended to reduce the Cabinet to subservience.'[60]

It was noted above that Mrs Thatcher on becoming prime minister had ritualistically expressed an intention to rely upon the advice of her cabinet. James Prior[61] confirms that 'in her early years as Prime Minister Margaret adhered closely to the traditional principles and practices of Cabinet government.'[62] This honeymoon period did not last long and may have been little more than keeping up appearances. When Mrs Thatcher entered Downing Street in 1979 she conformed to the now accepted practice that prime ministers would be accompanied by some personal aides. Initially she did not surround herself with a team of fiercely loyal political appointees responsible only to herself, although she did, like an American president, seek advice from more outside sources than had been the custom of her predecessors. Gradually during her period in office, whilst she continued to consult a variety of alternative advisory bodies, she also expanded her personal staff to enable her to intervene in all major aspects of government policy. By 1983 she had increased the size of her Policy Unit from three to nine, enabling its members to specialize in distinct policy areas and to keep an eye on what the departments were proposing. Francis Pym complained:

> . . . my final criticism of the Government . . . is that its style of operation has steadily become less flexible and more centralized. This process stems from the Prime Minister's tendency to think that she is always right . . . This leads her to believe that she can always do things better that other people, which then encourages her to try to do everything herself. The two consequences of this are, first, that central government now exercises direct control over more and more aspects of our lives and, second, that within the Government the Prime Minister exercises direct control over more and more Departments.[63]

Pym goes on to note that in order to facilitate such interventionism the prime minister had expanded her Downing Street staff '. . . to include experts in every major area, thus establishing a government within a government.' Pym's anxieties were echoed by political commentators at the time. In 1984 James Naughtie, writing about the appointment of David Young, questioned whether he might be a 'Haldeman-style Chief of Staff'and noted that critics '. . . point to an unhealthy concentration of power in a Presidential office, lurking behind the homely facade of Downing Street.'[64] On the same subject, and in a similar vein, a leading article in the *Scotsman* asserted that, '. . . departmental Ministers see the threat of a presidential office in Downing Street which would be a competing and sometimes conflicting source of power; the departments themselves share that view and worry lest it would undermine their traditional roles.'[65]

Advice is power in a system of government by conversation. Ministers and mandarins shared a concern that they were in danger of being excluded from the private conversation between the prime minister and her personal advisers. The prime minister was constructing an alternative advisory system which could enable her to ignore the accepted constitutional sources of advice. The cabinet feared that it was fast coming to resemble its American counterpart, in which cabinet members were often only the frontmen for policies decided elsewhere. The resignations of Nigel Lawson and Sir Geoffrey Howe may have been prompted by a variety of private motives, but this does not invalidate the public explanation: they balked at being the salesmen for policies decided by the prime minister and her personal advisers. The prime minister, like an American president, was becoming surrounded by an expanding team of personal aides and advisers, some of whom were tasked with monitoring the progress of the prime minister's policies through the government machine, in a similar manner to the way in which WHO aides 'ride herd' on the federal bureaucracy. Many, although not all, of what Simon Jenkins describes as 'a changing cast of political freelancers'[66] were outsiders, representing no wider constituency than themselves and in some cases deliberately chosen for their lack of public service tradition.[67] They owed their position and their loyalty to the prime minister and had no wider responsibility than that of serving her. Joan Smith describes Lord Young,[68] for example, as '. . . above all else, Mrs Thatcher's creature . . . owing his political career to her in a way that has never been true of the Tebbits, the Howes, or the Heseltines of this world.'[69] She goes on to assert that 'his appointment as Minister without Portfolio in 1984 was an affront to democracy, made possible only by his simultaneous elevation to the House of Lords . . . ' She describes Lord Young as '. . . a politician with a constituency of one – the woman who had appointed him'[70] and notes that he was 'unashamed of her patronage,' quoting him as saying 'I am the Prime Minister's footsoldier. I do as she wishes.'[71] These were words which could easily have been put into the mouth of more than one of the Nixon aides who went to gaol.

The advances in the presidentialization of the advisory system that took place under Mrs Thatcher showed signs of penetrating beyond the narrow confines of her personal staff within or attached to No.10. When an American president enters the White House he is not only accompanied by a personal entourage but he also has within his patronage a considerable number of policy advisory positions throughout the EOP and beyond into the higher reaches of the departments of state and regulatory agencies. Although the positions to be filled are too numerous, and in many cases too lowly, to warrant his personal involvement, they are nevertheless, regarded as 'political' posts and are expected to be filled by his supporters. Whilst no one would claim that the British prime minister had the same powers of appointment as those of an American president on entering office, an incumbent able to retain office for as long as Mrs Thatcher does exercise considerable patronage over a wide variety of public appointments. This prompted some to argue that she was endangering the political neutrality of the civil service.[72] Although, in the crudely party political sense, the claim that Mrs Thatcher had politicized the civil service remained unproven,[73] during her long occupancy of No.10 she was able to become personally involved in the appointment of almost the entire top two echelons of the civil service. Mrs Thatcher admits she took a close personal interest in these appointments and that 'the idea that the civil service could be insulated from a reforming zeal that would transform Britain's public and private institutions over the next decade was a pipe-dream.'[74] Whilst she had little choice over the names on the short lists she was in some cases able to select a preferred type of candidate. This would act as a signal to others in the higher ranks of the service as to the kind of candidate who could expect to receive preferment. It was not, then, simply a question of party political allegiance, the dangers of politicization were '. . . more subtle and insidious than appointments at permanent secretary level.'[75] The danger was that the traditional civil service virtues of impartiality and caution would be sacrificed as a result of the preferment of 'Thatcherite', 'can do' candidates, who enthusiastically embraced the government's policies.

In 1964, Richard Neustadt, engaging in the presidentialization debate, noted two major impediments to the British prime minister's presidentializing the system: the insistence on the present doctrines of the cabinet responsibility, and the insistence on the relative autonomy of the establishment work in the Treasury.[76] He noted that whilst the prime minister had some power of review over senior appointments, '. . . he has no independent source of advice save his own knowledge and knowledge of his ministerial associates . . .'[77] Neustadt went on to suggest that if a prime minister really wished to make himself the master of the government machine, he could do it by selective use of his own non-career people. To do this he would need to bring in a few key people who would build up networks with able and sympathetic civil servants, 'then rapidly but quickly you'd have to use Prime Ministerial authority over the posting of senior civil servants to ensure not passive subordinates but, rather, people of such temperamental affinity that your own people and they work well together easily.'[78] To some extent Mrs Thatcher did this and was able to Thatcherize, even if not exactly politicize, key positions in the civil service in the American manner. Michael Jones, reflecting on Mrs Thatcher's stewardship after the publication of her memoirs in 1993, commented:

> With Charles Powell at her elbow, she made her own foreign policy. With Alan Walters, she harried Geoffrey Howe and alienated Nigel Lawson. With Bernard Ingham, she propagated a personality cult that we in the media were happy to nurture. With Tim Bell and Gordon Reece, she burnished her image and won elections. Her mistrust of regular channels reinforced the power of these men, which surpassed that of most ministers. The Foreign Office attracted her unfailing scorn, but no department was safe. She had her own informants in the Treasury who told her of Lawson's budget plans. Powell ran his own diplomatic network. Ingham gave her advice on matters well outside his official responsibilities. Permanent secretaries who obstructed her were replaced by appointees who knew their place.[79]

Mrs Thatcher's advisory system was presidential but which presidential model did it resemble most closely? Did Mrs Thatcher seek advice from a plurality of competitive sources in the manner of FDR or did she become isolated by cronies, creatures and public relations experts in a manner reminiscent of Richard Nixon?

To answer this question a time dimension has to be taken into account. A changing pattern is discernible in the advisory system Mrs Thatcher developed during her eleven years in Downing Street. At the outset, in many respects, Mrs Thatcher's advisory system resembled that of FDR. Not only did she call upon the advice of the traditional sources of Whitehall, No.10 and Westminster, but she continued to consult the Economic Seminar established by James Callaghan, she convened brain-storming seminars, she maintained the links she had established whilst in opposition with policy think tanks, and she consulted a number of individual experts as and when required. John Vincent, in 1987, noted, 'the Prime Minister's appetite for advisers and intellectuals is the same as her appetite for anything else: intense, over-serious and insatiable.'[80] After Vincent made this judgement, however, towards the end of her long period in office, Mrs Thatcher became increasingly isolated and came to rely on a few close advisers. The most prominent of these were her Press Secretary, Bernard Ingham, and her Private Secretary, Charles Powell. As permanent civil servants neither started out as a crony or a creature, although they may have shown signs of becoming so.[81]

Mrs Thatcher's acute awareness of the importance of public relations was a match for any occupant of the Oval Office.[82] As an outsider she knew her power base was located beyond Westminster in the Tory grass roots, and for that matter, among Labour voters in the electorate at large. Public relations were more than news management, they were the key to delivering the public support which legitimized increased prime ministerial interventionism: the imperial premiership, like the imperial presidency, was founded on good PR. This dictated the need for direct communication between herself and 'her people' in order to convince them of the rightness of her policies and mobilize their support to bully the institutions impeding the realization of her agenda. James Prior, for example, asserts,

> One of the interesting features about Margaret as leader of the Opposition, and subsequently to a certain extent as Prime Minister, was the way she overcame resistance from her colleagues to her own wishes on Party policy. . . she tended to make policy very much by shooting from the hip. The reason was that she did not find it easy to get her own way round the Shadow Cabinet table, so she tended to make policy – usually of the more extreme kind – on television, or at Prime Minister's Question Time in the Commons. She was afraid of being pushed off what she wanted to do if there was much consultation with her colleagues beforehand, so she reckoned it was better to make the policy and argue about it afterwards.[83]

This was a tactic for which FDR was famous and Ronald Regan turned into an art form.[84] At election time Mrs Thatcher was advised by her own public relations team[85] and during the 1987 elections even employed her own personal campaign team to rival the official Conservative Party campaign run by Party chairman, Norman Tebbit. It would be wrong to assert that Mrs Thatcher became dependent upon, or isolated by, public relations advisers. In the 'business as usual' periods between elections, however, she did come to rely on the advice and good offices of her 'good and faithful servant', Bernard Ingham.

The almost casual manner in which Mrs Thatcher chose Bernard Ingham to be her Press Secretary[86] gave no indication of the close relation that was to develop between them or of the key and controversial role he was to play in her advisory system. Bernard Ingham spent almost as long in No.10 as Mrs Thatcher did. During that time he succeeded in centralizing control in Downing Street over the entire government information service to the extent that he became in the view of some critics, 'Minister for Information' in all but name:[87] the marketing director of Thatcher plc. Ingham effectively exploited his Downing Street position as much to provide the prime minister with inside information on departmental activities as to control and co-ordinate the public relations of the government. Robert Harris asserts, 'Ingham acquired his own network of appointees throughout Whitehall who kept him – and through him, the prime minister – well-informed of what was happening in their departments.'[88] This impressions is largely corroborated by Ingham's own description of his 'finishing school'.[89] In addition, by means of his daily unattributable lobby briefings, Ingham provided the prime minister with a channel to speak and leak to the media, enabling her indirectly to express views on dissident ministers and dissociate herself from any unwelcome policies that the cabinet might be trying to force upon her.[90] Ingham's role became sufficiently controversial to become the subject of two House of Commons debates. In the second of these in April 1986 Tam Dalyell described Ingham as '. . . no Press Secretary . . . [but] a man who is an adviser on central decisions of Government in Britain and whose power has grown exponentially . . . with the years during which he has occupied the office'.[91] Dalyell went on to claim that Ingham was '. . . with the arguable exception of Sir Robert Armstrong (Cabinet Secretary) . . . the most important man making decisions in British politics.'[92] Ingham was so powerful, indeed, that for him to describe a minister as 'semi-detached' was the kiss of death.[93]

A civil servant of a more orthodox kind than Bernard Ingham to have a prominent and controversial place in Mrs Thatcher's advisory system, was Charles Powell. In 1984 Powell joined Mrs Thatcher's Private Office. He was a diplomat from the Foreign Office on temporary attachment to No.10, whose job it was to advise the prime minister on foreign affairs. Powell quickly assumed a position of all-round adviser and prime ministerial favourite. The almost unlimited scope of his brief, coupled with the exclusive relationship that developed between him and Mrs Thatcher soon aroused criticism and controversy.[94] Hugo Young claims that Powell '. . . manned a barrier between Downing Street and the Foreign Office with an assiduity, many felt, that had contributed to the fateful divide between Mrs Thatcher and Sir Geoffrey Howe.'[95]

By the time Richard Nixon resigned from the presidency he had become cut off from the usual sources of advice and had come to rely exclusively on the counsel of members of his immediate family, his crony, Bebe Rebozzo, and his press spokesman, Ronald Ziegler. Nixon, it seemed, had succumbed to the temptation of the holders of great office. He had allowed favourites and good news bearers to insulate him from unwelcome political truths which should have been reaching him in the centre of the advisory wheel. Margaret Thatcher appears to have succumbed to the same temptation. Nigel Lawson asserts that, whilst in the short term Mrs Thatcher had weathered the storm of the Westland affair, its long term effects were wholly adverse. 'The lesson Margaret took from it was that her colleagues were troublesome and her courtiers were loyal. From then on she began to distance herself even from those Cabinet colleagues who had been closest to her – certainly those who had minds of their own – and to retreat to the Number 10 bunker, where the leading figures were Charles Powell and Bernard Ingham.'[96] Lawson notes that the prime minister no longer read newspapers, relying instead on Ingham's daily press summary, and he complains that Charles Powell '. . . never saw it as his role to question her prejudices, merely to refine the language in which they were expressed.'[97] In the end they contributed to the development of a bunker mentality in No.10. When faced with the political crisis of the Chancellor's resignation, Mrs Thatcher did not consult her party colleagues or her deputy, Sir Geoffrey Howe, but turned instead for advice to her two favourites, Ingham and Powell. Ranelagh describes that as '. . . yet another sign that Thatcher was isolated in power, unable to confide in her Ministers and depending for personal support and advice on her people, who were her appointees.'[98] This was a pattern that was repeated when Michael Heseltine finally challenged her leadership in 1990. Lawson notes that:

> Margaret, in her last days at No.10, was evidently bitterly lamenting how the Party had turned against her. 'Don't worry about, them Prime Minister' he [Ingham] claimed to have told her, 'we're right behind you'. That his perspective could be so distorted as to say this in the final stages in a leadership election in which it was the colleagues (them) who had the voting power, and the courtiers, on whose behalf he spoke, who had none, is in its way even more revealing.[99]

Mrs Thatcher's advisory system at the outset could be described as reminiscent of FRD but by the time she left Downing Street it had come to resemble the system of Richard Nixon. (Although it is important to stress that this is not to suggest that Mrs Thatcher's aides behaved illegally as had been the case with those of Nixon in respect of Watergate.)

According to Young:

> . . . that was its great weakness: its signal difference from the world
> the leader had created in her early years in Downing Street. Then she
> had devoted close attention to the world beyond her personal frontier,
> especially the world of the Commons' tea-room and the different
> pulses of the party detectable within it. She never forgot that politics
> was an insecure profession, and leadership sometimes the least secure
> of all political positions. But now, by the time true insecurity stared
> her in the face, she had grown more reckless, or at least less
> sensitive. She became less diligent with the party as she became more
> preoccupied with the world and her place in it. By mid-1990 she was
> living for much of the time in a bunker of the mind, with a small
> band of over-familiar figures posted at the gates, who saw their
> function as keeping the world at bay rather than admitting the breezes
> of alarm and dissent into the ante chambers of their mistress.[100]

Informed opinion seeking to evaluate Mrs Thatcher's stewardship has
frequently drawn attention to her 'style'.[101] John Greenaway for instance
asserts, 'Mrs Thatcher's domineering personality, together with her strong
strategic sense and firm opinions, ensured that her Governments had an
aura of presidentialism about them.'[102] This conveys the impression that
Mrs Thatcher dominated the government in appearance only, behaving
presidentially, whilst fundamentally upholding the constitutional
conventions of cabinet government. Hennessy, however, notes that 'ours
is a system without maps. It is built on convention, precedent, procedure,
not on a set of written constitutional principles . . . '[103] In such a system
there comes a point at which style becomes substance. Mrs Thatcher, by
behaving in a presidential way, acting like a singular executive, by-passing
the collective decision-making procedures of the cabinet, set precedents
which could be transformed into conventions of the constitution in the
future. Martin Burch asserts that 'overall under Thatcher . . . what
emerged was a distinct move towards a more singular style of executive
government'[104]: presidential government by any other name. That Mrs
Thatcher was able to conduct her government in an interventionist
presidential manner may be partly attributed to her forceful personality but
it would not have been possible had she not advanced the process of
presidentialization that was already apparent in the prime ministerial
advisory system.

Mrs Thatcher was an outsider. She behaved presidentially in a system
that was not presidential. Soon after the 1987 election Mrs Thatcher
claimed 'I think I have become a bit of an institution'.[105] David Willetts,

evaluating the role of the CPRS as an antidote to orthodoxy, asserted: 'institutional innovations at the centre may have an inherently short life. The grit in the machine is worn smooth.'[106] For a while Mrs Thatcher and her people introduced some new grit into the machine but eventually the system grinds down or rejects foreign bodies. After eleven years in power this was Mrs Thatcher's fate. The very personal nature of her triumphal election victories reinforced a view that she could dispense with the niceties of cabinet government. But in Britain the chief executive must never forget that her position depends not only on her electoral appeal but also on the support of a majority in the House of Commons, (although these two are of course connected), and this needs to be nurtured by the leader and mediated by leading members of the party in the cabinet. Mrs Thatcher, listening only to her personal staff, ignored this at her peril.

In 1990 Mrs Thatcher lost the confidence of her Parliamentary party. She came to be seen as an electoral liability, and was therefore, pushed out. Public policy failure contributed to her downfall.[107] Mrs Thatcher's interventionist conduct of government meant that public policy failure translated into prime ministerial policy failure, in a manner that reminds us of the personal responsibility for the executive borne by an American president. The prime minister had constructed a personal advisory system to pursue a personal policy agenda. This changed policy failure from being a matter of collective responsibility of the cabinet to one of individual responsibility of the presidentialized premiership.

Notes

1. Ranelagh, John, *Thatcher's People* (London: Fontana, 1992) p. 24.
2. Baker, Kenneth, 'The Last Days' *Sunday Times* 24 October, 1993, p. 6.3.
3. See Lawson, Nigel, *The View from Number Eleven* (London: Bantum Press, 1992) pp. 1062–4.
4. See Coleman, Terry, 'Downwardly mobile with Sir Alan Walters' *Independent* 30 July, 1990, p. 18. See also Ridley, Nicolas, *My Style of Government* (London: Hutchinson, 1991) p. 216.
5. Young, Hugo, *One of Us* final edn (London: Pan Books, 1993) p. 562.
6. For the full text of Heseltine's statement see *The Times* 10 January, 1986 p. 2. For comment see Hennessy, Peter, 'Why Mr Heseltine finally snapped' ibid., p. 10.
7. Brittan accepted individual ministerial responsibility for the action of one of his department's press officers, Colette Bowes. The latter had leaked to the press the contents of a confidential letter between

the Solicitor General and Heseltine, discrediting the latter.

8. Jones, Bill, 'The Thatcher Style' (Politics Association Resource Bank, 1989) p. 18. For full discussion of the Westland Affair and some of its possible constitutional implications see Pyper, Robert, 'The Westland Affair' in Robins, Lynton, ed. *Topics in British Politics* (London: Politics Association, 1987) pp. 20–37.

9. Harris, Robert, *Good and Faithful Servant* (London: Faber, 1990) p. 136.

10. Harris, Robert, op.cit., see for example, p. 92, p. 144 and p. 149.

11. Hennessy, Peter, *Whitehall* (London: Fontana, 1990) p. 652. Hennessy notes that the Foreign Secretary, Francis Pym '. . . took it badly and saw it as direct prime ministerial interference in Foreign Office matters.' Ibid. See also Rightie, Rosemary, 'Thatcher's diplomat at No.10' *Sunday Times* 24 October, 1982 p. 11.

12. For example, the CPS, the Adam Smith Institute, the Conservative Philosophy Group. See for instance Stothard, Peter, 'Who thinks for Mrs Thatcher' *The Times* 31 January, 1983 p. 10 and Kavanagh, Dennis, *Thatcherism and British Politics the End of Consensus?* (Oxford: University Press, 1987) pp. 89–98.

13. See Lawson, op.cit., pp. 467–8.

14. For text of speech see *The Times* 14 November, 1990 p. 3.

15. Cit. Young, op.cit., p. 579.

16. Young described some of the briefings which preceded the Madrid Summit in 1990, and notes that Mrs Thatcher held a pre summit meeting '. . . which included the entire advisory staff serving in Downing Street . . . outsiders like Alan Walters . . . and anyone else who might make a contribution to the question of what she should say in Madrid.' He goes on the assert 'never before had she called such a wide group of advisers together, and one in which as if to emphasise her embattled position *vis-a-vis* her ministerial colleagues, no other politician was present.' Young, op.cit., p. 557.

17. See for example, 'Denting the Contraption' *Economist* 10 March, 1984 p. 20 and 'Whitehall Fears on Think Tank' *Guardian* 17 June, 1983, p. 26.

18. Ranelagh, op.cit., p. 20, see also p. 158.

19. Hennessy, *Whitehall* op.cit., p. 632.

20. Parliamentary Secretary at the Ministry of Pensions 1961–4; Secretary of State for Education 1970–4.

21. Thatcher, Margaret, *The Downing Street Years* (London: HarperCollins, 1993) p. 129.

22. See Ranelagh, op.cit., p. 213 and Young, op.cit., p. 71 and p. 154. Mrs Thatcher's outsider status and attitudes to the Establishment are reminiscent of those of presidents Nixon and Carter, both of whom assumed the role of the outsider come to Washington to sort out the failures of the governing elite. See, Foley, Michael, *The Rise of the British Presidency* (Manchester: University Press, 1993).

23. Jenkins, Simon, 'Judging the Thatcher decade' *Sunday Times* Colour Supp. 30 April, 1989 pp. 22–35, p. 25.

24. Young, op.cit., p. 155.

25. See Ranelagh, op.cit., p. 213. Such views offer parallels with the kind of suspicion with which Richard Nixon and his aides viewed the federal bureaucracy. See Cronin, Thomas, 'The Swelling Presidency' in Bach, Stanley and Sulzner, George, T., eds *Perspectives on the Presidency* (New York: D.C. Heath, 1974) p. 185.

26. Sir Douglas Wass Permanent Secretary of the Treasury since 1974 was a known Keynesian.

27. 'One of us' was a designation applied by Mrs Thatcher herself to '. . . the politicians and other advisers on whom she felt she could rely. Collectively those graced with the privilege of belonging formed a cadre who, as she saw it, would change the face of the Conservative Party and launch the recovery of Britain.' Young, op.cit., p. ix. Young notes that of the probable cabinet only two members Keith Joseph and Norman St. John Stevas had voted for her in the secret ballot for the leadership election. Ibid., p. 138.

28. Young, op.cit., p. 154.

29. Sir Douglas Wass was marginalized and a new chief economic adviser to the Treasury, Terence Burns was appointed from entirely outside the Whitehall world. See Young, op.cit., pp. 156–7. Young notes that 'Treasury men more malleable than Wass began to be treated more seriously than him.'

30. Hoskyns had founded his own computer company which had expanded into the Hoskyns group, of which he was the chairman and manager director. A member of the CPS, he had been introduced to Mrs Thatcher by Sir Keith Joseph. He was well-know for his iconoclastic views about the civil service and his insensitivity to Whitehall was reminiscent of that of Thomas Balogh in the 1960s. (See above, chapter four.)

31. See Hennessy, *Whitehall* op.cit., p. 628.

32. Hennessy, ibid., p. 640. For a full account of the activities of the Efficiency Unit during and after Rayner's time, see pp. 589–627.

33. Thatcher, op.cit., p. 46.

34. Young, op.cit., p. 230.

35. Walters was given an office in No.10, that crucial prerequisite of access, but he did not become part of the Policy Unit.

36. Sir John Hoskyns and his deputy Norman Straus had both been members of the CPS, for example.

37. Sherman was a journalist, a former communist, and the first director of the CPS. Like Hoskyns, Sherman was well-known for his scepticism regarding the quality of Whitehall advice.

38. See Lawson, op.cit., p. 680 and p. 384.

39. 'Thatcher Style Wars' *Economist* 18 January, 1986, p. 13.

40. Something Bernard Donoughue said he had strongly resisted doing. Lord Donoughue, interview, 19 May, 1994. For a full discussion of Mrs Thatcher's Policy Unit see Willetts, David, 'The role of the Prime Minister's Policy Unit' *Public Administration* Vol.65, Winter 1987 pp. 443–54.

41. Although Ingham had been a provincial journalist and newspaper editor first and civil servant second, entering Whitehall in 1967 at the age of thirty-five. For details of Ingham's appointment see Ingham, *Kill the Messenger* (London: HarperCollins, 1991) pp. 1–9.

42. 'Thatcher Style Wars' *Economist* op.cit., p. 11.

43. Vincent, John, 'The Thatcher Governments 1979–1987' in Hennessy, Peter and Seldon, Anthony, eds *Ruling Performance* (Oxford: Blackwell, 1987) p. 279.

44. Thatcher, op.cit.,p. 26.

45. Secretary of State for Defence 1979–81; Leader of the House of Commons 1981–2; Secretary of State for Foreign and Commonwealth Affairs 1982–3.

46. Pym, Francis, *The Politics of Consent* (London: Hamish Hamilton, 1984) p. 17.

47. For an account of Mrs Thatcher's early relations with the CPRS see Hennessy, *Whitehall* op.cit., pp. 640–2.

48. Robert Young, on secondment from Vickers, and David Pascall, on secondment from British Petroleum, transferred from the CPRS to the Policy Unit.

49. See, for example, Norton-Taylor, Richard, 'Whitehall fears on Think Tank' *Guardian* 17 June, 1983 p. 26; 'Thatcher strengthens personal "think tank"' *The Times* 2 July, 1983 p. 2. For academic analysis see Blackstone, Tessa and Plowden, William, *Inside the Think Tank* (London: Heinemann, 1988) pp. 182–4, Hennessy, Peter 'The Firework that Fizzled' *New Society* 3 January, 1985 pp.

10–12.

50. See Thatcher, op.cit., p. 277 and p. 30.
51. Hennessy, *Whitehall* op.cit., p. 658.
52. See Burch, Martin, 'Prime Minister and Cabinet: from Thatcher to Major' *Talking Politics* Vol.7, No.1, Autumn 1994 pp. 27–33, p. 28.
53. Jenkins, Peter, *The Thatcher Revolution* (London: Cape, 1987) p. 184.
54. Sampson, Anthony, *The Essential Anatomy of Britain* (London: Hodder & Stoughton, 1992) p. 20.
55. 'Denting the contraption' *Economist* op.cit., p. 20.
56. Harris, *Thatcher* op.cit., p. 132.
57. Pym, op.cit., p. 17.
58. Ibid., p. 18.
59. Leader of the House of Commons and Minister for Arts 1979–81.
60. St John-Stevas, Norman, 'Prime Ministers rise and fall but the Cabinet abides' *Telegraph* 7 August, 1986 p. 16.
61. Secretary of State for Employment 1979–81; Secretary of State for Northern Ireland 1981–4.
62. Prior, James, *A Balance of Power* (London: Hamish Hamilton, 1986) p. 133, see also p. 117.
63. Pym, op.cit., pp. 16–17.
64. Naughtie, James, 'Thatcher throws a spanner in the political works' *Scotsman* 6 April, 1987 p. 11 op.cit., p. 11.
65. 'Help for No.10' leading article *Scotsman* 6 April, 1984 p. 10.
66. Jenkins, Simon, op.cit., p. 29.
67. For example, Sir John Hoskyns; Sir Alfred Sherman; Ferdinand Mount; Sir Alan Walters; Sir David Wolfson; David Young.
68. David Young became Lord Young of Graffham in 1984.
69. Smith, Joan, 'Lord Young' *Independent* Magazine 23 June, 1990, p. 54.
70. Ibid.
71. Cit. ibid.
72. See Hennessy, *Whitehall* op.cit., pp. 635–41 see also Young, Hugo, 'Purging the devil's advocates' *Sunday Times* 24 October, 1982 p. 11.
73. See Hennessy *Whitehall* op.cit., p. 635.
74. Thatcher, op.cit., p. 48 see also p. 46.
75. Bancroft, cit. Hennessy, *Whitehall* op.cit., p. 638.
76. Neustadt, Richard, E., '10 Downing Street' in King, Anthony, ed. *The British Prime Minister* 2nd edn (London: Macmillan, 1985) pp. 141–54, p. 150.

77. Ibid.
78. Ibid., p. 151.
79. Jones, 'Thatcher – the renegade at war behind enemy lines' *Sunday Times* Review 17 October, 1993 p. 6.
80. Vincent, op.cit., p. 288.
81. In Ingham's case the conversion to Thatcherism had occurred before exposure to the lady herself. See Ingham, *Kill the Messenger* op.cit., pp. 151–4. Powell, on the other hand, went native during his time in No.10. According to Ranelagh, Powell's conversion was so complete he was reported to have turned down an ambassadorship in order to stay on with Mrs Thatcher in No.10. See Ranelagh, op.cit., p. 11.
82. See Cockerell, Michael, Hennessy, Peter and Walker, David, *Sources Close to the Prime Minister* (London: Macmillan, 1984).
83. Prior., op.cit., p. 107.
84. See Reagan, Ronald, *An American Life* (London: Hutchinson, 1990) p. 234.
85. Headed by Tim Bell and Gordon Reece.
86. See Ingham, op.cit., pp. 1–9.
87. See 'Off the Record, the voice behind the view from No.10' *The Times* 14 January, 1983 p. 10.
88. Harris, Robert, op.cit., p. 170.
89. See Ingham, op.cit., pp. 370–1.
90. See Harris, Robert, op.cit., p. 150 and 'Profile of Bernard Ingham' *Independent* op.cit.
91. Cit. Harris ibid., p. 140.
92. Ibid.
93. A description applied by Ingham to John Biffen, Leader of the House of Commons, at a lobby briefing on 10 May 1986. Biffen was sacked shortly afterwards.
94. See Lawson, op.cit., p. 680.
95. Young, op.cit., p. 584.
96. Lawson, op.cit., p. 680.
97. Ibid., p. 680.
98. Ranelagh, op.cit., p. 281. By March 1990 Alan Clark notes that 'a number of "heavy" backbenchers of the "Centre" of the Party have let it be known that her "Decision-making Circle" should be widened, that they are uneasy about the "privileged access" enjoyed by "certain key and unelected advisors."' Clark, Alan, *Diaries* (London: Phoenix, 1993) p. 289.
99. Lawson, op.cit., pp. 467–8.
100. Young, op.cit., pp. 583–4.

101. See, for example, Hennessy, *Whitehall* op.cit., p. 317 and Kavanagh, Dennis, 'Prime Ministerial Power Revisited' *Social Studies Review* March, 1991 pp. 131–5, p. 135 and *Economist* 'Thatcher's style wars' op.cit.
102. Greenaway, John, 'All Change at the Top?' *Social Studies Review* March 1991 pp. 136–40, p. 136.
103. Hennessy, 'How much room at the top?' op.cit., p. 25.
104. Burch, 'Prime Minister and Cabinet Thatcher to Major' op.cit., p. 29.
105. Cit Hennessy, *Whitehall* op.cit., p. 628.
106. Willetts, op.cit., p. 445.
107. Particularly in respect of Europe and the Poll Tax.

9   Conclusion

> Liberties can be taken with a constitution written in invisible ink, within the rules of law and commonsense, without apoplectic consequences[1]

> The British constitution has long been a source of fascination to political scientists and indifference to everyone else . . . The machinery is notoriously short on brakes: the checks and balances which are a feature of written constitutions. The symptoms of trouble are an accident-prone cabinet [and] leaks and rumblings of non-consultation from government ministers . . . [2]

At least since James I, the struggle for influence has been continuous and so has the struggle to define legitimate sources of influence. The politics of advice thus forms part of the continuous dialogue of government. In America the constitutional separation of powers requires that it is a dialogue conducted between the legislative and executive branch of government, with the judicial branch occasionally being called upon to adjudicate between the two. In Britain, since the nineteenth century, a secret constitutional separation of powers has existed between the permanent government in Whitehall and the transitory government from Westminster.[3] In Britain, therefore, it is a dialogue conducted within the executive branch itself.

The key question in this debate is, on whose advice should executive power be exercised? It is a question that is all the more keenly contested because on it the written constitution in both countries remains silent. From time to time the dialogue erupts into a public argument.[4] Public controversy is usually taken as an indication that previously accepted practices are no longer being observed. An unsettled period then ensues in which both sides claim legitimacy of constitutional precedent. When such controversy subsides, and the dialogue about advice continues, but no longer tops the political agenda, then it can be assumed that a new, provisional constitutional settlement has been reached.

The provisional nature of each phase of the institutionalized separation of powers ensures that such settlements can only be temporary. The absence of written constitutional rules about advice has enabled new generations of political actors to reach new accommodation on the matter.

This should not be regarded as a problem, that is, a danger to constitutional government. It forms part of the normal business of constitutional politics which attempts to reach a balance between the political need for new sources of advice and policy initiatives, and the constitutional need for accountability. The outcome of this process has been continuously mutating executive advisory systems, in which advice can be seen as a mechanism for restoring equilibrium between the increasing political expectations placed upon the executive and the formally static constitutional powers. In both Britain and America the executive has been repeatedly forced to stretch, bend and circumvent the constitution in order to respond to political expectations.

In America in 1828 the president was transformed from the oligarch of the oligarchies into the tribune of the people. This re-opened questions about advice to the executive that the Founding Fathers thought they had settled, implicitly at least, at Philadelphia in 1787. Popular support which secured the presidency for Andrew Jackson in 1828, had by the 1930s placed the president in the intolerable position of having to satisfy political expectations that far outweighed his constitutional powers. It was President Franklyn D. Roosevelt who was eventually able to convince Congress of the need for reform and innovation in the presidential advisory system to help bridge this gap. Congress responded by passing the 1939 Reorganization Act which established the Executive Office of the President (EOP), designed to provide the chief executive with additional policy advice. The White House Office (WHO), a sub-division of the EOP, was created to provide the president with institutionalized personal political support. The president was expected to receive advice from a plurality of sources. The EOP and the WHO were intended to facilitate this process; they were not expected to become an insulating layer interposed between the president and the wider policy-making community. Advisory systems, however, continuously mutate and during the presidency of Richard Nixon the potential for presidential isolation implicit in the 1939 arrangements was realized. This gave rise to a 'corrupted' model of the presidential advisory system in which the president appeared to have become a captive of his cronies and creatures who manned WHO barricades against the traditional sources of public policy advice.

Presidentialization of the American political system eventually led to the presidentialization of American government: presidents were compelled to seek institutional change and push the constitution to its limits in order to try to meet their burgeoning responsibilities. A similar pattern can be discerned in Britain. Universal adult suffrage, two world wars and a series of economic crises, combined to place increasing demands on the government, and, as in America, the executive branch acquired the lion's share of new responsibilities. Britain in contrast to America, has a collective executive, the cabinet. A collective executive, whilst appearing to offer the advantage of sharing the growing burden of executive responsibilities among several individuals, had the disadvantage of being less well suited to respond to the modern demands for instant government. Under the influence of the media, the electorate was coming to expect government to involve rapid responses from an identifiable, individual decision-maker. In Britain the executive branch as a whole did acquire new powers in the form of Acts of Parliament enabling government departments to become increasingly interventionist. It was the prime minister, however, at the head of the executive, who carried the increased responsibilities in electoral terms, but acquired no formal change in constitutional power, and little by way of increased institutional support, with which to meet them.[5] By the time Harold Wilson was elected in 1964, the growing dominance of the prime minister in the government combined with the advent of tele-politics, helped to substantiate claims that British politics had become presidentialized. In the eyes of the constitution, government was a collective responsibility of the cabinet; in the eyes of the electorate it had become the personal responsibility of the prime minister.

If prime ministers were to be held responsible for the winning and losing of general elections, they needed to appear to dominate their government. In 1964, prime ministers were expected to be almost entirely dependent on the advice of their cabinet. The accepted constitutional position regarding advice to the prime minister being that the prime minister, at the top of a hierarchical advisory system, received policy and political advice from their cabinet colleagues, who in turn were advised by their departmental civil servants. Whitehall acted as a filter for advice from experts, interest groups and any other outside sources. Prime ministers, then, needed alternative sources of advice, advice, that is, from sources other than those mediated by their cabinet colleagues, to enable them to monitor all major aspects of government and to compete on an equal footing with ministers, who were themselves briefed and supported by their departmental civil servants.[6] It also had to be 'their' advice, that is, advice sensitive to the prime minister's political fortunes in the new presidentialized circumstances.

Harold Wilson attempted to change the advisory system by appointing a number of personal political aides. Advice being a constitutional matter, this was for the prime minister to introduce constitutional change unilaterally. Wilson's innovations were, therefore, resisted by those having a particular view of constitutional propriety and a vested interest in the existing arrangements: senior policy advisers in the civil service and senior cabinet ministers. The largely unwritten nature of the British constitution means that the constitutionality of political behaviour is at least partly determined by the opinion of contemporary political actors.

Inevitably, by provoking senior members of both the permanent government and the government for the time being, Harold Wilson's strategies aroused much controversy and many claims that constitutional propriety had not been observed. Wilson to some extent retreated into the arms of traditional policy advisers from the civil service. They in turn attempted to meet him halfway by responding to the prime minister's new needs. They recognized that political reality compelled the prime minister to demand advice from sources other than the cabinet, and therefore tried to safeguard the voice of Whitehall by collaborating with the prime minister. The Cabinet Secretary and the No.10 Private Office, attempted to improve the briefing service offered by themselves in the hope of countering the influence of 'kitchen cabinets' of unofficial advisers and favourites. If the prime minister was provided with a *parallel*[7] source of advice he would not resort to an *alternative*[8] advisory system. This attempt at accommodation by the civil service, whilst increasing the sources of advice available, failed to provide the kind of personal political advice that prime ministers now required. Wilson, therefore, continued to maintain a Political Office of unofficial, partisan advisers and gave recognition to the growing influence of the media in prime ministerial politics by increasing the size and partisan nature of the No.10 Press Office.

These changes were consolidated under Edward Heath. Initially Heath appeared to reject the advisory strategies of his predecessor. He established the Central Policy Review Staff (CPRS), ostensibly to restore the cabinet to its traditional constitutional place in the prime ministerial advisory system. However, Heath, like Wilson, seemed to be forced by political expectations into a presidential style of policy making in which the collective responsibility of the cabinet became the dignified facade behind which the efficient workings of prime ministerial power was exercised. The new advisory system that was evolving during Harold Wilson's premiership became more firmly established and the CPRS, instead of serving to underpin the collective executive, became the instrument of the man in No.10. Whilst the cabinet failed to regain its former position, the senior policy-makers of the civil service did go some way towards reclaiming theirs.

By the mid 1970s there were some clear signs that, at least in respect of advice, the premiership was becoming presidentialized. A new pattern was emerging in which advice to the prime minister arose from a plurality of sources, only one of which was the cabinet, but over all of which the civil service was struggling to retain a monopoly. The increased orientation of the Cabinet Office towards serving the prime minister and the establishment of the CPRS offer some parallels with the EOP, and the

Political Office created by Wilson, and continued by Heath, was a modest step in the direction of providing the prime minister with the kind of personal political advice and support American presidents receive from the WHO.[9]

This already discernible presidentialization of the advisory system was further advanced when Harold Wilson returned to office in 1974. A four year period in opposition, exposed to party and electoral politics and cut off from the seductive influence of Whitehall, had prompted Wilson to reappraise his position. He entered office in 1974 prepared for a more frontal assault on the old constitutional settlement. This time he succeeded in avoiding the kind of controversy that his advisory system had provoked in the 1960s by institutionalizing alternative advisory support in the form of the Prime Minister's Policy Unit.

Under Wilson's successor the presidentialization process marked time. James Callaghan, was less interested in the mechanics of the advisory system. He retained the system-in-place which he had inherited from Wilson, but the sea change that was then taking place in economic policy from Keynesianism to monetarism, prompted him to establish a new advisory body, the Economic Seminar. This was an innovation that provoked no controversy at the time since its membership included the most senior mandarins and its existence was unknown to most cabinet ministers.

By the time Mrs Thatcher entered office the prime ministerial advisory system was considerably more complex than the traditional hierarchical model that had been recognized as constitutionally legitimate in 1964. By 1979 the prime minister was at the centre of an advisory network in which the cabinet was only one among many sources of advice the prime minister could call upon. The traditional distinction between parallel sources of advice (constitutionally legitimate), and alternative sources of advice (constitutionally dubious), was becoming less clear. The presidentialization of the advisory system that had been continuous, if spasmodic, since 1964, was considerably advanced during Mrs Thatcher's long period in Downing Street. Mrs Thatcher paid little regard to the traditional sensitivities of Whitehall and Westminster about advice. She directly consulted experts, convened *ad hoc* seminars, consorted with outside policy think tanks, expanded her personal staff in No.10 and in some instances replaced government by cabinet and cabinet committees with government by informal prime ministerial groups.

By 1990 the traditional hierarchical model of the British prime ministerial advisory system showed clear signs of convergence with the American presidential model established during the incumbency of FDR. The evolution that had taken place in the advisory system to reconcile the growing incompatibility between the constitutional power and political role of the prime minister, resembled the changes that had taken place in America during and since the 1930s. By the end of Mrs Thatcher's period in office, however, there were also some signs that the new prime ministerial advisory system was, like its American counterpart, vulnerable to the weakness of isolating the person with the power to make public policy decisions from exposure to legitimate sources of policy advice.

The thesis of this book has been that the presidentialization of electoral politics in Britain has brought in its wake a presidentialization of Britain's governing institutions, specifically there has been a presidentialization of the premiership in respect of advice. An examination of the advisory systems of four prime ministers, whilst demonstrating a great deal of flexibility in these matters, also pointed to the existence of constitutional limits. Former ministers of both Wilson's and Thatcher's cabinets typically articulated their complaints about their respective prime minister's advisory systems in constitutional terms. In doing so they were clearly appealing to shared ideas about accepted constitutional norms about advice. Cabinet government is constructed on a set of tacit agreements. If members of the cabinet are to be bound by collective responsibility they have a strong claim to be involved in the policy discussion and decision-making process. Loyal execution of government decisions bestows on the civil service the right to be consulted on the formulation of policy.[10] The implication of these tacit agreements is that ministers and mandarins claim a constitutional right to advise the prime minister.

According to Kevin Sharpe, '. . . ideas are often asserted at the very moments when they are being undermined in practice.'[11] The same, perhaps, can be said of constitutional rules. The hue and cry raised when prime ministers fail to observe the constitutional rules about advice confirms not only the existence of those rules but signals the start of a period of constitutional change during which prime ministers 'pummel the constitutional modelling clay'[12] to accommodate a shift in political expectations. New advisory bodies emerge and a process of socialization and colonization by the traditional advisers of Whitehall begins. This process, whilst eventually bestowing constitutional legitimacy on new advisory bodies, at the same time reduces their usefulness. Alternative advice becomes domesticated. It attracts and develops vested interests and becomes bureaucratized. This compels the next radical tenant of No.10 to be 'unconstitutional' in the name of political necessity, to seek alternative advice and once again initiate a process of constitutional change. Constitutional rules about advice to the executive do exist, but they are not fixed. It is this flexibility that has permitted constitutional change to keep pace with political change.

The presidentialization of electoral politics in Britain has been accompanied by a presidentialization of the premiership in respect of advice. A degree of convergence between the prime ministerial advisory system with the American presidential model is observable. Although individuals, in particular Harold Wilson and Margaret Thatcher, accelerated the process, no reverse took place under either Edward Heath or James Callaghan. Indeed, looking forward briefly to John Major, Martin Burch claims, 'overall under Major there has been a move to a more collegiate . . . executive. . . '[13] Burch also notes, however, that 'Many of the changes brought in under her [Mrs Thatcher] have survived, but they have been regularized and drawn more into the formal structure.'[14] This suggests that the presidentialization of the prime ministerial advisory system has been a change prompted by long term changes in the political system, specifically the presidentialization of electoral politics, rather than a process dependent upon particular office holders. Personalities have had an impact only on the pace at which change has taken place.

Some convergence has taken place between the advisory systems of Britain and America, but it is important to note that some constitutional and institutional differences exist which, at present, limit the presidentialization process in Britain. Despite the presidentialization of electoral politics, the formal constitutional position of the prime minister remains unchanged. The British prime minister is not supposed to be a singular executive assisted by a purely advisory cabinet, but the head of a collective executive in which the cabinet share executive responsibility. This formal constitutional position on its own would not be an insurmountable barrier. The diaries of former cabinet ministers and the memoirs of prime ministers indicate that if classic cabinet government, in which policy is the outcome of collective discussion and collective decisions, ever existed, it does so no longer. The formal constitutional position, however, is buttressed by institutional factors which continue to thwart full-scale presidentialization. The British party system, and the manner in which prime ministers are chosen, ensure that cabinet ministers remains a force to be reckoned with.

Whilst there has been an increasing tendency for British party leaders to 'capture' their political party and stamp their own authority on it in the manner of American presidents,[15] British parties are not in the state of decomposition noted in respect of American national parties. To retain the party leadership prime ministers must appear to be electoral assets. This indeed has been an impetus to the presidentialization of the advisory system, but, unlike American presidents, British prime ministers are not directly elected. Prime ministers owe their position to the fact that they are supported by a majority of members of the House of Commons. This is a constituency that needs to be nursed, a process in which the British cabinet plays its part. An American president is assisted by a cabinet composed predominantly of political unknowns who owe their position almost entirely to the president's favour. Members of a British cabinet depend on the prime minister's patronage for their jobs but it is always mutual, a two way relationship. Prime ministers face around the cabinet table the barons of their party who mediate the votes of the majority in Parliament which are an essential basis of the prime minister's position. Mrs Thatcher's demise can be seen as a testament to the ambiguity of presidentialization. This relationship of inter-dependence is not the only significant difference between the two systems. Unlike American presidents, who in effect create a presidential wing often seeming to share little more than a name with the Congressional party, prime ministers share a close working relationship with their party colleagues. It is a relationship which has developed over a period of years in which they have climbed to the top of the governmental and party ladder together. It is important, therefore, not to exaggerate the extent to which divergence of interests may exist between a prime minister and his or her party and its leaders in the cabinet.

A time dimension also has to be considered in respect of differences in the manner of electing presidents and prime ministers. Two months elapse between the election of an American president and the day he takes over executive power. This long hand-over period allows the president's personal political aides to exercise a good deal of power. Stephen Benn asserts that 'in the absence of any formal authority during this period the effective political power of the President-elect is transmitted through his staff. This pattern, once established, has in recent times proved to be a dominant if not decisive influence on the future structure of decision-making in that Presidency.'[16] There were hints that this kind of pattern was beginning to develop before Mrs Thatcher took office. According to Ranelagh, 'by the time she became Prime Minister in 1979, Thatcher people (as opposed to Ministers) had become absolutely central to the implementation of Thatcherism.'[17] However, whilst some 'Thatcher people' from the policy think tanks subsequently received positions in Downing Street they remained few in number. More importantly, the British electoral system places a newly elected prime minister immediately in Whitehall's embrace and this limits the opportunity for aides to acquire the kind of powerful brokerage positions assumed by the aides of a president-elect.

Not only does the way in which a prime minister is elected ensure that cabinet members still count because they mediate the political support of their party's backbenchers in Parliament, cabinet ministers also help to deliver the cooperation of the civil servants in the Whitehall departments. Whitehall itself represents a powerful barrier to further presidentialization of the advisory system if, as seems likely, it would result in a weakening of Whitehall's monopoly over public policy advice. British prime ministers, in contrast to American presidents, exercise only limited patronage over the civil service. Even in the case of Mrs Thatcher the debate about politicization remains inconclusive. That it arose at all was due partly to the fact that she succeeded in retaining office for such a long period. British civil servants owe loyalty to which-ever government has been elected, they owe no fealty to any particular occupant of No.10. The Whig view of British political history is the long story of liberty-loving Englishmen being obliged to teach foreign kings a lesson in English constitutionalism. Whitehall has become the custodian of this Whig tradition and perpetuates the motif by instructing modern prime ministers and their advisers on the limits of presidentialization. Cabinet government, underpinned by the convention of collective responsibility, has given ministers and officials a mutual interest in this process. Neustadt notes that '. . . the great boon in the Cabinet system for the civil servant is that through his minister, who needs his advice, it secures for him a voice in the decisions he must carry out.'[18] Collective responsibility increases the likelihood that ministers, excluded from the discussion and decision-making process, will make a public fuss when they bear public responsibility for unpopular policies which they have not themselves made. Ministers, defending their own constitutional rights, thereby also defend those of their Whitehall policy advisers, whose anonymity requires public silence in such matters. Despite the inclusion of greater numbers of outsiders in the advisory network, Whitehall, by a process of infiltration (eg. CPRS; Policy Unit), isolation (Balogh), condemnation (Williams; Walters) and accommodation (William Armstrong; Economic Seminar; Parsons; Ingham; Powell; and the greater orientations of the Cabinet Secretary and Secretariat towards serving the prime minister), has succeeded in giving a good account of itself in the struggle.

It is not by chance that advice to the executive becomes of both political and constitutional significance when a radical prime minister enters office. In Britain, the civil service assumes a monopoly over advice on which the public policy it will have to administer is based. The civil service, however, in the late twentieth century, is still according to the Fulton Report, '. . . fundamentally the product of the nineteenth-century philosophy of the Northcote-Trevelyan Report'. Northcote-Trevelyan[19] could, by 1854, understand the implications of 1832: it was only the first step into the democratic age, others would surely follow. Like the Founding Fathers in 1787, they wanted to avoid rule by either the ignorant mass or rule by a caesar. Their answer was to install a permanent government of philosopher kings in Whitehall that would act as a check on any radicalism of politicians bidding for the popular vote. The civil service in Shirley Williams's view is '. . . a beautifully designed and efficient braking mechanism. It produces a hundred well-argued answers against initiative and change.'[20] It can be said to have been successful in performing the function for which it was intended.

The corollary of the tacit agreement which gives civil servants the right to be consulted is that, once their political masters have taken a decision it will be loyally executed. This side of the agreement appears to break down if the political masters are intent upon introducing the kind of radical constitutional or institutional change that Whitehall is designed to check. Young, for example, asserts that '. . . ranged against the politician's claim to break with the past is the belief in the civil service that it represents and personifies the seamless integrity of the past, present and future rolled indistinguishably into one. Whitehall is the custodian of the very continuity that the new keepers of Westminster think they have been elected to rupture.'[21] In such circumstances, prime ministers intent upon a radical programme like Margaret Thatcher, feel the need to seek alternative advice in order to overcome the obstacles Whitehall places in the way of change. In doing so prime ministers are not only obliged to undermine Whitehall's monopoly over advice, they are also less inclined to pay attention to their cabinet colleagues who are essentially the channel of advice from this constitutionally legitimate source. This gives rise to a shared sense of grievance in Whitehall and Westminster that the constitutional rules about advice are not being observed. Prime ministers are accused of behaving presidentially, of assuming freedoms about advice that are alien to accepted British constitutional norms.

In the seventeenth century Parliament feared that a pension from the French king would enable Charles II to dispense with its services and rule absolutely. In the twentieth century advice has become the currency of politics. Whitehall and Westminster fear that a presidentialized premier listening to alternative sources of advice will have the wherewithal to impose personal rule. Alternative advisers, therefore, remain suspect. The mandarins and ministers fear that they will be excluded from making the policy decisions they must administer and carry political responsibility for respectively. They therefore have a shared interest in raising a hue and cry. At such times questions about advice top the political agenda and complaints are typically articulated in constitutional terms.

British government is a duopoly of Westminster and Whitehall. Advice is the hyphen that links the public constitution with the secret constitution. When prime ministers appoint alternative advisers they are signalling that they suspect the civil service of failing to uphold the tacit agreement of the duopoly. A period of constitutional turbulence ensues which usually results in both sides ceding some ground. The civil service attempts to accommodate the prime minister's new needs for advice and begins to cooperate with some radical initiatives, and prime ministers allow their alternative advisers to be absorbed or expelled.[22] This dialogue about advice that can be seen as forming part of the normal discourse of English politics over the last thousand years, has also been the motor of constitutional change. The rule of feudal monarchs gradually gave way to the rule of constitutional monarchs, the rule of kings gradually gave way to the rule of cabinets and prime ministers. The discernible convergence between the advisory system of the British prime minister with that of an American president may be an indication of the next round of constitutional change. Precedents de-radicalize 'radical' innovations. Wilson and Thatcher have set precedents for any further presidentialization of the premiership in the future.

Notes

1. Deedes, W.F., 'Reinforcements for No.10?' *Telegraph* 15 November, 1982 p. 14.
2. 'Denting the contraption' *Economist* 10 March 1984 p. 20.
3. See Neustadt, Richard, E., '10 Downing Street' in King, Anthony, ed. *The British Prime Minister* 1st edn (London: Macmillan, 1969) pp. 119–30, p. 126.
4. In America, for example, over the role of Sherman Adams in President Eisenhower's White House or the status of executive privilege in connection with the Watergate scandal during President Nixon's incumbency. In Britain, for example, over the role of Marcia Williams in Harold Wilson's advisory system or over the part played by Professor Alan Walters as Mrs Thatcher's economic adviser.
5. See Hunt, Sir John, 'Cabinet Strategy and Management' Royal Institute of Public Administration Conference, Eastborne, 1983, (London: RIPA, 1983) pp. 90–4, p. 92, for discussion of the gap between the prime minister's 'role' and 'power'.
6. See Willetts, David, 'The role of the Prime Minister's Policy Unit' *Public Administration* Vol.65, Winter 1978 pp. 443–54.
7. Advice to the prime minister directly from Whitehall unmediated by members of the cabinet.

8. Advice from outside sources unmediated by either members of the cabinet or civil servants.
9. Although these parallels should not be over-stated. See Willetts, op.cit., pp. 452–3.
10. See Neustadt, Richard, E., 'White House and Whitehall' in King, op.cit., pp. 131–47, pp. 134–5.
11. Sharpe, Kevin, *Political Ideas in Early Stuart England* (London: Pinter, 1989) p.
12. Hennessy, Peter, *Whitehall* (London: Fontana, 1991) p. 314.
13. Burch, Martin, 'The Prime Minister and Cabinet from Thatcher to Major' *Talking Politics* Vol.7, No.1, Autumn 1994 pp. 27–33, p. 32.
14. Ibid. See also Greenaway, John, 'All Change at the Top?' *Social Studies Review* March, 1991 pp. 136–40, p. 136.
15. See Foley, Michael, *The Rise of the British Presidency* (Manchester: University Press, 1993) p. 265.
16. Benn, Stephen, *The White House Staff* (Unpublished doctoral thesis, University of Keele, 1984) p. xi.
17. Ranelagh, John, *Thatcher's People* (London: Fontana, 1992) p. 223.
18. Neustadt, '10 Downing Street' op.cit., p. 126.
19. Well Trevelyan at least, see Hennessy, op.cit., pp. 31–4.
20. Williams, Shirley, cit., Hennessy, op.cit., p. 1.
21. Young, Hugo, *One of Us* final edn (London: Pan Books, 1993) p. 154.
22. See Watt, David, 'Civil Servants and Kitchen Cabinets' *Financial Times* 27 October, 1972 p. 23.

Appendix

Diagrammatic representation of the American presidential advisory system and the changing advisory system of the British prime minister

The models below are intended to illustrate the gradual presidentialization of the prime ministerial advisory system that has occured since 1964.

The models are not comprehensive, they include only the main advisory sources in each system. This, however, is sufficient to demonstrate that a degree of convergence between the two systems has taken place during the period covered.

American Presidential Model – Roosevelt/Kennedy – The Wheel Model[1]

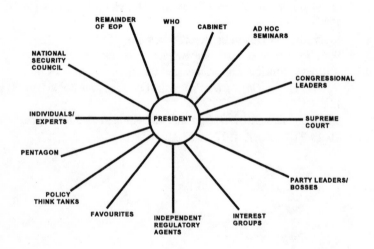

---

1   Derived from an idea about the organization of the White House Office in Dr Stephen Benn's thesis, `The White House Staff' (Keele University, 1986, unpublished) p. 435.

Presidential Model – Nixon – `Corrupted' Model

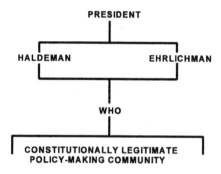

The Brownlow Committee Report (1939) which recommended the establishment of the EOP and its sub-section, the WHO, specified that the latter should *not* become a layer interposed between the president and the heads of his departments.[2]

---

2 See above, chapter three.

British Prime Ministerial Model – 1964 – The `Hierarchical' Model

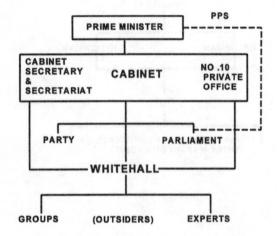

Wilson Model 1964–70

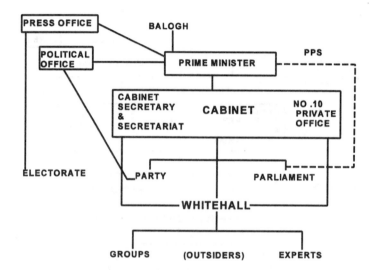

Heath Model 1970–74

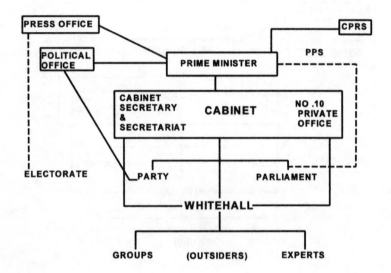

Wilson Model 1974–76

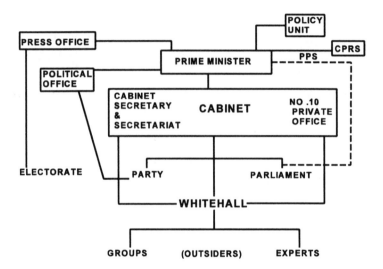

Callaghan Model 1976–79

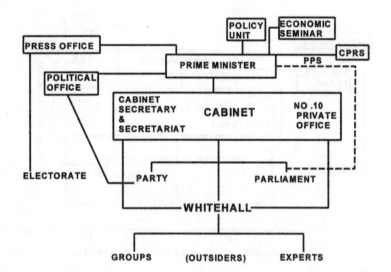

Thatcher Model 1979–88 approx.

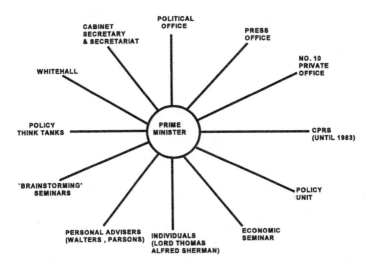

Thatcher Model after 1987–88 approx. possibly

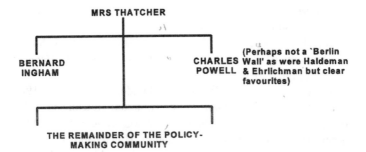

Bibliography

Alexander, Andrew and Watkins, Alan, *The Making of the Prime Minister, 1970* (London: Cape, 1970).

Aitken, Ian, 'Mr Haines's real scandal' *Guardian* 14 February, 1977, p. 10

Ashworth, John, M., 'On the Giving and Receiving of Advice (in Whitehall and Salford)'(Manchester: Statistical Society, 1982)

Ayling, Stanley, *George the Third* (London: History Book Club, 1972)

Bach, Stanley and Sulzner, George, T., eds *Perspectives on the Presidency* (New York: Heath & Co, 1974)

Bagehot, Walter, *The English Constitution* Fontana edn (London: Fontana, 1963)

Baker, Kenneth, 'The Last Days' *Sunday Times* 24 October, 1993, p.6.3

Balogh, Thomas, 'The Apotheosis of the Dilettante: The Establishment of Mandarins' in Thomas, Hugh, ed. *Crisis in the Civil Service* (Tonbridge: Anthony Blond, 1968) p. 11–52

Barber, James, *The British Prime Minister Since 1945* (Oxford: Blackwell, 1991)

Beloff, Nora, 'How Wilson sees Premier's job' *Observer* 1 March, 1964, p. 6

Beloff, Nora, *The Transit of Britain* (London: Collins, 1973)

Benn, Stephen, 'The White House Staff' (unpublished doctoral thesis, University of Keele, 1984)

Benn, Tony, 'Manifestos and Mandarins' in *Policy and Practice: the experience of government* (London: Royal Institute of Public Administration, 1980) pp. 57–78

Benn, Tony 'The Case for a Constitutional Premiership' in King, Anthony, ed. *The British Prime Minister* 2nd edn (London: Macmillan, 1982) pp. 220–41

Benn, Tony, *Out of the Wilderness* (London: Hutchinson, 1987)

Benn, Tony, *Office Without Power* (London: Hutchinson, 1988)

Benn, Tony, *Conflicts of Interest* (London: Hutchinson, 1989)

Benn, Tony, *Against the Tide* (London: Hutchinson, 1992)

Berkley, Humphrey, *The Power of the Prime Minister* (London: Allen & Unwin, 1966)

Berrill, Kenneth, 'Strength at the Centre – the case for a Prime Minister's Department' in King, Anthony, ed. *The British Prime Minister* 2nd edn (London: Macmillan, 1982) pp. 242–57

Bevins, Anthony, 'Government in turmoil as Chancellor resigns' *Independent* 27 October, 1989, p. 1

Binkley, Wilfred, E., *The President and Congress* (New York: Vintage Books, 1962)

Binkley, Wilfred, E., 'The President as Chief Legislator' in Bach, Stanley and Sulzner, George, T., eds *Perspectives on the Presidency* (New York: Heath & Co., 1974) pp. 302–19

Binkley, George, T., *The Man in the White House* 2nd edn (New York: Greenwood Press, 1978)

Blackstone, Tessa, 'Ministers, Advisers and Civil Servants' Hugh Gaitskell Memorial Lecture, Nottingham University, 1979, in Morgan, John, ed. *Politics and Consensus in Modern Britain: Lectures in Memory of Hugh Gaitskell* (Basingstoke: Macmillan, 1988) pp. 65–81

Blackstone, Tessa and Plowden, William, *Inside the Think Tank: Advising the Cabinet 1971–1983* (London: Heineman, 1988)

Blum, John, et al *The National Experience: History of the United States* 2nd edn (New York: Harcourt, Brace & World Inc., 1968)

Brown, George, *In My Way* (Harmondsworth: Penguin, 1972)

Bruce-Gardyne, Jock, *Whatever Happened to the Quiet Revolution?* (London: Charles Knight, 1974)

Bruce-Gardyne, Jock, *Ministers and Mandarins: Inside the Whitehall Village* (London: Sidgwick & Jackson, 1986)

Burch, Martin, 'Power in the Cabinet System' *Talking Politics* Vol.2, No.3, Spring 1990, pp. 102–8

Burch, Martin, 'Prime Minister and Cabinet: from Thatcher to Major' *Talking Politics* Vol.7, No.1, Autumn 1994, pp. 27–33

Butler, David and Pinto-Duschinsky, Michael, *The British General Election of 1970* (London: Macmillan, 1971)

Butler, David and Stokes, Donald, *Political Change in Britain* (London: Macmillan, 1974)

Butler, David and Kavanagh, Dennis, *The British General Election of 1979* (London:Macmillan, 1980)

Butler, David 'British Politics 1945–1987' in Hennessy, Peter and Seldon, Anthony, eds *Ruling Performance* (Oxford: Blackwell, 1987) pp. 324–30

Butt, Ronald, 'Tories must find a way out of their own trap' *The Times* 7 March, 1974, p. 16

Callaghan, James, *Time and Chance* (London: Collins, 1987)

Campbell, John, *Edward Heath: a biography* (London: Cape, 1993)

Castle, Barbara, 'Mandarin Power' *Sunday Times* 10 June, 1973, p. 17 & p. 19

Castle, Barbara, *The Castle Diaries* (London: Papermac, 1990)

Cheshyre, Robert, 'Wilson's new outsiders worry Whitehall' *Observer* 24 March, 1974, p. 4

Chester, Lewis, et al *Watergate: the Full Story* (London: Deutsch, 1973)

Childs, David, *Britain Since 1945* 2nd edn (London: Routledge, 1986)

Chitterden, Maurice and Clarke, Steve, 'Dirty tricks row over TV's pursuit of Thatcher man' *Sunday Times* 4 November, 1991, p. 15

Chrimes, S.B., *English Constitutional History* 4th edn (Oxford: University Paperbacks, 1973)

Clarke, Alan, *Diaries* (London: Phoenix, 1993)

Coates, David, *Labour in Power? A Study of the Labour Government 1974-1979* (London: Longman, 1980)

Cockerell, Michael, Hennessy, Peter, and Walker, David, *Sources Close to the Prime Minister* (London: Macmillan, 1984)

Coleman, Terry, 'Downwardly mobile with Sir Alan Walters' *Independent* 30 July, 1990, p. 18

Conservative Party, 'A Better Tomorrow' (London: Conservatice Central Office, 1970)

Cronin, Thomas 'The Swelling Presidency' in Bach, Stanley and Sulzner, George, T., eds *Perspectives on the Presidency* (New York: Heath & Co, 1974)

Cronin, Thomas 'A Resurgent Congress and the Imperial Presidency' *Political Science Quartley* Vol.95, No.2, Summer 1980, pp. 209-37

Crossman, R.H.S., 'Introduction' in Bagehot, Walter, *The English Constitution* Fontana edn (London: Fontana, 1963)

Crossman, R.H.S., *Inside View* (London: Jonothan Cape., 1974)

Crossman, R.H.S., *Diaries of a Cabinet Minister Vol.1 Minister of Housing 1964-66* (London: Hamish Hamilton & Jonothan Cape, 1975)

Crossman, R.H.S., *Vol.2 Lord President of the Council and Leader of the House of Commons 1966-68* (London: Hamish Hamilton & Jonothan Cape, 1976)

Crossman, R.H.S., *Vol.3 Secretary of State for Social Services 1968-70* (London: Hamish Hamilton & Jonothan Cape, 1977)

Crowther-Hunt, Lord, 'Mandarins and Ministers' *Parliamentary Affairs* Vol.33, No.4, 1980, pp. 373-99

Davies, Joseph, *The Prime Minister's Secretariat 1916-1920* (Newport: R.J. Johns, 1951)

Deedes, William, 'Reinforcements for No.10?' *Telegraph* 15 November, 1982, p. 14

Dell, Edmund, 'Collective Responsibility: fact, fiction or facade?' in *Policy and Practice* (London: RIPA, 1980) pp. 27-48

Donoughue, Bernard, 'The Conduct of Economic Policy 1974-79' in King, Anthony, ed. *The British Prime Minister* 2nd edn (London: Macmillan, 1982) pp. 47-71

Donoughue, Bernard, *Prime Minister: the Conduct of Policy under Harold Wilson and James Callaghan* (London: Cape, 1987)

Donooughue, Bernard, Interview with this writer, 19 May, 1994

Economist Leading article, 20 June, 1970, p. 9

Economist 'Denting the Contraption' 10 March, 1984, p. 20

Economist 'Thatcher Style Wars' 18 January, 1986

Elton, G.R., *The Tudor Constitution* (Cambridge: University Press, 1960)

Falkender, Lady Marcia, 'Letter to the Editor' *The Times* 31 May, 1976, p. 9

Falkender, Lady Marcia, 'Eyes and Ears for Harold Wilson' *Observer* 20 February, 1977, p. 26

Falkender, Lady Marcia, *Downing Street in Perspective* (London: Weidenfeld & Nicolson, 1983) See also Williams, Marcia, below.

Fay, Stephen and Young, Hugo, 'The Fall of Edward Heath' Parts 1 & 2 *Sunday Times* (Weekly Review) 22 & 29 February, 1976, pp. 33–4

Foley, Michael, *The Rise of the British Presidency* (Manchester: University Press, 1993)

Fox, James, 'The brains behind the throne' *Sunday Times* (Colour Supp.) 25 March, 1973, pp. 46–57

Frost, David, *'I Gave Them a Sword'* (London: Macmillan, 1978)

Fulbright, J.W. (Senator), 'Decline and Possible Fall of Constitutional Democracy in America' in Bach, Stanley and Sulzner, George, *Perspectives on the Presidency* (New York: D.C. Heath & Co., 1974) pp. 355–64

Fulton Report, 'Report of the Committee on the Civil Service 1966–1968' Cmnd. 3638, (London: HMSO, 1968)

Goodman, Arnold, *Tell Them I'm On My Way* (London: Chapmans, 1993)

Goodman, Arnold, 'The Power and the Vain Glory' *Observer* (Review) 8 August, 1993, pp. 41–2

Gordon Walker, Patrick, *The Cabinet* (London: Cape, 1970)

Greenaway, John, R., 'The Higher Civil Service at the Crossroads: the Impact of the Thatcher Government' in Robins, Lynton, ed. *Political Institutions in Britain* (London: Longman, 1991) pp. 38–57

Greenaway, John, R., 'All Change at the Top?' *Social Studies Review* March 1991, pp. 136–40

Greenstein, Fred, I., 'Change and Continuity in the Modern Presidency' in King, Anthony, ed. *The New American Political System* (Washington: American Enterprise Institute of Public Policy and Research, 1978)

Greenstein, Fred, I., 'Nine Presidents In Search of a Modern Presidency' in Greenstein, Fred, I., ed. *Leadership in the Modern Presidency* (Harvard: University Press, 1988)

Guardian Leading article, 'Boys in the back room' 29 June, 1974, p. 8

Guardian 'Whitehall fears on Think Tank' 17 June, 1983, p. 26

Haight, David, E. and Johnson, Larry, D., eds *The President: Roles and Powers* (New York: Rand McNally, 1965)

Haines, Joe, *The Politics of Power* (London: Coronet Books, 1977)

Hanham, H.J., *The Nineteenth Century Constitution 1815-1914* (Cambridge: University Press, 1969)

Harris, Kenneth, 'Mr Wilson's Job 2: A Year of Power' *Observer* (Colour Supp.) 24 October, 1965, pp. 6-10

Harris, Kenneth, *Thatcher* (London: Fontana, 1989)

Harris, Robert, *Good and Faithful Servant* (London: Faber, 1990)

Harris, Robert, 'Hard Man at No.10' *Sunday Times* 2 December, 1990, p. 3.1 and p. 3.14

Hart, D., 'The President and his Staff' in Shaw, Malcolm, ed. *Roosevelt to Reagan: Development of the Modern Presidency* (New York: Hurst & Co., 1987)

Harvey, J. and Bather, L., *The British Constitution and Politics* 5th edn (London: Macmillan, 1982)

Hattersley, Roy, 'Lord of Misrule?' *Sunday Times* 3 October, 1993, p. 3

Heale,M.J., *The Making of American Politics* (London: Longman, 1977)

Healey, Denis, *The Time of My Life* (Harmondsworth: Penguin, 1990)

Heasman, D.J., 'The Prime Minister and the Cabinet' in King, Anthony, ed. *The British Prime Minister* 1st edn (London: Macmillan, 1969) pp. 44-65

Heath, Edward and Barker, Anthony, 'Heath on Whitehall Reforms' *Parliamentary Affairs* Vol.31, No.4, Autumn, 1978, pp. 363-90

Hennessy, Peter, 'Whitehall Hostility into Overseas Staff Inquiry' *The Times* 26 April, 1977, p. 9

Hennessy, Peter, 'The Firework that Fizzled' *New Society* 3 January, 1985, pp. 10-11

Hennessy, Peter, 'The Quality of Cabinet Government' *Political Studies* Vol.6, 1985, pp. 15-45

Hennessy, Peter, 'Why Mr Heseltine finally snapped' *The Times* 10 January, 1986, p. 10

Hennessy, Peter, *Cabinet* (Oxford: Blackwell, 1986)

Hennessy, Peter, *Whitehall* (London: Fontana, 1990)

Hennessy, Peter, 'How much room at the top? Mrs Thatcher, the Cabinet and Power Sharing' in Norton, Philip, ed. *New Directions in British Politics* (London: Edward Elgar Ltd., 1991) p. 31

Hennessy, Peter, Morrison, Susan and Townsend, Richard, 'Routine Punctuated by Orgies: the Central Policy Review Staff 1970-1983' Strathclyde Papers on Government No.31 (Strathclyde: University, 1985)

Heseltine, Michael, 'Resignation Statement' *The Times* 10 January, 1986, p. 2

Hill, Christopher, *The Century of Revolution 1603-1714* (London: Reinhold, 1980)

Hodgson, Geoff, *Labour at the Crossroads* (Oxford: Martin Robertson, 1981)

Hodgson, Godfrey, *All Things to All Men: the false promise of the modern Presidency* (New York: Simon & Schuster, 1980)

Hodgson, Godfrey, 'Now is the time for all Right-thinking men . . . ' *Sunday Times* 4 March, 1984, pp. 44–52

Hodgson, Godfrey, 'After the Parties Break Up' *Independent* 17 June, 1992

Hofstadter, Richard, *The American Political Tradition and the Men Who Made It* (New York: Alfred Knopf, 1973)

Hogg, Sarah, interview with this writer, 31 January, 1992

Holden, Anthony, 'After Marcia and Joe' *Sunday Times* 27 February, 1977, p. 32

Holmes, Martin, *The Labour Government 1974-1979* (London: Macmillan, 1985)

Hoskyns, Sir John, 'Whitehall and Westminster: An outsider's view' *Parliamentary Affairs* Vol.36, No.2, Spring 1983, pp. 137–47

Howard, Anthony and West, Richard, *The Making of the Prime Minister* (London: Cape, 1965)

Hughes, Ann, ed. *Seventeenth Century England: A Changing Culture. Volume 1, Primary Sources* (London: Ward & Lock, 1980)

Hunt, Sir John, 'Cabinet Strategy and Management' (London: Royal Institute of Public Administration, 1993)

Hunt, Lord Hunt of Tanworth 'The United Kingdom' in Plowden, William, ed. *Advising the Rulers* (Oxford: Blackwell, 1987)

Hunt, Lord Hunt of Tanworth, Interview with this writer, 28 April, 1994, and letter 5 May, 1994

Hunt, Norman, 'Whitehall and Beyond' *Listener* 5 March, 1964, pp. 379–81 'Post-experince interview with Harold Wilson' in King, Anthony, *The British Prime Minister* 1st edn (London: Macmillan, 1969) pp. 93–115

Hurd, Douglas, *An End to Promises* (London: Collins, 1979) Hutchinson, George, *Edward Heath: a Personal and Political Biography* (London: Longman, 1970)

Hutchinson, George, 'After the fiasco of Sir Harold's list, can the honours system now survive?' *The Times* 29 May, 1976, p. 14

Independent 'What she thought, he said: Profile of Bernard Ingham a source close to the Prime Minister' 24 November, 1990, p. 16

Ingham, Bernard, *Kill the Messenger* (London: HarperCollins, 1991)

Irving, Clive, 'Whitehall: The Other Opposition' *New Statesman* 22 March, 1974, pp. 383–4

James, Dorothy, Buckton, *The Contemporary Presidency* 2nd edn (Indianapolis: Bobbs-Merrill Co., 1974)

James, Simon, *British Cabinet Government* (London: Routledge, 1992)

James, Simon, 'The Central Policy Review Staff, 1970–1983' *Political Studies* Vol.34., 1986, pp. 423–40

Jenkins, Peter, *The Battle for Downing Street* (London: Charles Knight, 1970)

Jenkins, Peter, 'Heat in the Kitchen' *Guardian* 5 April, 1974, p. 9

Jenkins, Peter, 'Epitaph for a Prime Minister' *Guardian* 30 March, 1979, p. 17

Jenkins, Peter, *Mrs Thatcher's Revolution* (London: Cape, 1987)

Jenkins, Simon, 'Judging the Thatcher decade' *Sunday Times* (Colour Supp.) 30 April, 1989, pp. 22–35

Jennings, Sir Ivor, *Cabinet Government* (Cambridge: University Press, 1969)

Jensen, Merrill, *The Articles of Confederation* (Wisconsin: University Press, 1959)

Jones, Bill, 'The Thatcher Style' (Politics Assoc. Resource Bank, 1989)

Jones, G.W., 'The Prime Minister's Power' in King, Anthony, ed. *The British Prime Minister* 1st edn (London: Macmillan, 1969) pp. 168–90

Jones, G.W., 'The Prime Ministers' Advisers' *Political Studies* Vol.21, 1973, pp. 363–75

Jones, G.W., 'Harold Wilson's policy-makers' *Spectator* 6 July,1974, pp. 12–13

Jones, G.W., 'Development of the Cabinet' in Thornhill, William, ed. *The Modernization of British Government* (London: Pitman, 1975)

Jones, G.W., 'The Prime Ministers' Secretaries: Politicians or Administrators?' in Griffith, J.A.G., ed. *From Policy to Administration* (London: Allen & Unwin, 1976)

Jones, G.W., 'The Prime Minister's Aides' in King, Anthony, ed. *The British Prime Minister* 2nd edn (London: Macmillan, 1985) pp. 72-95

Jones, G.W., 'The United Kingdom' in Plowden, William, *Advising the Rulers* (Oxford: Blackwell, 1989) pp. 36–66

Jones, Michael, 'Thatcher – the renegade at war behind enemy lines' *Sunday Times* (Review) 17 October, 1993, p. 6

Kaufman, Gerald, *How to be a Minister* (London: Sidgwick & Jackson, 1980)

Kavanagh, Dennis, 'The Heath Government 1970–1974' in Hennessy, Peter and Seldon, Anthony, eds *Ruling Performance* (Oxford: Blackwell, 1987) pp. 216–40

Kavanagh, Dennis, *Thatcherism and British Politics: the End of Consensus?* (Oxford: University Press, 1987)

Kavanagh, Dennis, 'Prime Ministerial Power Revisited' *Social Studies Review* March 1991, pp. 131–5

Kavanagh, Dennis, 'Changes in the political class' in Jones, Bill and Robins, Lynton, eds *Two Decades of British Politics* (Manchester: University Press, 1992) pp. 79–93

Keir, D.L., *The Constitutional History of Modern Britain* 9th edn (London: A & C Black, 1969)

Kellner, Peter and Hitchins, Christopher, *Callaghan: the Road to Number Ten* (London: Cassell, 1976)

Kellner, Peter and Crowther-Hunt, *The Civil Servants: an Inquiry into Britain's Ruling Class* (London: MacDonald & Jane, 1980)

Kenyon, J.P., ed. *The Stuart Constitution 1603–1688* (Cambridge: University Paperback, 1976)

King, Anthony, 'Margaret Thatcher: the style of a Prime Minister' in King, Anthony, ed. *The British Prime Minister* 2nd edn (London: Macmillan, 1985) pp. 96–140

Klein, Rudolf and Lewis, Janet, 'Advice and Dissent in British Government: the case for Special Advisers' *Policy and Politics* Vol.6, No.1, September, 1977, pp. 1–25

Koenig, Louis, W., *The Invisible Presidency* (New York: Rinehart, 1960)

Koenig, Louis, W., *Congress and President* (Illinois: Scott, Foresman & Co., 1965)

Koenig, Louis, W., *The Chief Executive* 5th edn (New York: Harcourt Brace Jovanovich, 1986)

Labour Party, 'Labour's Programme' (London: the Labour Party, 1973)

Lapping, Brian, *The Labour Government 1964–70* (Harmondsworth: Penguin, 1970)

Lawson, Nigel, *The View from Number Eleven* (London: Bantum Press, 1992)

Lees, John, D., *The President and the Court* (London: British Assoc. for American Studies, 1980)

Leuchtenburg, William, E., 'Franklin D. Roosevelt: the First Modern President' in Greenstein, Fred, I., *Leadership in the Modern Presidency* (Harvard: University Press, 1988)

Listener 'Thinking about the Think Tank' 28 December, 1972, p. 880

Listener Leading article, 22 April, 1976

Mackintosh, John, *The British Cabinet* 2nd edn (London: Metheun, 1968)

Mackintosh, John, 'Harold Wilson' in Mackintosh, John, P., ed. *British Prime Ministers in the Twentieth Century Vol.II Churchill to Callaghan* (London: Weidenfeld & Nicolson, 1978) pp. 171–215

Macmillan, Harold, *Riding the Storm* (London: Macmillan, 1971)

Madgwick, P.J., 'Prime Ministerial Power Revisited' *Social Studies Review* May 1986, pp. 28–35

Madgwich, P.J., Steed, D. and Williams, L.J., *Britian Since 1945* (London: Hutchinson, 1982)

Madison, James, Hamilton, Alexander and Jay, John, *The Federalist Papers* (1788) Penguin edn (Harmondsworth: Penguin, 1987)

Margach, James, 'My Plans by Harold Wilson' *Sunday Times* 18 October, 1964, pp. 41–2

Margach, James, 'When we win power: Edward Heath talks to James Margach' *Sunday Times* 3 October, 1965, pp. 11–12

Mather, Ian, 'Wilson's crisis shooter' *Observer* 17 March, 1974, p. 5

McClelland, John, S., *The Crowd and the Mob* (London: Unwin, 1989)

McGuinnis, Joe, *The Selling of the Presidency 1968* (London: Trident Press, 1968)

McKay, David, *Politics and Power in the USA* (Harmondsworth; Penguin, 1994)

Moorehead, Caroline, 'Profile of Lady Falkender: Part 1 From a secretary's chair to a seat in the House of Lords' *The Times* 23 July, 1974, p. 18 and Part 2 The Battle for Downing Street won, her political future is assured' *The Times* 24 July, 1974, p. 16

Morgan, Kenneth, ed., *Oxford Illustrated History of Britain* (Oxford: University, 1984)

Morgan, Kenneth, *Labour People: Leaders and Lieutenants Hardie to Kinnock* (Oxford: University Press, 1987)

Moseley, R.K., *The Story of the Cabinet Office* (London: Routledge & Kegan Paul, 1969)

Mount, Ferdinand, *The Constitution Now* (London: Heineman, 1992)

Naughtie, James, 'Thatcher throws a spanner in the political works' *Scotsman* 6 April, 1987, p. 11

Neustadt, Richard E., '10 Downing Street' and 'White House Whitehall' in King, Anthony, ed. *The British Prime Minister* 1st edn (London: Macmillan, 1969) pp. 119–30 and pp. 131–47

Neustadt, Richard, E., *Presidential Power – Politics of Leadership with Reflections on Johnson and Nixon* (New York: John Wiley & Sons, 1976)

Norton-Taylor, Richard, 'Callaghan shields advisers' *Guardian* 2 August, 1976, p. 1

Pares, Richard, *King George III and the Politicians* (Oxford: University Press, 1967)

Parker, Alan, 'The Organization of the US Presidency 1933-1972: the Politics of Advice' (unpublished doctoral thesis, University of Nottingham, 1977)

Pimlott, Ben, *Harold Wilson* (London: HarperCollins, 1992)

Plumb, J.H., *Sir Robert Walpole* Vol.2, Penguin edn., (Harmondsworth: Penguin, 1972)

Plumb, J.H., *England in the Eighteenth Century* (London: Pelican, 1990)

Political Quarterly 'Mr Wilson's Leadership' editorial Vol.42, No.4, 1971, pp. 353-62

Pollitt, C., 'The CPRS 1970-1974' *Public Administration* Winter 1974, pp. 375-92

Polsby, Nelson, 'Some Landmarks in Modern Presidential-Congressional Relations' in King, Anthony, ed. *Both Ends of the Avenue* (Washington DC., 1982)

Ponting, Clive, *Breach of Promise: Labour in Power 1964-1970* (London: Harmish Hamilton, 1989)

Powell, Enoch, J., *The Times* 4 October, 1993, p. 35

Prior, Jim, *A Balance of Power* (London: Hamish Hamilton, 1986)

Pym, Francis, *The Politics of Consent* (London: Hamish Hamilton, 1984)

Pyper, Robert, 'The Westland Affair' in Robins, Lynton, ed. *Topics in British Politics* (London: Political Education Press, 1987) pp. 20-32

Ramsey, R., 'Wilson and the Security Services' in Copley, R., Fielding, S. and Tiratsoo, N., eds *The Wilson Governments 1964-1970* (London: Pinter, 1993) pp. 152-61

Ranelagh, John, *Thatcher's People* (London: Fontana, 1992)

Raphael, Adam, 'At the Court of Queen Maggie' *Observer* 7 October, 1979, p. 11

Reagan, Ronald, *An American Life* (London: Hutchinson, 1990)

Redhead, Brian, 'James Callaghan' in Mackintosh, John, P., ed. *British Prime Ministers in the Twentieth Century Vol.II Churchill to Callaghan* (London: Weidenfeld & Nicolson,1978) pp. 216-39

Reedy, George, *The Twilight of the Presidency* (New York: NAL Books, 1980)

Riddell, Peter, *The Thatcher Government* 2nd edn (Oxford: Blackwell, 1985)

Ridley, F.F., 'What happened to the Constitution under Mrs Thatcher?' in Jones, Bill and Robins, Lynton, *Two Decades of British Politics* (Manchester: University Press, 1992) pp. 111-28

Ridley, Nicholas, *My Style of Government* (London: Hutchinson, 1991)

Rightie, Rosemary, 'Thatcher's diplomat at No.10' *Sunday Times* 24 October, 1982, p. 11

Robbins, Caroline, ed., *Two English Republican Tracts* (Cambridge: University Press, 1969)

Rossiter, Clinton, *The American Presidency* 2nd edn (London: Harvest, 1960)

Rothchild, Lord, 'A useful exercise with interest' *The Times* 2 July, 1983, p. 8

Roth, Andrew, *Heath and the Heathman* (London: Routledge & Kegan Paul, 1972)

Routledge, Paul, 'Revolutionary move by minister in creating aide attacked' *The Times* 9 October, 1972, p. 3

Rush, Michael, *The Cabinet and Policy Formation* (London: Longman,1984)

Samson, Anthony, *The Essential Anatomy of Britain* (London: Hodder & Stoughton, 1992)

Sayles, G.O., *The King's Parliament* (London: Arnold, 1975)

Schlesinger, Arthur, Jr., *The Age of Jackson* (London: Mentor, 1945)

Schlesinger, Arthur, Jr., *Age of Jackson* (Boston: Little, Brown & Co., 1945)

Schlesinger, Arthur, Jr., *The Imperial Presidency* 2nd edn (Boston: Houghton Mifflin Co., 1989)

Scotsman Leading article, 'Help for No.10' 6 April, 1984, p. 10

Seymour-Ure, Colin, 'Institutionalization and Informality of Advisory Systems' Plowden, William, ed. *Advising the Rulers* (Oxford: Blackwell, 1989) pp. 175–84

Sharp, Andrew, *Political Ideas of the English Civil Wars 1641–1649* (London: Longman, 1983)

Sharpe, Kevin, ed. *Faction and Parliament – essays on early Stuart history* (London: Metheun, 1978)

Sharpe, Kevin, *Politics and Ideas in Early Stuart England* (London: Pinter, 1989)

Shore, Peter, *Entitled to Know* (London: Macgibbon, 1966)

Sked, Alan and Cook, Chris, *Post-War Britain: a political history* 3rd edn (Harmondsworth: Penguin, 1990)

Smith, Joan, 'Lord Young' *Independent* 23 June, 1990, p. 54

Sorensen, Theodore, C., 'Presidential Advisers' in Cronin, Thomas, E. and Greenberg, Sanford, D., eds *The Presidential Advisory System* (New York: Harper, 1969)

St John-Stevas, Norman, 'Prime Ministers rise and fall but the Cabinet abides' *Telegraph* 7 August, 1986, p. 16

Stothard, Peter, 'A new mix for the cocktail cabinet' *The Times* 4 April, 1982, p. 11

Stothard, Peter, 'Who thinks for Mrs Thatcher?' *The Times* 31 January, 1983, P10

Tanner, J.R., *English Constitutional Conflicts of the Seventeenth Century 1603-1689* (Cambridge: University Press, 1971)

Tebbit, Norman, *Upwardly Mobile* (London: Weidenfeld & Nicolson, 1988)

Telegraph Leadering article, 'Your obedient masters' 29 June, 1974, p. 14

Thatcher, Margaret, *The Downing Street Years* (London: HarperCollins, 1993)

The Times Leading article, 20 June, 1970, p. 11

The Times 'Off the record, the voice behind the view from No.10. Portrait of Bernard Ingham' 14 January, 1983, p. 11

The Times 'A very good resignation' 10 January, 1986, p. 11

Thomson, David, *England in the Twentieth Century* (London: Pelican, 1969)

Tocqueville, Alexis, *Democracy in America* Vol.1, (1835) Fontana edn trans. Lawrence, George, (London: Fontana, 1968)

Trevor-Roper, Hugh, 'Nixon – America's Charles I?' *Spectator* 11 August, 1973, pp. 176-7

Vile, M.J.C., *American Historical Documents: The Presidency* (London: Harrap, 1976)

Vile, M.J.C., *The Politics of the USA* 4th edn (London: Pelican, 1987)

Vincent, John, 'The Thatcher Governments 1979-1987'in Hennessy, Peter and Seldon, Anthony, eds *Ruling Performance* (Oxford: Blackwell, 1987) pp. 274-300

Walker, David, 'The First Wilson Governments 1964-1970' in Hennessy, Peter and Seldon, Anthony, eds *Ruling Performance* (Oxford: Blackwell, 1987) pp. 186-215

Wapshott, N. and Brock, G., *Thatcher* (London: Fontana, 1983)

Wass, Douglas, *Government and the Governed: BBC Reith Lectures 1983* (London: Routledge & Kegan Paul, 1983)

Watkins, Alan, 'The conservatism of Mr Wilson' *Spectator* 3 December, 1965, p. 731

Watkins, Alan, 'Cronies and Kitchen Cabinets' *Sunday Telegraph* 7 April, 1974, p. 9

Watt, David, 'Civil servants and kitchen cabinets' *Financial Times* 27 October, 1972, p. 23

Weller, Patrick, *First Among Equals: Prime Ministers in Westminster Systems* (Australia: Allen & Unwin, 1985)

Weller, Patrick, 'Types of Advice' in Plowden, William, ed. *Advising the Rulers* (Oxford: Blackwell, 1987) pp. 149–57

White, Theodore, *Breach of Faith: the fall of Richard Nixon* (New York: Atheneum, 1975)

Whitehead, Philip, 'The Labour Governments, 1974–1979' in Hennessy, Peter and Seldon, Anthony, eds *Ruling Performance* (Oxford: Blackwell, 1987) pp. 241–74

Wigg, George, *George Wigg* (London: Michael Joseph, 1972)

Willetts, David, 'The Prime Minister's Policy Unit' *Public Administration* Vol.65, Winter 1987, pp. 443–54

Williams, Glyn and Ramsden, John, *Ruling Britain – A Political History of Britain 1688–1988* (London: Longman, 1990)

Williams, Marcia, *Inside Number 10* (London: Weidenfeld & Nicolson, 1972) (see also Falkender, above)

Williams, N., *The Eighteenth Century Constitution* (Cambridge: University Press, 1960)

Wilson, Harold, *The Labour Government 1964–1970: a personal record* (London: Weidenfeld & Nicolson and Michael Joseph, 1971)

Wilson, Harold, *The Governance of Britain* (London: Weidenfeld & Nicolson, 1976)

Wilson, Harold, *Final Term: the Labour Government 1974–1976* (London: Weidenfeld & Nicolson and Michael Joseph, 1979)

Wilson, Harold, *Memoirs 1916–1964* (London: Weidenfeld & Nicolson and Michael Joseph, 1986)

Wintour, Charles, 'Edward Heath speaking frankly: My Style of Government' *Evening Standard* 1 June, 1972, pp. 24–5

Wolff, Michael, 'The power of the Prime Minister: should he pick up the ball and run with it?' *The Times* 24 May, 1976, p. 14

Wood, David, 'Public spending cuts, Six talks, in Conservatives' first priorities' *The Times* 20 June, 1970, p. 1

Woodhouse, Diana, 'Mr Lawson and the 'Ill-concealed Iceberg'' *Social Studies Review* Vol.6, No.2, November, 1990, pp. 79–81

Young, Hugo, 'Purging the devil's advocates' *Sunday Times* 24 October, 1982, p. 11

Young, Hugo, *One of Us* final edn (London: Pan Books, 1993)

Ziegler, Philip, *The Authorized Life of Lord Wilson of Rievaulx* (London: Weidenfeld & Nicolson, 1993)

Index